AF553699

SCIENCE CURRICULUM

ENCYCLOPAEDIA OF SCHOOL CURRICULUM - 10

SCIENCE CURRICULUM

By

Dr. Marlow Ediger
M.S. Education, Ph.D.
Professor Emeritus in Education
Truman State University
Box 417, 201 W, 22nd St
North Newton KS 67117
United States of America

&

Dr. Digumarti Bhaskara Rao
M.Sc., M.A., M.A., M.Ed., Ph.D.
Reader & Research Director
R.V.R. College of Education
Srinivasa Nagar Colony
Guntur–522 006
(India)

DISCOVERY PUBLISHING HOUSE PVT. LTD.
NEW DELHI-110 002

First Published - 1996

Reprinted - 2018

ISBN: 978-93-5056-597-1 (Set)

ISBN: 978-81-7141-321-8

Science Curriculum

Published by:

DISCOVERY PUBLISHING HOUSE PVT. LTD.
4383/4B, Ansari Road, Darya Ganj
New Delhi-110 002 (India)
Phone: +91-11-23279245, 43596064-65
Fax: +91-11-23253475
E-mail: discoverypublishinghouse@gmail.com
sales@discoverypublishinggroup.com
web: www.discoverypublishinggroup.com

Printed at:
Infinity Imaging Systems
Delhi

PREFACE

Science has become an important organ of human life. It has greatly effected the mankind and one cannot even imagine a world without the contributions of science. No one can live luxuriously, or atleast happily, without applying the scientific knowledge in day-to-day activities.

Science, considering the inseparable bond between scientific contributions and human life styles, has made a compulsory part of school curriculum. Many innovations around the globe are adding year by year to the existing science education programmes. Still there are lacunae in science curriculum which are contributing to the failure of science education.

Science education, under these circumstances, needs a thorough diagnosis and treatment to improve its quality and potentiality. In its treatment, at one place or other we have to have a good science curriculum. So we have expressed our views on science curriculum and its allied aspects. The components of this book will aid the science educators in bringing out a quality science curriculum. We will be very happy if the personnel and pursuers of science utilise these perceptions and encourage us to improve this work by contributing their valuable suggestions.

Marlow Ediger
Bhaskara Rao

CONTENTS

CONTENTS (CONTD.)

SCIENCE

Science has helped the man to acquire supremacy over nature. It has greatly affected the way the people view themselves and the world around them. The wonderful achievements of science has glorified the modern world and illuminated the human creative potential.

In ancient times, most of the people believed that natural events and everything that happens to them are because of the actions of the God and Spirits. But the ancient Greeks were among the first to use systematic observation and reasoning to analyse natural happenings. As scientific thinking gradually developed, nature has seen less and less as the product of mysterious spiritual forces. Moreover, people began to feel that nature could be understood and even controlled through science.

Science, in literal sense, means 'the pursuit of knowledge'. The word 'Science' comes from the Latin word 'Scientia' which means 'Knowledge'. The term science in the sense of knowledge was used for long to include the entire subject matter of study. Though it is correct, it does not imply that, all knowledge is science. This is very clear by the fact that all the branches of social sciences and humanities are universally excluded from the purview of sciences. The reason offered for this is that the conclusions in social sciences and humanities are beyond verification and quantification.

The Post-war efforts by various people to elevate the status of humanities and social sciences to science, proved to be a futile effort. Again the reason was the inability to measure, quantify and verify the human mind and behaviour. Thus, the facility to measure, quantify and verify the object in question is the part of Science, its conclusions are universal. The body of knowledge is factual and verifiable, and the results are data-based.

Science is usually defined as a systematized knowledge. It is not a casual heap of disconnected scraps, but the bonds of union and the principles of arrangement is knowledge and it is mainly practical and social.

The knowledge is ordered, but it is not ordered from the stand point of and for the sake of knowledge. Not, thus, the presence of systematization characterizes science, but the presence of a peculiar principle and method of systematized from the stand point of and for the sake of knowledge as distinct from the stand point of practice and social intercourse. Specifically, this means that the subjects matter of knowledge is selected, formulated and arranged. With special reference to the exhibition of relations of intellectual dependence which its various parts sustain one another.

Many efforts, hence, were made to arrive at a precise meaning and definition of the word science by avoiding the loopholes. Let us see some of the important definitions to understand the science.

The Columbia Encyclopaedia defined science as "......accumulated and systematized learning, in general usage, restricted to natural phenomenon. The progress of science is marked not only by an accumulation of facts, but by the emergence of scientific method of the scientific attitude."

According to Frederic Fitzpatrick, "Science is cumulative and endless series of empirical observations which result in the formation of concepts and theories, with both concepts and theories being subject to modification in the light of further empirical observation. Science is both a body of knowledge and a process of acquiring it."

Albert Einstein felt that 'Science searches for relations, which are thought to exist independently of the searching individual." White-head, the famous philosopher, defines science as "an attempt to systematize our knowledge of the circumstances in which recognitions occur." Ames, M.V. says "Science is more than a compilation of facts. It is a method of thinking and working, a way of solving problems." Conant defines that, "Science is an interconnected series of concepts and theories. Science is a body of knowledge and the process of acquiring and refining knowledge."

Paul Hurd opined that "Facts themselves do not make a science. Science is not simply an abstraction from empirical data, but an intellectual occasion often suggested by data. It is the discerning of order among the data that makes the science. Science is an intellectual activity which arises from personal experience and takes place in the minds of men. It is simply a way of using human intelligence to achieve a better understanding of nature and nature's laws."

B. F. Skinner, a great psychologist, defined science as "First of all, sciences is a set of attitudes. It is a deposition to deal with facts rather than with what some one has said about them." Green, A. W. says that "Science is a way of investigation". In the words of Poincare, "Science is built of facts as a house is built of stones, but an accumulation of facts is no more a science than a heap of stones." According to Weinbeg and Shabat, "Science is a certain way of looking at the world".

Since life in the present world invariably warrants, to variable degrees, knowledge of scientific facts and laws, science has now become everyday science for everybody. Teaching of everyday science for everybody has become an unavoidable part of general education. Science takes its place side by side with other subjects as an essential element of one's education. It affords a knowledge of certain facts and laws and an insight into methods and dates peculiar to the domain of science.

The teaching of science like any other subject as school stage can be justified for various reasons. The very nature of the subject justifies its inclusion in the school curriculum. Science prepares pupils to think and sharpen their intellect making them more careful and systematic in reasoning. It provides unique training in truth, inculcates a spirit of inquiry, develops the capacity to know the unknown and gives strength to face failures.

The report of the Education Commission (1964-66) laid much emphasis on science-based education. In its own words, "There is one thing about which we feel with no doubt of hesitation, that is, science-based education in coherence with Indian culture and values can alone provide the foundation as an instrument for the nation's progress, security and welfare."

In its recommendations on "Education and Productivity", the Commission further mentions that "Science Education should become an integral part of school education, and ultimately some study of science should become a part of all courses in humanities and social sciences."

Science education in daily life, specially at the school stage, is necessary for several reasons. Firstly, the rapid growth of science and technology is influencing almost all walks of life. In fact, this rapid growth is resulting in the production of altogether new materials, new uses of old materials as well as providing the society with powerful tools capable of bringing about changes in the environment. Secondly, significant portions of the students terminate their studies after primary education and therefore there is an imperative need to provide them education, informally or non-formally, on continuing basis about the ongoing developments in the areas of science and technology having direct relevance to life. Thirdly, in view of the nature of science, the scientific laws and principles being generalisation of common experiences, the need for relating science with the life of community becomes quite obvious. A comparison between the processes of science and those used in agriculture, health and hygiene revealing the similarity between them also endorses the same view. Lastly, only the important objectives of education will bring about desired behavioural change. If science is taught in isolation, as a body of facts and principles alone, it can hardly meet the above objectives. It is therefore, all the more, necessary to make deliberate efforts to devetial science education with life.

REFERENCES

Bhaskara Rao, D. and D. Pushpa Latha (1994). Achievement in Biology. New Delhi : Discovery Publishing House.

Bhaskara Rao, D. and K. Vijaya (1995). A Text Book Evaluation. Ambala Cantt : The Associated Publishers.

Bhaskara Rao, Digumarti, editor (1996). Encyclopedia of Education for All, 5 vols. New Delhi : APH Publishing Corporation.

CURRICULUM

Curriculum is the soul of the process of education. It is the heart of the educational institution and mind of the course and all that only goes with it. Identifying the place of curriculum in educational process Cunningham one said that "Curriculum is the tool in the hands of the artist (the teacher) to mould his material (the pupils) according to his ideals (aims and objectives) in his studies (the school)."

The word curriculum is derived from a Latin word 'currere' which means 'to run'. So, "the curriculum means a course to be run for reaching a certain goal." This meaning does not inform enough specifically and intelligently. In fact, the term curriculum has a rich past which in itself is an interesting subject of study. An important definition of curriculum states the role and characteristics of a curriculum.

'The requisite content of knowledge arranged systematically for progressive acquisition; the total living of the child so far as the school can influence it or should take responsibility for developing it; the specialised environment deliberately arranged for directing the interests and abilities of children toward effective participation in the life of the community and the nation; concerned with helping children, enrich their own lives and contribute to the improvement of the society through the acquisition of useful informations, skills and attitudes; the learning experiences which children and youth have under the direction of school; the sequence of potential experience set up in the school for the purpose of disciplining children and youth in group; ways of thinking and acting; the continuous activity of the individual interacting with the environmental factors about him, the learnings or changes in behaviour that occur in the chain of series of experiencing; the systematic arrangement of course designed to meet the needs of a pupil or a group of pupils; the complete school environment involving all the courses, activities, readings and associations furnished to the pupils in the guidance of the school; all the learning experiences provided by the school, class study, health, recreation services and guidance services; social inheritance organised for its rapid assimilation by immature minds; the means to attain the aims of education, viz., the complete manhood for the attainment of a full life; and all the experiences which take place under the sponsorship of the school.'

According to the Secondary Education Commission's Report, 'Curriculum is much more than the boundaries by the academic subjects taught traditionally'. It should include totality of experiences that pupil receives through the manifold activities that go on in the school, in the classroom, library, laboratory, workshop, playgrounds and in the numerous informal contacts between teachers and pupils. In this sense, the whole life of the school becomes the curriculum......and helps in the evolution of balanced personality'.

These explanations rule out the possibility of a nation-wide curriculum for all pupils of all people if one considers the individual differences among pupils not only at various age levels but also at the same as well. In a report, Half Our Future : A Report of the Central Advisory Council for Education, on the education of average pupils in England says :

We should neither draw up a fixed table of information, subject by subject, what all pupils should master, nor even presecribed beyond the minimum essentials set out in the preceding paragraph a set list of subjects which all should study. A universal subjects curriculum ought to be ruled out if only because of the wide range both of capacity and of taste among the pupils with whom we are concerned. At the bottom end of the scale, it is a matter of finding a very few things in which the pupils show interest and can make progress and working outwards from them. Near the top of our terms of reference, half-way up of the whole scale of ability, it is a matter of selecting from, fairly large number of possibilities those that are likely to be more valuable to the individual pupils. The selection will vary from group to group. On the pupil's side, a prime consideration will often be relevance to what they are going to do when they leave school; on the school's side, the selection is bound to be affected by the strengths and weaknesses of the staff. An historian turned reluctant geographer, or vice versa, is not likely to inspire pupils who take a great deal of rousing at the best of times. Both subjects can, as we shall see later, offer many of the same values. If the head decides that the cobbler had better stick to his last, we shall neither be surprised nor unduly distressed.

We can say that the curriculum is an evolving concept. It is always in the making, being more in the nature of a process than a finished product. It informs us what to teach before we can consider methods and approaches to teaching and the age at which the various ideas are to be introduced (Vaidya). It is futile to talk 'how' and 'when' to teach without first deciding 'what' to teach.

There are four significant dimensions essentially to be considered when one talks of curriculum development. They are the determination of educational directions, the choice of principles and procedures for selecting and ordering the potential experiences comprising the instructional programme, the selection of a pattern of curriculum organisation and the determination of principles and procedures by which changes in the curriculum can be made (Smith, Stanely and Shores).

VARIABLES OF CURRICULUM

A curriculum does not exist in isolation. It comes about as a resultant of many variables having varying degrees of mutual interaction which impinge on it. Some of the most important variables are teacher, pupil, examination and evaluation, instructional and illustrative material and research (Vaidya).

PURPOSES OF CURRICULUM

The curriculum serves the following purposes since it is the source of all activities of the institution.

i) To provide pupils continuous as well as sequential experienc-

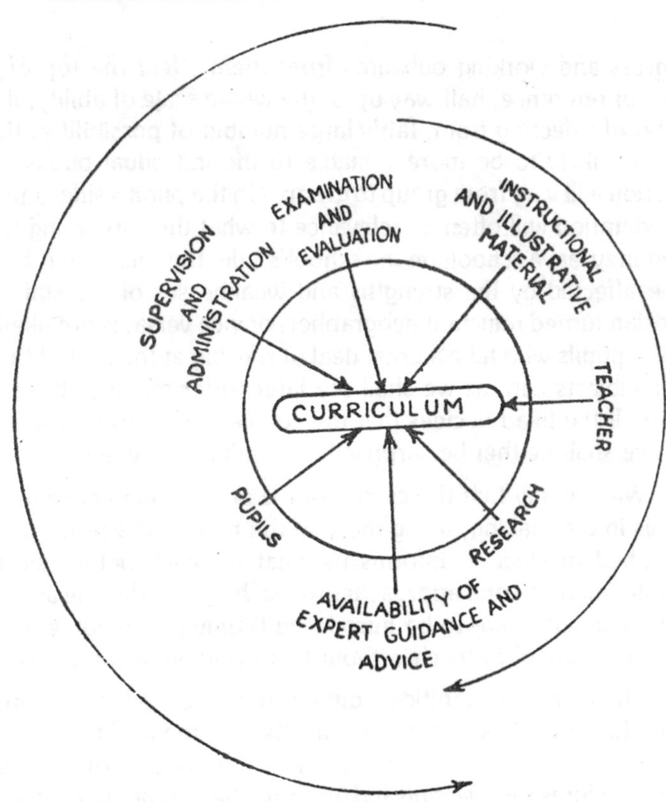

es right from the very beginning of the school onward, that is, through the secondary school on into the college;

ii) To approach science conceptually rather than factually as well as with somewhat less emphasis on the technical application of science;

iii) To use those methods of instruction which familiarize students not only with the nature of scientific enterprise but also with various processes of science (measuring and counting precisely, hypothesizing, setting up control experiments, recognising assumptions, testing and evaluating evidence, generalising and applying concepts and principles) which lie at the heart of scientific method;

iv) To provide deeper insights into the schema of the structure of science, that is, its philosophy, history and methods of inquiry;

v) To provide effectively for dividual differences, ability, needs and interests;

vi) To make maximum use of local skills and resources; and lastly

vii) To provide for built in mechanisms which provide for its continuous and critical re-evaluation.

CURRICULAR REQUIREMENTS FOR EXCEPTIONAL CHILDREN

Usually, the curriculum will be developed considering the class children as average. But, in any class one can see gifted as well as backward children. The existing curricula do not at all take into consideration their felt needs, interest, capacities, capabilities, aspirations, etc. We now mention below the significant considerations of the educational programmes (Vaidya).

Significant considerations	Gifted	Backward	Remarks
1. Individual Instruction.	It should be adapted to their potentialities. There should be, then, increasing emphasis on self-education.	They respond better when taught individually in small groups of two, three or four.	Backward pupils need continuous individualised attention throughout the school period.
2. Education based upon immediate experience.	It should only be in the beginning. This, then becomes their take-off point.	Their education should centre on concrete experience. They can thus check their thoughts against experience.	——
3. Emphasis on subject matter and the development of personal curriculum.	Subject matter should receive increasing emphasis.	Subject matter is of secondary importance. Development of personality is of paramount importance.	——
4. Utilitarian type of work.	Not essential.	Essential	——
5. School as 'home base'	Not necessarily.	It strengthens their self-confidence and reinforces self-respect.	——
			Contd.

Significant considerations	Gifted	Backward	Remarks
6. Teacher strong in one of the disciplines	Essential.	Broad based and trained in psychology and guidance.	—
7. Elastic time-table	It is highly desirable.	It is highly desirable.	—
8. Use of psychological tools for identification purposes.	Their use is highly desirable. Their problems can be easily identified and relevant steps taken in advance. Teacher can also plan their instructional and educational programmes on secure grounds in the light of their potentialities.	Their use is highly desirable. Their problems can be, thus, easily determined and the corresponding measures can be easily applied.	—
9. Rapport between teacher and pupil.	Even less rapport at a later stage can work without suffering any loss in efficiency. If teacher is a researcher, then first class rapport between the teacher and pupil is a must, Generally speaking, the goal should be : pupils should depend less and less on the teacher as they go up the school ladder.	More highly desirable. In fact, the same teacher should work with them throughout the school.	—
10. Motivation	It is desirable in the beginning but, later on, they can motivate themselves.	They require more of it. Motivation needs to be reinforced quite frequently.	—

Contd.

Significant considerations	Gifted	Backward	Remarks
11. Methods of teaching.	Expository discourse and techniques of explanation. Teaching techniques largely based upon language activities, lecture, method and question-answer method, etc.	Their teaching teaching needs to be approached through concrete methods of teaching. They respond very effectively to methods involving self-activity.	—
12. Deliberate social direction.	It is desirable but not essential.	It is highly desirable and essential.	—
13. Examination	Choice of subjects should be theirs but the examination standards should be highly exacting and demanding.	It should be optional for them. Foucs should be on the development of wholesome personality.	—
14. Immediate opportunities for success.	Immediate opportunities for experiencing success are not essential. High standards can be fixed for them.	They need immediate success experiences otherwise they lose interest in their work.	—
15. Individual and group work.	It is highly desirable.	It is essential. They hardly benefit from ordinary classroom teaching.	—
16. Role of the teacher.	They demand high standards from the teacher.	They demand emotional understanding and dedication from them.	Teacher should enjoy more professional freedom in his local situations.
17. Emphasis on environmental studies.	These should receive general emphasis. Productive thinking and theory-building need to be increasingly stressed.	Their curriculum should be organised around their centres of interest. Environmental studies vitalize their learning.	—
			Contd.

Significant considerations	Gifted	Backward	Remarks
18. Field trips.	Field trips are essential as these vitalize their subject matter knowledge and, thus, lead to the deeper understanding of facts, concepts and principles.	They play a significant part in their lives. These should be dovetailed with their vocational plans.	—
19. Repetition and drill.	It should only be to a limited extent.	They need more of it.	—
20. Education for life, more of the basic education variety.	It is highly desirable but of secondary importance. They are expected to dig more and more of new knowledge and develop highly sophisticated skills. They will be our future pace-setters in national affairs.	It is essential.	—

CHARACTERISTICS OF CURRICULUM

The curriculum considers many aspects such as course objectives, institutional facilities, individual needs, societal requirements and so on. Hence it possesses certain characteristics.

Smith, Stanely and Shores have felt the need of a progressive curriculum. The main characteristics of it are :

1) It must be mostly based upon the first hand experiences of the pupils from all the significant areas of human living. These experiences are characterized by newness, novelty, challenge, stimulation and creativity. Content receives increasing emphasis as the children move to the higher grades.
2) It should emphsize intellectual structures; and conceptual themes.

3) It should provide sufficient scope for observation, experimentation, independent work, drawing of inferences and criticism of experimental results obtained in the laboratory. Further, it should provide pupils sufficient experiences in formulating problems not only pinpointedly but more and more productively as well. Pupils will thus gain practice in the use of scientific method indirectly at their level of development.
4) It should provide sufficient scope for the cultivation of skills, interest, attitudes and appreciations.
5) It should be psychologically sound. It should take into account the theories of learning relevant to science teaching (Gestalt psychology, Geneva School and the work of those psychologists and educators which relates to the Acceleration of Mental Development in particular). Further, children's capacities and capabilities, if taken into account, will lead to the development of differentiated curriculum (for meeting individual differences). Incorporating geographical difference in it will be another innovation.
6) It should aim at bringing about an intelligent and effective adjustment with the environment itself. Further, it should enable pupils to acquire relevant scientific information of subsequent use in the significant areas of human living.
7) It should foster the growth or development of attitude and skills required for maintaining a planned social order of democratic type. To put more concretely, it should contribute towards democatic living.
8) It is tested and improved through research.
9) Lastly, it should not be narrowly conceived, should not be static but dynamic and forward looking; sample adequately both the scientific content and the abilities of the pupils to be developed, should cater to the right use of leisure later on and should be related to the environment in which the children live. Consequently, it will then become exciting, real and imaginative.

Sharma wants the following reorientation to the curriculum.

i) The content chosen should be in conformity with the aims and objectives of teaching science.

ii) It should be related to the interests of different age groups and everyday iife and the needs of the community. It should bear direct significance to life's problems and activities. There should be a wide range of scientific subjects which will emphasise the unity of scientific approach to meaningful and socially significant human problems. They should not be meaningless disconnected fragments but should be sought for social understanding and develop desirable social behaviour and are learnt through child's experience.

iii) Mastery of the subject-matter should not be made an end in itself. Teaching pupils 'how to think' is more important than teaching them 'what to think'.

iv) It should consist of a variety of physical and mental activities that will lead to those knowledge, skills, interests and attitudes which are necessary for proper adjustment to the social and physical environments.

v) The content that is used in giving pupils experiences in scientific thinking must be interesting, informative and free from inaccuracies of superficialities.

vi) Opportunities should be provided for first hand experience and for application of scientific method, acquired knowledge, skills, and attitudes to life situations, but various experiences that are educative should not be neglected.

vii) It should be flexible and should suit the varying needs of the children and the community.

viii) It should also include the material which helps in the appreciation of the work and sacrifice of great scientists in their search for truth.

ix) It should be such as can be adequately dealt with under stipulated conditions, such as available time, staff, equipment etc.

x) The learning activities should be organised in order to difficulty so that the pupils through reasonable effort may gain the satisfactions of accomplishment. This will afford opportunity for the exercise of creative abilities of pupils which in turn will make the students self-confident, self-reliant and independent. He will pursue science as a hobby and not something forced upon him.

xi) The course should be divided into units, each should contain essentially a major problem of everyday life. Each unit should again be divided into subordinate problems to facilitate learning by the pupils. These units or topics should be organised in such a way that the succeeding units will call for the understanding of larger and larger relationships and conceptions. Though for the sake of convenience the topics may be listed under different branches of science but it should always be borne in mind that topics should not be dealt as isolated items but should be so inter-related and integrated that their independence and their usefulness to mankind may be stressed thoughout.

xii) Provision should be made for science societies, visits to places of scientific interests and projects, etc.

Since curriculum development is a dynamic process and must never be static, the curriculum should always be in a process of revision leading to modernisation, refinement and enrichment.

REFERENCES

Bhaskara Rao, D. (1993). *Vignanasashtra Bhodhana (Teaching of Science).* Guntur: Nagarjuna Publishers.

Bhaskara Rao, D. and K. Vijaya (1995). *A Text Book Evaluation.* Ambala Cantt: The Associated Publishers.

Sharma, R. C. (1995). *Modern Science Teaching.* Delhi: Dhanpat Rai & Sons.

Smith, Stanely and Shores (1957). *Fundamentals of Curriculum Development.* New York: Harcourt, Brace & World, Inc.

Vaidya, Narendra (1971). *The Impact Science Teaching.* New Delhi : Oxford & IBH Publishing Co.

CURRICULUM DEVELOPMENT

The prime aim of education has shifted to totality of experiences from acquisition of knowledge. As education is regarded as a dynamic process so the aims and objectives have changed. In order to justify the aims and objectives of a subject as well as a course it is essential to know what to teach ? So vast is the field of science that it is no small problem to decide what facts should be taught ? Since curriculum is the totality of experiences of a child, and the experiences of each child are different from others, so the curriculum will be different for each pupil. It is, therefore, very essential to develop or prepare or construct or organise curriculum which should meet the requirement of each individual, necessities of the society and aims and objectives of the course. The curriculum is developed in different countries in different ways.

I. STYLES OF CURRICULUM DEVELOPMENT

Three specific styles are followed, in the United States, namely instrumental, interactive and individualistic. The specific needs for more and better-prepared students led to the development of instrumental type of curriculum in 1950s. In mid-sixties, it is followed by interactive style as curriculum reform which extended to other aspects of the school programmes and other sectioins of

Styles of Curriculum Development

Styles	Instrumental	Interactive	Individualistic
Major Goals	Utilitarian Job/career oriented	Society oriented, Social development.	Personal or individual development
Implicit Values	People as things (competition)	People as social animals (Interaction and cooperation)	People as individuals (idioswncratic/ self-development)
Subject Domains	Disciplinary	Interdisciplinary (humanities, G. sciences, social studies)	Gross inter-disciplinary (Science and humanities mix)
Taxonomic Domains	Cognitive	Affective	Creative
Materials	Highly structured (Teachers handbooks, students workbooks, prescribed texts etc.)	Loosely structured (Students packages, teachers guides, multimedia etc.)	Unstructured (Modular based, resource banks, retrieval system).
Teacher's Role	As Director	As Manager	As Assistant
Teaching Techniques	Lecture, Discovery, Inductive, Inquiry	Group projects, Problem Solving, Discussions.	Self-instructional techniques, practical tasks
Evaluation Techniques	Teacher evaluation—mainly objective (Prespecified goals)	Teacher evaluation mainly Subjective	Self-evaluation (goals identified during the process of learning)

the school community. By the end of 1960s, a third style called individualistic which aimed at the development of the individual. Each style has its own specific characteristics.

II. APPROACHES TO CURRICULUM DEVELOPMENT

The curriculum can be organised depending on the objectives to be achieved. Majority five approaches, viz., Integrated or Disciplinary, Flexible or Structured, Conceptual or Factual, Process or Content, and Teacher-centred or Pupil-centred. Any one or a combination of these approaches can be used in developing the curriculum.

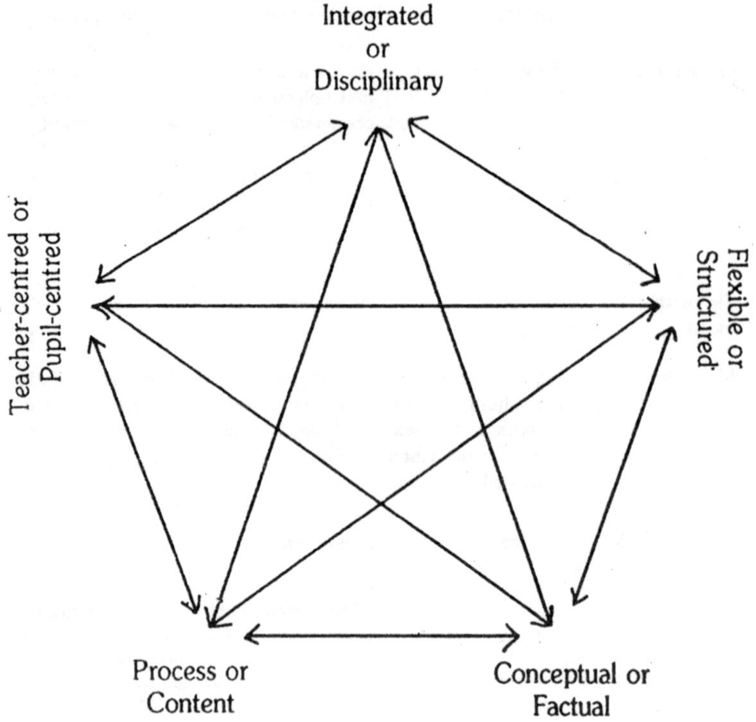

Approaches to Curriculum Development

III. PATTERNS OF CURRICULUM DEVELOPMENT

Curriculum can be organised by following different patterns, namely, Subject-centred, Activity-centred, and Core-centred. These patterns can be used independent of each other or can be mixed-up, depending on the content, subject and purpose.

IV. TRENDS IN CURRICULUM DEVELOPMENT

Many trends are followed in developing the curriculum. But, Individualised, Inter-disciplinary, and Social-issues Oriented trends are followed mainly at the time of curriculum organisation.

CHARACTERISTICS	PATTERNS OF CURRICULUM ORGANISATION			
Distinctive Characteristics	Subject centered	Activity centered	Core centered	Additional remarks
1. Research scientists classify total knowledge into its different branches so as to master atleast one branch of knowledge. It is assumed that after schooling is over, one may continue mastering the rest.	Present	—	—	
2. Four kinds of exposition are used: Simple to complex, whole to part, chronological, and pre-requisite learnings.	Present	—	—	
Teaching techniques stressed are : lectures, discussions, questions and answers, written exercises, oral reports, term papers, only relevant laboratory work in science and activities, like painting, cartooning, modelling, designing and constructing (in broader sense) receive less emphasis.	Present	—	—	Emphasis is on the mastering of facts, principles and laws rather than for the evidence of growth in habits of thinking and social processes. Development of critical thinking is not ruled out, knowledge is not arranged to increase the practical intelligence and wisdom.
				Contd.

CHARACTERISTICS	PATTERNS OF CURRICULUM ORGANISATION			
Distinctive Characteristics	Subject centered	Activity centered	Core centered	Additional remarks
3. Solely depends upon interest and purposes of children what is taught and how it is approached depend upon the realisation of children's purposes.	—	Present	—	—
4. Common learnings result from the pursuit of common interests by particular groups of children. At its best, teacher does not hesitate to develop personal curriculum for each child.	—	May or may not be present	Present	—
5. Curriculum emphasizes social values.	May or may not be present	May or may not be present	Present	It is woven around themes of social living, for example. protection and conversion of life, property and natural resources, felt needs of the individual for social adjustment in a variety of circumstances. Further, it fosters social integration.

Contd.

CHARACTERISTICS	PATTERNS OF CURRICULUM ORGANISATION			
Distinctive Characteristics	Subject centered	Activity centered	Core centered	Additional remarks
Essential Characteristics				
6. Curriculum is planned in advance.	Present	—	Only minimum common learnings are insisted upon for all students regardless of their ability and socio-economic status.	In subject curriculum, help is sought from experts and some times teachers are co-opted. Individual differences are met through optional subjects and designing differentiated assignments.
7. Mastery in one of the school subjects at a very advanced level is important.	Present	Present	Present	—
8. Activities are planned co-operatively by students and teachers	—	Present	Present	—
9. Problem-solving is employed as a dominant method of teaching. Teacher does not short circuit the learning process. Project method is preferred.	—	Present	Present	—

Contd.

CHARACTERISTICS	PATTERNS OF CURRICULUM ORGANISATION			
Distinctive Characteristics	**Subject centered**	**Activity centered**	**Core centered**	**Additional remarks**
10. Children's individual needs and interests are met within the programme—special pursuits or subjects provide for differentiated interests.	—	Present	Present	—
11. Teachers having broad general education with specialized training in child and adolescent psychology and guidance are required.	—	Present	Present	—
12. Availability of flexible teaching facilities in abundance for carrying out various types of activities (individual, small group and class) is required.	—	Present	Present	—
13. Availability of equipment and materials consistent with children's interest and requirements at various age levels.	—	Present	Present	—

Contd.

CHARACTERISTICS	PATTERNS OF CURRICULUM ORGANISATION			
Distinctive Characteristics	Subject centered	Activity centered	Core centered	Additional remarks
14. Availability of transport facilities.	Present	Present	Present	For enriching subject matter knowledge in case of subject curriculum and development of interest etc. in case of the other two.
15. Length of the period	As necessary and then fixed.	Flexible	Flexible	—
16. Grouping of students is allowed.	Rarely	Frequently	Frequently	—

1) *Individualised Trend*

Individualised trend is widely supported by educationists as it allows the student to engage in activities or programmes or instruction uniquely appropriate to his own style and pace of learning. The instruction in this type promotes independence and provides opportunities for study beyond resources. This trend meets the individual requirements of each child at his peculiar level of ability, achievements and progression. But this trend consumes lots of resources and requires high quantities of manual and material facilities.

2) *Interdisciplinary Trend*

The trend has presently shifted from uni-disciplinary to inter-disciplinary as there is increasing co-relation among various subjects or branches of curriculum. The recent efforts to develop curricula in the areas of environmental and population education indicate a trend towards inter-disciplinary approach in curriculum construction. These areas are challenging in the sense that they require consideration in the context of biological, sociological, historical, economical and political realities. There are, however, certain problems to implement inter-disciplinary curriculum. We need expert teachers to co-relate different disciplines. Team teaching serves better in this trend. There must be inter-disciplinary training in teacher educatio n.

3) *Social-issues Oriented Trend*

There is an increased trend in developing curriculum to emphasize in social implications. There are many social issues, norms or problems, which must be included in the curriculum. Because of this only, many subjects are having concepts on population, pollution, health, mental health, agriculture, etc. This trend in constructing the curriculum would require an open classroom format for teaching. It emphasizes self-discipline, free choices of instructional materials and format by the pupils and social relevance. It will take teachers and taught some time to get comfortable in the less structured teaching and learning (Sharma). Teacher education programmes will have to be changed drastically to meet the challenge.

V, PRINCIPLES OF CURRICULUM DEVELOPMENT

Curriculum development involves certain principles which need to be considered to fulfill the requirements of the individual and the society and to achieve the aims and objectives of the course and institution. Those principles are :

1. Principles of the Nature and Objective of the Course

As every course is started to achieve certain aims and objectives depending on its nature, the curriculum should be in confirmity of those goals.

2. Principle of the Duration of the Course

Every course will have its times duration. Depending on the availability of time the curriculum must be constructed.

3. Principle of the Availability of Resources

The curriculum implementation requires both manual and material resources. Hence the curriculum must be practical by considering the availability of teachers, laboratories, equipment, text books, evaluation tests, etc. If one aims highly, there will be a total failure.

4. Principle of the Totality of Experiences

The curriculum must be facilitator of total experiences needed for a child.

5. Principle of the Individual Interests

a) *Principle of Utility* : The curriculum should meet the daily needs of the children. It should give practical knowledge so as to enjoy the life and to adjust to the changing conditions of life and society.

b) *Principle of Vocational Requirement:* The curriculum should prepare the pupils for future life by providing information about their future vocational requirements, otherwise the schooling will result in a waste.

c) *Principle of Creativeness*: Every child will have some creativity. The curriculum must provide opportunities to utilize and promote creativeness of the pupils.

d) *Principle of Development of Innate Powers* : The innate powers of the children must be drawn out and sharpened by the curriculum. The pupils can be kept in place of a scientist so as develop their innate powers.

e) *Principle of Child Centredness:* No two children will be alike in this universe as the knowledge, achievement, interests, abilities, attitudes, social status, and physical conditions change from individual to individual. Hence the curriculum should meet the individual requirements by having the characteristic of child-centredness.

f) *Principle of Elasticity and Variety* : The curriculum shall create dis-interest in it if it is rigid and narrowly conceived. So it should balanced by giving emphasis to cultural values, interests, abilities and by permitting a variety of skills, habits, hobbies, etc.

g) *Principle of Leisure Time Pursuits* : We are well aware of the proverb that 'an idle man's brain is a devil's workshop'. So the curriculum should provide work for the leisure time of the children. This can be achieved by nature study, collection and preservation of specimens, photography, gardening, socially useful productive work, and such other activities.

h) *Principle of Activity Centredness* : Emphasis should be there in the curriculum on learning by doing. Elaborate provision should be there for laboratory activities and field experiences.

j) *Principle of Forward Looking* : The curriculum should help a child in adjusting and preparing for a full and effective adult life.

k) *Principle of Moral Values* : To live in the society as a successful citizen the curriculum should develop the social norms and mores.

5. Principle of the Society Interests

a) *Principle of Vocational Requirements* : Society is a complex organisation. For its effective functioning agencies such as transport, communication, productivities, electricity, agriculture, health, water, etc., are required in a good way and to achieve these we need trained personnel. Hence the curriculum should have provisions to meet these vocational requirements.

b) *Principle of Progress of the Society* : The progress of a society depends on its people who have scientific knowledge as the scientific knowledge develops a complete personality in a man. So the curriculum should be in a position to improve the scientific knowledge of the learners.

c) *Principle of Integrity of the Society* : The existence of any society mainly depends on its integration. By providing opportunities of learning about the advantages derived by integration the curriculum can develop integrative attitude in the minds of pupils.

d) *Principle of Conservation* : The curriculum should preserve and transmit the customs, traditions, standards of conduct, social norms, etc., on which the culture and civilization depend.

e) *Principle of International Consciousness* : Though one belongs primarily to his birth nation, he is no more limited to one nation and he is indebted to the constitutions of many nations. So one must feel that he is first a man and a world citizen and hence this should be achieved by the curriculum. The knowledge about the contributions of scientists to mankind, the interdependence of nations, etc., can help the children in developing in them the international consciousness.

VI. SYSTEMS OF ORGANISING CURRICULUM

The content organisation in the curriculum needs a careful consideration depending on the objectives to be achieved and facilities that are available. The content can be organised in different ways.

1. Logical Order Method

In logical order method, the topics or lessons will be arranged in an orderly manner from simple to complex stages. The arrangement of lessons will be in the same class or it can be spread to some other classes of the course.

2. Concentric Method

The topics, in this method, will find a place in different classes of different years of a course in a progressive manner. The content will be included from simple to complex as the classes progress so as to make the pupils understand the content according to capabilities that present in chronological and mental ages. This method is useful in primary and secondary school levels.

3. Topic Method

In this method, the content selected will be explained in detail in the same class at the same point. Once completed, there will be no future learning about his at any stage. Usually, this method will be of use at higher stages of learning.

4. Psychological Method

The subject matter, in this method, will be selected basing on the psychological level of the pupils. Depending on the mental ages, the content will be chosen.

5. Historical Method

Arrangement of subject matter takes place as per its historical development. The content will be linked with contemporary issues, inventions, kingdoms, etc.

6. Seasonal Arrangement of Lessons Method

The lessons will be arranged in the curriculum according to availability of natural resources. It will be absurd to teach about rain in summer or about a frog's life history in non-seasons. Hence the arrangement or content follows the seasons.

VII. MODERN EMERGING TRENDS IN SCIENCE CURRICULUM DEVELOPMENT

Science education is now major concern all over the world as it is expanding beyond our imagination both quantitatively and qualitatively. It is gratifying the needs and desires of the human populations. Now, since the beginning the century, many new trends in the construction of science curriculum.

1. Establishment of State Institutes of Science Education

Many parts of the world, of course many parts of a nation too, are witnessing seperate institutions of science education which are responsible the development of science curriculum, planning and implementation of science education in schools, and training the teachers of science.

2. Emphasis on Conceptual Learning

There is a shift to conceptual understanding of science from the traditional learning of facts. The curriculum is also so planned and implemented in many states.

3. Integrated Science

The present trend is towards unified or integrated approach to the organisation of content within various branches of science, rather than studying seperate branches. In some countries, attempts are underway to integrate science with social sciences and humanities. In India also, there are such subjects of learning at under-graduate level.

4. Decentralised Curriculum

The curriculum is developed centrally in the traditional systems. No doubt it helps in utilizing the resources of expenditure and ensuring qualitative and equal standards, but the class teachers are unable to teach effectively as the local needs and resources differ from place to place. So now the curriculum construction is decentralised and such curricula are developed including the local needs and interests.

5. Pupil-centred Instruction

Now, it is well recognised that first hand experiences are very effective in teaching-learning process, and it is only possible through active involvement of students in the learning process through discovery and inquiry approaches. Provisions are now made in curriculum for heuristic method, problem-solving method, project method, etc.

6. Self-learning Materials

In addition to the traditional instructional material, multimedia learning packages are developed. Self-learning kits, modules, programmed instruction/learning materials, computers, etc., are under use to a great extent.

7. Low-Cost Materials

There is great emphasis on developing low-cost or no-cost science materials rather than lying on expensive and sophisticated equipment. Certain centres are established to design and develop low-cost science materials. The teachers can also develo their own materials getting locally available material.

8. Non-formal Science Education

There is a trend towards providing non-formal science education to the people who are outside the reach of formal science education. There are many such programmes in many countries including India and the United States of America.

9. Indigenous Curriculum

Now many countries are developing their own curriculum rather than importing it from developed countries based on their past experiences. This indigeneous curriculum is helping in meeting the local needs and interests utilizing local manual and material resources.

10. Teachers Involvement

In many occasions, the practising teachers are made part of curriculum development rather putting the so-called experts on the panel. The teacher, in turn, with their practical experiences, either way, contributing well to the development of quality curriculum.

REFERENCES

Bahskara Rao, Digumarit. *Teaching of Science* (in-Press)

Bhaskara Rao, D. (author) and Marlow Ediger (editor (1995). *Scientific Attitude vis-a-vis Scientific Aptitude.* New Delhi : Discovery Publishing House.

Sharma, R. C. (1993). *Modern Science Teaching.* Delhi : Dhanpat Rai & Sons.

Vaidya, Narendra (1971). *The Impact Science Teaching.* New Delhi : Oxford & IBH Publishing House.

SCIENCE IN THE CURRICULUM

A quality science curriculum needs to be in evidence in the school/class setting. Each person lives in a world of science. The natural environment with its plants and animals reflects subject matter in science. Inventions and technology to improve the lot of each person truly emphasizes the methods and content of science.

To life effectively in society, students individually need to experience the wonders and contributions of science and scientists. A vital program of science instruction should be the lot of each student.

THE USE OF EXPERIMENTS

A modern program of elementary school science will have much in the area of experiments that pupils will perform with teacher guidance. This will mean that learners should actually be involved in conducting these experiments whenever possible. Almost all units taught in elementary school science can emphasize experimentation. For example, if pupils are studying a unit on "Magnetism and Electricity," the following objects and items can be placed on a learning center to initiate the unit:

1. Containers which contain shreds of paper, pieces of wood, a piece of plastic, and different kinds of cloth.
2. Nails, paper clips, different size coins, a piece of copper, and other kinds of metals.

Pupils can notice which objects and items on the learning center are attracted and which are not attracted by the use of magnets.

Scientists engage in conducting many experiments. This is a way of gaining new knowledge. It is a way of identifying new problem areas. Once these problems areas have been clearly defined; information can be gathered to solve these problems. A hypothesis or hypotheses are then developed which pertain to an answer or a solution to the problem. The hypothesis or hypotheses are tentative and not final or fixed. Only through testing can elementary school pupils develop some degree of certainty as to the correctness or accuracy of the hypothesis. Too frequently when science experiments are conducted, pupils want to jump to hasty conclusions as to the outcomes. An experiment or experiments are conducted to test a hypothesis or serval hypotheses. In the preceding example pertaining to the unit "Magnetism and Electricity," pupils could hypothesize as to which kinds of objects and items will be attracted by the magnets. This is only a hypothesis and not a fact. The hypothesis, of course, is based on knowledge. Pupils could then test the hypothesis with the actual using of the magnets. Different kinds of magnets should be utilized to test the hypothesis. Hypotheses are substantiated, modified, or refuted based on testing. As time goes, on with the further study and thought, new concepts and generalizations may be developed pertaining to previously held conclusions.

Very early in the experiences of elementary school pupils, the concepts of "experimental" and "control groups" should be emphasized. Pupils on the kindergarten level, for example, may be studying a unit on "Plants in Our community." The questions may arise as to what plants need in order to grow well. On a learning center, two potted plants can be placed. It is important to have these plants as alike as possible in terms in quality. The soil should be as comparable as possible for the two potted plants. The amount of moisture that each potted plant is to receive should be held constant also. In other words, both potted plants should receive the same treatment except for one variable which will be tested. This variable will be that one of these potted plants has a cardboard box placed over it. This plant will represent the experimental groups whereas the other potted plant will be the control group. Pupils can then test their hypothesis as to what will happen to the plant in the experimental group if it receives no sunshine. The plant in the experimental groups can be compared with the plant in the control group at selected intervals. Experiments such as these should be a an experimental groups as well as a control group. If the outcomes are always the same in this experiment, pupils can achieve accurate generalizations.

In the unit previously mentioned pertaining to "Plants in Our Community," other variables can be tested also as to what plants need in order to grow. Let us again assume for purposes of discussion that the two potted plants are as similar as possible in terms of quality. They receive the same amount of sunshine due to their location. The soil of these potted plants is similar. The one variable that will now be tested will pertain to amount of moisture that one plant will receive as compared to the other plant. Desert plants would not be involved in this experiment. On of the potted plants will receive no moisture while the other receives a proper amount. Pupils can observe what happens at different intervals when the experiment is being conducted. The plant receiving no moisture for a period of time would be in the experimental groups whereas the plant which is receiving the normal treatment is in the control group. Again, pupils should have ample opportunities to observe what actually happens when the one variable is tested. Another variable that could be tested in the experiment would be the soil that is used the potted plant. All other variables would remain the same. Pupils could use three kinds of soil; sandy soil, clay and loam. Thus, with several experiments such as these, pupils could generalize as to which kind of soil is most beneficial to plants.

Pupils must have opportunities to identify problems and questions; secondly, information or data needs to be gathered; thirdly, a hypothesis or hypotheses are developed; and finally, the hypothesis or hypotheses are tested and subject to revision and modification. These steps may bot necessarily be followed rigidly. However, pupils should use the methods of science in conducting experiments so that results are unbiased and objective.

THE IMPORTANCE OF SCIENCE

More time, no doubt, is devoted to teaching elementary school science than ever before. The writer can well remember attending a five teacher rural elementary school when science was taught once a week on the intermediate and upper grade levels in the 1930's and early 1940's. The science curriculum then consisted largely of reading about science from a specific series of textbooks. The reading was generally done orally with each pupil taking his turn. Many students in graduate and undergraduate classes of the writer attending the elementary school years in the 1930's and 1940's mention similar learning experience learning experiences. The use of experiments in elementary school science has been discussed previously; experimentation should be central in a modern program of science. The time, of course, devoted to the teachings of science has increased much.

There is much for pupils to learn in science in a scientific age. The space age, jet planes, cars, trucks, buses, ships, refrigerators, rangers, washers, and driers—to mention a few of man's achievements—require that pupils understand and develop major concepts, principles, and generalization of science.

Many elementary schools have adequate time devoted each day to the teaching of science. To be sure, ample time given to teaching a specific curriculum area will not automatically make for optimum achievements on the part of pupils. However, if pupils are to realize carefully selected objectives, the proper amount of time needs to be given to provide for quality learning activities in elementary school science and evaluate if stated goals have achieved.

Thus, society has realized the importance of science for pupils in the elementary school. If learners are to do well in science on the secondary level, they need to experience an excellent science program on the elementary level. Young children are curious about their natural environment. Selected pupils have come to school late on the kindergarten and first grade levels due to being curious about insects, rocks, plants, snow, puddles of water, and other natural phenomenon while walking of school.

Teachers have been amazed about the items children will bring to school for a science learning center. Little or no coaxing needs to be done here. Pupils voluntary want to bring objects to school pertaining to the curriculum area of science. They may bring rocks, insects in containers, tadpoles in jars, plants magnets of different kinds, and other items related to science. Pupils can raise many important questions on what has been brought for the science learning center. Pupils may reveal their interest by asking questions such as the following:

1. What do insects feed on?
2. How are rocks formed?
3. How do tadpoles change into frogs?
4. What do plants need in order to grow?
5. Why do magnets "pick up" certain things but not other materials?

Pupils with teacher leadership can discuss possible answers to these questions. Research also will need to be done to get need information in solving problem areas. The area of science offers many occasions for pupils to develop interest in and become curious about natural phenomena. It almost appears that pupils are naturally interested in science. Thus, it is not wonder that elementary school science is receiving more emphasis than ever before in the elementary curriculum. Also, in an industrial, automated society, pupils must understand contributions that science has made to improve the quality of living for human beings.

IN-SERVICE EDUCATION IN SCIENCE

With more science taught in the elementary school curriculum than ever before, it has become very important to conduct an adequate number of workshops and hold an ample number of faculty meetings to update science in the elementary school.

An elementary school or several elementary schools conducting workshops in the teaching of science must, first of all, determine what facet or facets of the science curriculum need to be emphasized in this approach in in-service education. Cooperatively, then, faculty members should decide upon the theme of the workshop. The theme can be decided upon only by studying trends in elementary school science and evaluating where one's school is presently in this important curriculum area. Thus, a gap will generally exist between where the school is presently and where it should be in elementary school science. The following areas may represent some of these gaps:

1. objectives of elementary school science.
2. selection of unit titles.
3. proper sequence in the science curriculum.
4. conducting experiments.
5. using a science equipment effectively.
6. using a variety of learning activities.
7. assessing pupil achievement effectively.
8. developing a philosophy for teaching science.
9. assisting pupils in reading science content.
10. identifying the scope of the science curriculum
11. learning by discovery in science.

Committees can be developed based on decisions made in the general session pertaining to problem areas that need solution in the area of elementary school science. It is excellent if each participant in the general session can select the committee he or she wishes most of participate in. Committee members need to sense purpose in work that is done. In other words, if participants can voluntarily select the committee they wish to serve in and sense that purpose is involved in solving problem areas, energy levels should be high for optimum achievement. The following resources should be available for all committee members:

1. knowledgeable resource personnel who can work effectively with people.
2. a professional library from which participants can get needed information.

Thus, members of the different committees involved in working to gain more insight into a effective elementary school science program should have resources available which will help in gaining quality results from efforts put forth.

It is necessary for participants in workshop to work on problems and area of interest of their very own choosing. This would then provide for individual differences among committee members. It may be that one participant alone has the following problem pertaining to the teaching of elementary school science:

assisting pupils in working on committees where responsibility of each member commensurate with ability is in evidence (this teacher may have had difficulty in getting certain committee member to do their share of the work). Thus, the individual participant in the science workshop can work in the direction solving a relevant problem in the teaching of science. Consultant help and resources materials would be available to help participants on an individual basis.

Faculty meetings in an elementary school should also be devoted to improving the elementary school science curriculum. An agenda committee composed of three or four faculty members can arrange items for discussion at the next faculty meeting. It is good to rotate the members of this committee provide for a broad base of participation on the part of faculty members of elementary school. Every faculty member should have equal rights to present items to agenda committee for discussion at faculty meetings. The agenda should be in the hands of participants two to three days before the meeting is held. This should give all participants ample opportunities to think about the various alternatives and possibilities when discussing solutions to questions and problem areas. Individuals can volunteer or be assigned to serve on committees to solve selected problem areas. Some of the problems areas that may be identified in faculty meetings pertaining to the teaching of elementary school science could be the following:

1. How can the inquiry approach be utilized when teaching science?
2. How does one write objectives which are behaviorally stated?
3. How can pupil achievement be effectively evaluated when using the problem solving approach?

Much thought, research, and discussion can go into the solving of each of these questions or problems. Some faculty members, no doubt, will need to visit other schools and observe teachers, for example, using the inquiry approach in teaching, as well as observe other innovations.

DEVELOPING CURRICULUM GUIDES

Each public school system should develop curriculum guides which can be utilized by teachers in teaching the different curriculum areas of the elementary school. Curriculum guides should be used in terms, of providing suggestions for teaching. They should definitely not be prescriptive. In the early history of curriculum guides, it was felt that these were to be followed rigidly. Today, the emphasis definitely is upon selection, in terms of good criteria or standards, as to what will be utilized from a curriculum guide. The curriculum guide, along with other reference sources, can assist the science teacher to do better job of planning of teaching elementary school pupils.

The question arises as to what are the salient parts of good curriculum guide. The format followed in developing these guides may vary from school system to school system. However, there will be some basic agreements as to which essential parts to include in a curriculum guide. The following are important parts of a curriculum guide in terms of the section devoted to elementary school science:

1. statements pertaining to a philosophy of teaching science.
2. suggestions for using for guide.
3. general and specific objectives for teaching different units of study.
4. scope and sequence of science units for each grade in elementary school.
5. suggested learning activities for each science unit.
6. suggested evaluation techniques to use in evaluating pupil achievement.
7. a listing of child growth and development characteristics.
8. suggestions for implementing committee work, and teacher-pupil pupil planning.
9. suggestions for helping pupils learn inductively, use the problem solving approach, and learn through the inquiry approach.
10. a good bibliography listing teacher references and pupil references.

From the preceding parts that could go into the developing of a curriculum guide, it is quite obvious that the teacher can have a valuable source of ideas to use in planning the science curriculum. For example, the teacher can evaluate and selected objectives which pupils should achieve in a specific unit. The teachers also has numerous opportunities to select learnings activities from the curriculum guide which should help a given set of learners achieve to their optimum. The evaluation section of the guide should give the science teacher some new approaches to utilize in effectively evaluating pupil achievement. Again, curriculum guides must be used as guides and not as a holy book which must be followed precisely.

USE OF TELEVISION IN SCIENCE

Educational television has made many important contributions in upgrading the science curriculum. Elementary schools that have access to closed circuit television generally will have listings of programs which teachers will have well in advance of their showing. These programs will relate directly to ongoing units being taught in science. For each unit of study, guides have been or should be developed pertaining to the different telecasts. For each broadcast, a listing of objectives for pupils to achieve is important. The teacher can sense then what each broadcast will emphasize in terms of objectives. Suggestions for learning activities are presented in the guide which will provide readiness within learners for viewing the telecast. The teacher can them select which activities would do the best job of providing readiness for learning so that adequate background knowledge will be developed within pupils. If pupils do not the have the needed concepts, facts, terms and generalizations necessary for understanding the telecast, optimum achievement cannot result. The readiness activities should also assist pupils in developing interest in the broadcast. An inward desire should exist on the part of the learner in wanting to watch the telecast. Certainly, learners should have identified some questions which they would want to have answered when viewing the broadcast.

After the telecast, follow-up activities are necessary so that pupils can use what has been learned. Answers to questions raised before the broadcast can be discussed. Experiments may need to be performed in order that pupils can get needed data in answer to questions. Pupils may volunteer to develop reports on selected topics which relate to the broadcast using science encyclopedias or regular encyclopedias. Taking an excursion may help to answer additional questions raised after the telecast. In other words, there are many learning activities for pupils which will assist them to "branch out" in broadening their thinking and interests after having viewed a telecast.

USING KNOWLEDGE OF CHILDREN

Science teachers who do a poor job of teaching may not be using knowledge pertaining to important child growth and development characteristics. Teachers need to study each of their pupils carefully so that the best quality of learning activities can be provided. Educational psychologists have long emphasized the importance of providing for individual differences in a class. Too frequently, however, little has been done in this area by practitioners. A very clear violation of providing for individual differences exists when science teachers want to kept all pupils "together" by having the whole group study the same thing at the same time. Perhaps, science has become a reading course where pupils spend much time in reading content from a series of elementary school science textbooks. As educators should be well aware of, this activity will be too difficult for some pupils': for others it is too easy. Very few pupils will find that the content is written on their reading level. Pupils also desire new experiences and want variety in learning activities they are participating in.

Many statements have been written on child growth and development characteristics. Faculty members of an elementary school need to study these contributions written by psychologists and educators realizing that pupils differ from each other in many ways within a class, such as interest, intelligence, abilities, past experiences, motivation, appearance, height, and weight.

VARIETY IN LEARNING ACTIVITIES

It is important for the science teacher to provide a variety of learning activities for pupils. This would be important for the following reasons:

1. pupils have different learning styles.
2. different levels of achievement in science exist within any class of pupils.
3. not all pupils, of course, benefit equally from the same

activity.

4. teachers have different teaching styles.
5. selected learning activities capture the interests of pupils more than do other kinds of experiences.
6. individuals desire new experiences.
7. monotony in activities hinders pupils in developing proper motivation toward learning.

There are many learning activities in elementary school science which would assist pupils in gaining needed concepts, main ideas, facts, and generalizations. These learning activities could help pupils in the area of problem solving. The following, among others, could become purposeful learning activities for pupils in elementary school science: conducting experiments and demonstrations, taking excursions, reading from a series or several series of elementary school science textbooks, getting information from a set or several sets of general encyclopedias and/or science encyclopedias, reading from library books, working at learning centers, using pictures, using transparencies and the overhead projector, constructing objects, making models, utilizing filmstrips and films, listening to tape recordings. Interviewing resource personnel, viewing slides, visiting museums, having discussions, giving oral reports to the class, writing reports. Engaging in dramatic activities, making dioramas, developing friezes, completing murals, making graphs and charts, developing illustrations, and participating in panel discussions. There are many, many kinds of learning activities for pupil in elementary school science; there should basically be no boredom on the part of pupils when this curriculum area is being taught. It is important to select those learning activities which will help pupils to do the very best possible in elementary school science.

Approaches to teaching science can also be varied in terms of using the inductive versus the deductive approach to learning. Much has been written about the advantages of using the inductive approach as compared to the deductive approach. Some of these advantages are the following:

1. pupils have to do much responding so that generalizations and conclusions can truly be discovered.

2. learners reveal where they are presently in achievement when learning by discovery.
3. pupils can become actively involved in ongoing learning activities.
4. it keeps learners "on their toes" when doing much responding in ongoing learning activities.
5. pupils have many opportunities, to do critical and creative thinking.
6. a variety of learning activities can be utilized in the inductive approach.
7. pupils can become more self-directed with less reliance on the teacher dominating the classroom situation.
8. teachers become more flexible in their thinking when less reliance can be placed upon how pupils will respond.
9. learners can work more in the direction of using the methods and approaches of scientists, scientists gain much knowledge and information through discovery.

The science teacher can have pupils develop generalization deductively. For example, in a unit on "Liquids, Solids, and Gases," the teacher could perform an experiment whereby a bottle with a narrow opening would be filled with a few inches of water and placed on a hot plate. A balloon would be stretched over the narrow opening of the bottle before it is placed on the hot plate. Pupils would be encouraged to see what will happen. The balloon, of course, becomes larger. The teachers then proceeds to explain to the class why the balloon became larger and what happens when air is heated.

In the inductive approach utilizing the same experiment, the teacher could have pupils hypothesize freely as to what will happen when this same bottle, containing a few inches of water, with the attached balloon is placed on the hot plate. Reasons for the hypotheses can also be discussed thus giving the teacher much information on where learners are presently in achievement pertaining to the area now being taught in the unit "Liquids, Solids, and Gases." Following the discussion, the hypotheses need to be tested using the experiment. The experiment can be performed more than one so that pupils can sense than the outcomes in the experiment will have the same results. The size of openings of the bottles as well as the size of the balloons can vary when having pupils view the same kind or type of experiment when noticing that the results are similar in terms of generalizations or conclusions realised. Further research can be done using elementary science textbooks. Encyclopedias, films, filmstrips, and other resources to explain conclusions realized from conducting the experiment. In using the inductive approach, the teacher does a very small amount of explaining or lecturing. The teacher sets the stage for learning. Pupils identify problems, gather information, develop hypotheses, test hypotheses, and revise them when necessary. Active involvement on the part of pupils is of utmost importance in ongoing learning activities.

A science teacher could tape record his own teaching and evaluate the quality of experiences pertaining to pupils learning by discovery or using the inductive approach. If a portable video-tape making is available in the elementary school, teaching performance in science could also observe non-verbal facets of communication such as gestures, facial expressions, and body movements in the teaching-learning situation. Valuation feed-back from learners can come from viewing different facets of teaching on video-tape. The teachers can notice such factors as the following:

1. Do pupils appear interested or bored in the ongoing learning activities?
2. Are all learners actively involved in the lesson being presented?
3. Do a few pupils dominate the discussion while others refrain from participating?
4. Do pupils feel free to hypothesize pertaining to possible outcomes of science experiments?
5. Are pupils using variety of reference sources in gathering data to develop and/or test hypotheses?
6. Do pupils reveal curiosity in wanting to learning more about any unit of study in elementary school science?

If the teacher has access to video-taping teaching performance, or if a tape recorder is used only, he can analyze what kind of verbal interaction occurred between pupils and the teacher in a classroom situation. The teacher, for example, can notice the following in teaching-learning situations:

1. Do pupils have ample opportunities to hypothesize?
2. Does the teacher ask many relevant questions of learners pertaining to ongoing units of study in science?
3. Are these questions on the present achievement level of pupils?
4. Do pupils have need background information to develop meaningful hypotheses?
5. Is lecturing minimized much in ongoing learning activities?
6. Is the teacher praising pupils is achieving desired objectives in elementary school science?
7. Do learners identify relevant problem areas?
8. Does is appear that pupils individually are being challenged in developing an inward desire to learning?
9. Does the teacher give pupils adequate time to engage in hypothesizing when being involved in problem solving activities?
10. Does the teacher refrain from scolding or minimizing pupils is the class setting?

BEHAVIORAL OBJECTIVES IN ELEMENTARY SCIENCE

Elementary school science lends itself very well to having teachers state their objectives behaviorally. Selected educators advocate that objectives be stated precisely. Advantages of behaviorally stated objectives are the following:

1. These objectives very clearly state what learners are to learn.
2. It can definitely be measured if pupils have achieved these objectives.
3. Learning activities can be selected carefully which will guide learners to realize the objectives.
4. Teachers can be held accountable for pupils realizing the objectives

5. Learners can achieve these objectives at different rates of speed thus providing for individual differences.
6. Parents can notice specifically what their pupils have learned.
7. Principals and supervisors can have better basis for evaluating teacher performance.
8. Teachers could even be paid on the basis of achievement or lack of it in terms of learner performance (this could be a motivating factor for some teachers).
9. Objective criteria are used to assess pupil achievement; these criteria are the behaviorally stated objectives.

As in almost any innovation, there are also disadvantages to behaviorally stated objectives. The following, among others, are some of the disadvantages:

1. Too frequently, the trivial or unimportant is taught since the lowest level of cognitive objective are easiest to write.
2. No one can definitely be sure what pupil actually should learn when stating all objectives precisely prior to teaching.
3. Objectives should come from the learner also and not the teacher only.
4. Affective domain objectives may become minimized if all objectives need to be stated so that it can be measured precisely if pupils have achieved them.
5. Learners become rather passive individuals if all objectives are stated by the teacher prior to teaching.
6. By stating objectives in advance prior to teaching, the teacher is assuming that proper sequence in learning will be in evidence.
7. The teacher should focus more on the learning activity rather than the objectives since it is in this framework that interest and meaning is developed.
8. Behavioral objectives are very time consuming in writing.

The science teacher, the elementary school principal, and the supervisor need to study behavioral objectives carefully to determine if this plan of teacher is really wanted in elementary school science. Workshops and faculty meeting can be devoted to the study and implementation of behavioral objectives. Objectives which pupils are then to achieve should meet the following criteria:

1. they are important or relevant.
2. they stress key ideas or generalizations emphasized by specialists in the different areas or science such as in biology, chemistry, physics, zoology, botany, geology, and astronomy.
3. there is balance among understandings, skills and attitudinal objectives or among cognitive, psychomotor, and affective domain objectives.

All behaviorally stated objectives should follow the following standards:

1. the objectives should be clearly written so that little or no room exists in their interpretation.
2. it can definitely by measured if the objectives have been achieved.
3. it states what learners will learn as a result of teaching.

If pupils are studying a unit on "The Solar system," the following objectives may have been identified for pupils to realize:

1. The pupil will list in writing the nine planets in proper sequence from the sun.
2. The pupil will recite orally the names of the largest and the smallest planet.
3. The pupils will write a fifty paper on the possibility of life as we know it on a planet of his own choice (excluding the planet earth).
4. Pupils in their own words will define the meaning of the following concepts: solar system; universe; planet; satellite; asteroids; theory; hypothesis; magnetic pole; rotation; and revolution.
5. The pupil will demonstrate and discuss the causes of the different seasons of the year.

6. Learners will predict what will happen in the future in space exploration.
7. A model of the solar system will be made in committees of three; the model will be evaluated in terms of criteria discussed in class.

The first and second behaviorally stated objectives require recall of information which is the lowest level of cognition. Pupils would recall the names of the nine known planets in proper order, and be able to name the largest and smallest of these planets. The third objective may also involve simple recall of what has been learned previously by pupils. Pupils could recall from a discussion if there is or is not life as we know it on one of the planets and write on the selected topic. Pupils individually, however, could also be quite creative when writing a paper of at least fifty words pertaining to the possibilities of life existing on a planet which he chooses to write on. The paper could involve unique, novel, original, and constructive ideas which would involve synthesizing of knowledge. The fourth objective goes beyond recall of knowledge. It is true that the child would need to think of definitions he has heard of previously pertaining to such words so solar system, universe, planet, satellite, asteroids, theory, hypothesis, magnetic pole, constellation, rotation, and revolution. The learner, however, would need to reveal his understanding of these concepts by giving definitions in his own words. Comprehension of the meaning of these concepts would be important to pupils when achieving this objective. The fifth objective would generally involve applying what has been learned previously. The knowledge and information the child has developed previously is now utilized in demonstrating the causes of the different seasons of the year. The pupil could use a large globe to represent the earth and flashlight to represent the sun. The learner could also make drawings on the chalkboard and/or use pictures in clarifying the various causes for the different seasons for the year. In the sixth objective, creative thinking based on much knowledge is involved. Pupils would need to have considerable background information to make predictions as to what will happen in the future as far as space exploration is concerned. The last objective involves a psychomotor domain objective in that a construction activity is involved requiring the use of the muscles. To be sure, much thought and research will go into the making of an accurate model of the solar system. Pupils will need to check the accuracy of their model in terms of standards or criteria developed in class. The latter part of this objective (objective number seven) can involve a very complex level of thinking. Definite criteria will need to be developed in class so that the model of the solar system can be effectively evaluated in terms of these guidelines.

Thus, behaviorally stated objectives can be used effectively in a modern program of elementary school science. It is important when emphasizing these kinds of objectives that teachers have pupils go beyond the level of recall of information. The science teacher also needs to think terms of some kind of rational balance among cognitive, psychomotor, and affective domain objectives. Never should one category of objectives dominate teacher-learning situations. One category of objectives does affect the other category of categories.

ADJUSTING THE SCIENCE CURRICULUM TO THE CHILD

Too frequently, the teacher has objectives for pupils to achieve which are expressively complex. The science teacher may have felt that this is a way of setting high standards in a specific curriculum area. Many pupils then cannot achieve these objectives and develop feelings of an inadequate self. Pupil achievement goes downhill in situations such as these. Learners think and feel that they cannot do well in elementary school science and this becomes a reality. If pupils perceive that they cannot do well in science, this is the way that learners will behave. The teachers needs to have some kind of pretest in a new science unit to determine where learners are presently in achievement. Once this has been determined, objectives can be developed which are attainable. If objectives are attainable, learners can feel successful and develop feelings of an adequate self. The curriculum is then adjusted to where pupils are presently in achievement in different units of study in elementary school science.

Certainly, there is danger, too, in teaching pupils what they already know in a new unit of study. A pretest can give elementary science teachers data if objectives need to be made more complex. Again, the objectives should be attainable for learners. The science curriculum in this case is again adjusted to present achievement levels of learners.

IN SUMMARY

Conducting experiments is a very important tvpe or kind of

learning activity in a modern elementary school science program. Balance among the different curriculum areas in the elementary school must be stressed in teaching-learning situations. In-service education for teachers, principals, and supervisors is important to update the science curriculum. Curriculum guides can be a valuable source to utilize when selecting objectives, learning experiences, and evaluation techniques in a modern program of elementary school science. A variety of learning experiences should be provided for pupils in the elementary school. The science curriculum must be adjusted to the present achievement level of each learner. Inductive approaches should be emphasized by the teacher in teaching-learning situations; critical and creative thinking as well as problem solving should be emphasized. Attitudinal objectives are important for pupils to achieve. There must be proper balance among the following kinds of objectives for pupils to achieve.

1. understanding, skills, and attitudes or
2. cognitive, affective, and psychomotor domains.

Adequate emphasis needs to be placed upon microcomputer instruction in the curriculum. Wright and Forcier list the following general criteria in selecting computer courseware:

1. Content is accurate
2. Content is appropriate.
3. Presentation is clear.
4. Screen display is highly readable.
5. The computer's capabilities are effectively employed..
6. Program executes reliably.
7. Program is cost effective.
8. Program is easy to use.
9. Support materials are effective.
10. No racial or sexual discrimination implied.

REFERENCES

1. Edward B. Wright and Richard E. Forcier, The Computer : A Tool for the Teacher. Belmont, California : Wadsworth Publishing Company, 1985 page 158.

NEED OF SCIENCE

Science has occupied almost all spheres of human life. We are living in a society which is completely drawn into the scientific environment. Now, we can not think of a world without science. The wonderful achievements of science has glorified the modern world and transformed the modern civilization into a scientific civilization.

Science is no longer confined to a few seriously devoted persons. Since life in the present world invariably warrants, to variable degrees, knowledge of scientific facts and laws, science has now become everyday science for everybody. Teaching of everyday science for everybody has become an unavoidable part of general education. Nobody questions its inclusion as a subject in the school curriculum. It is included in a school's curriculum for the same reasons as any other subject, but in addition science inculcates certain special values peculiar to it and which no other subject can provide. But besides satisfying the usual needs for its inclusion as a subject in the curriculum such as intellectual, cultural, moral, aesthetic, utilitarian and vocational values—science learning provides training in scientific method and also helps to develop a scientific attitude of mind in the learner. The qualities imbibed by the learner through learning science are of great value to a citizen living in the society. Hence, science is now made a compulsory subject in every system of school education right from the elementary stage.

Science teaching in schools, can and should make a difference in the lives of children and the difference should be on the positive side of the educational ladder. Much has been said about the importance of children's understanding the nature of the scientific enterprise. In a free society, scientific advancement is dependent upon the will of the people, their will as decision-making citizens to support it and their will as individuals to become scientists. Therefore, liberally educated people in a free society should understand the nature of the scientific enterprise, the social, economic, and political factors that effect its development and the personal satisfactions that come to one who pursues a career in it.

Science has been referred to as a self-corrective process of finding out. Or as Niels Bohr expressed it, 'science includes the methods by which man puts limiting values on his preconceptions'. Or as Percy bridgeman opined it, the methods of science consist of doing your demands to get the answer with no holds barred. Regardless of whether we refer to them as the methods of science, as problem solving, as inquiry or as discovery, there are processes of investigation in science that have been found to be effective in advancing our understanding of natural phenomena. Elements of the process have been defined in various ways and research has clearly indicated that pupils can be taught how to perform them in conducting their own investigations. Furthermore, as they learn to perform the process, they become more independent or self directive in their learning. To become independent in these ways meets a basic need of all children and thus represents a kind of satisfaction that can be achieved in no other way. If properly taught, science can help all children learn how to learn.

In questions of science Galileo Galilei once said 'the authority of a thousand is not worth the humble reasoning of a single individual.' While learning science, the learner develops certain faculties through reasoning and experimentation which no other subject can provide.

Considering science from the intellectual point of view, it is the most inexhaustible storehouse of knowledge. Since Nature is an inexhaustible source of knowledge, science as a subject, offers the widest range of knowledge to the learners. It has exposed the mankind to infinite avenues of knowledge in nature, living and non-living, the world we perceive and also the world beyond human perception thereby makes us conscious of the unknown to be explored.

Science, besides satisfying the intellectual curiosity of man and providing materials and media for intellectual exercise, has disciplinary effect on the minds of individuals. Since science covers the widest range of knowledge, the learner wonders at the intricacies and mysteries of the Universe, the known and the unknown. These tend to create a broader outlook in the life of the learner.

Science is universal in character and it has no barrier of any kind. The scientific revolution began in Western Europe where modern science was born but its home is now the whole world. The fruits of scientific discoveries in one country are enjoyed by the people all over the world. Science is not concerned with caste, creed or colour nor recognizes territorial barriers. Such a pattern inherent in science will definitely have an impact on the minds of the learners and is expected to help to develop broad-mindedness in them.

The study of science has several other disciplinary values. For instance, science is an interest-awakening subject and its pursuit demands persistent efforts, diligence and patience. Any experimentation in science requires keen observation, concentration of mind as well as accurate representation of facts. There is no place for prejudice or bias in science. Scientific pursuits warrant objective observation and impartial judgement. Engagement in any scientific activity, be it theoretical or experimental, therefore, pre-supposed intellectual honesty, preserverance, concentration of mind and broad-mindedness. In science we do not conclude or predict any thing on the basis of superstition, traditional belief or hear-say, unless the facts are based on proof. In science there is no place for sentiment or emotion except rationality. A scientific result to be acceptable must be valid for all cases.

In pursuing a scientific problem, one has to define the problem, plan the process, collect relevant data, formulate necessary hypotheses, repeat the processes if necessary, apply to specific cases before generalizing. During the process, one has to be logical and objective at every step. Thus, scientific pursuits demand such qualities as minute observation, scientific attitude of mind, persistence, preserverance, concentration of mind, accuracy of measurement, patience; logical, objective and unprejudiced judgement; respect for other's opinions, respect for truth, etc. These disciplinary qualities of mind, if cultivated through the teaching of science, may be carried over to manifest in the general behaviour of the learner. This will prove useful for living as an efficient social individual in the society. No other subject provides opportunities for inculcation of so many disciplinary qualities of the mind of the learners.

It is hardly necessary to elaborate the utilitarian or practical values of science. The present world is a world of science and technology. Every thing or every event happening around us demands some knowledge of simple scientific facts or principles. Without the elementary knowledge and information of science, we will be at a loss. Science is now everyday science for everybody.

The achievements and the benefits of science touch all sectors and all levels of the modern society. The modern man has applied science and technology for the well-being of mankind by inventing machines and by harnessing the resources of nature. The gifts of science have been profitably used for making life comfortable and raising the standard of living. But the use or abuse of the wonderful gifts of science depends on man and his mind. The recent advances in the field of science and technology and the wide application of the achievements of science in industry, agriculture, medicine, transport and communication as well as their uses in domestic life justify, more than ever, the utilitarian values of science.

Science has opened innumerable avenues for pursuing different vocations. A student of science can study engineering and technology, medicine, agriculture or any similar subject and make his career in that profession. In addition, scientific activities have given rise to many varieties of crafts and allied services. Science, therefore, gives opportunities for career-making and pursuing professions and vocations. In fact, if we refer to preparation of the individual for the future as one of the aims of education, then science, as a subject, is rightly serving this purpose. In this age of science and technology there is a demand for technical personnel. The maintenance and creation of new departments, new establishments need the services of engineers, scientists and technicians and there will always be need for research workers in new fields of science. Educationist Paul Fredman once said, science is no longer the preserve of a few completely—perhaps abnormally devoted men; it is becoming and increasingly will become, one of the major professions open to any young man of ability, demanding no more in the way of special bent or devotion than medicine or law. But like those other professions, it too will continue to offer a life with characteristic flavor; it will have its own professional standards and its own typical type of thinking and will call forth its practitioners its own loyalties.

Science has made a tremendous impact on the cultural life of the present day society which is a product of science. The thinking, feeling and actions of a modern man are practically guided by the effects of science. There is an involvement of science, direct or indirect, in all works as well as leisure of a modern man. Our habits and attitudes have also been affected by science.

The study of science brings behavioural change in the learner and enriches his character and personality. Science gives opportunity for creative thinking and constructive imagination. Further, science is a subject where ideas can be experimented upon and verified. The learner develops the habits of searching for the truth. These qualities affect the pattern of behaviour of the learner. The significant aspect of science is that whatever the student learns has immediate application in the world around him. This is educationally very sound.

In society, there will always be problems to be solved. One of the very useful outcomes of learning science is the development of problem solving skill. If properly cultivated through the teaching of science, the student can apply this skill to solve problems in his personal or social life.

One of the aims of modern education is to provide means for utilization of leisure especially in the industrialized societies. There is no end to interesting pursuits in science, intellectual or otherwise. Scientific activities provide the best hobbies and pass times for proper utilization or leisure.

At higher levels, arts and science are no way different. There can be no good piece of art without application of science, and on the other hand there is artistic or aesthetic element in all scientific activities. The great thinkers have always been stressing the need for the unity of science and arts, for they originate from the same root. In the modern civilization, scientific creations glorify arts and aesthetics and science may be said to be the modern substitute for arts in the sense that it is the result of the same kind of creative thought and action which have generated arts.

Arts and aesthetics are components of culture and civilization. The creation of the universe is a great piece of art. There is aesthetics in the mysteries and harmonies of nature. Saunders felt that 'there is an aesthetic side to the scientist's activities and to his contribution to human culture. On the lowest level he has the satisfaction of adding to the sum of human knowledge; on a higher level he enjoys the subtle pleasure of devising some hypothesis which fits a diversity of facts opening up new areas of knowledge. Appreciation of 'fitness of purpose', the suitability of an apparatus for the job for which it was designed, can give great inward satisfaction. There is a pleasing skill in avoiding or eliminating sources of errors and in particular the errors of human observation. Wonder is aroused by neatness with which some material quality or some living activity, can be sorted out from other qualities or activities for examination and demonstration. There is an elegance that runs through the logic and handiwork of the scientists. It is seen in the formulae of mathematicians, it is equally seen in the experiments and observations of great naturalists. The very simplicity of great generalizations of science stirs the imagination. With microscope and telescope the scientist opens up new worlds of wonder and beauty. A speck of living matter becomes a creature of incredible beauty, a snow flake more lovely than diamonds and a distant star becomes a universe. It is at this level that science shares equally with the arts; the privilege of contributing to the aesthetic development of the human race.

Culture in addition to knowledge, includes all activities, thoughts, feelings, attitudes, patterns of individual or social life of men. The study of science gives opportunity for the development of favourable traits of human character which become a positive contribution to the cultural life of the society. For instance, with science gaining ground and spreading its influence in the life of man, there has been a profusion of literature based in science. Scientific fiction, being interesting, adds to the cultural heritage of man. Similarly, the literature on history and development of science is no less interesting. It is the study of the origin and development of civilization itself and has developed into a separate branch of study which contributes to the cultural heritage.

The biographies of scientists incorporated in the science course develop a scientific attitude among the learners. The description of the pursuits of scientists, their tenacity and preserverance, etc., are worth reading. Such a study brings out the scientists' attitude towards science and their hopes and frustrations on their way to discovery. Sometimes, even after their invention or discovery, it takes a long time for social acceptance. The facts about the sacrifices of the scientists for the benefit of mankind stir one's imagination. The lives of Galileo, Watt, Curies and others show how the scientist has to suffer to make an original discovery. The lives of the scientists can inspire the minds of the young learners. It is believed that the study of science and the life of the scientists engenders praise worthy humility.

The study of the scientist's way of discovery is more interesting. It gives the learners an opportunity to grasp the essential steps of scientific method or procedure. For example, the story of the discovery of the Laws of Gravity by Sir Isaac Newton or the story of the discovery of the cause of malaria by Sir Ronald Ross, will help to make the meaning of science clear. It is useful to give the pupils, the idea how scientists sacrifice their personal comfort for the good of society. Broad-mindedness and selfless service to mankind are characteristics of their lives.

A scientist is a seeker of truth and scientific facts give a true picture of nature. In a scientific pursuit, it requires intellectual honesty at each step. In an experiment, one has to record correct data, collect authentic information and make objective interpretation of observations. Any thing other than truth will lead to wrong results. For exploration of the unknown, scientists have to proceed carefully on the basis of the true picture at each stage of the process. Intellectual honesty and love for truth coupled with sincerity of purpose and virtues are prerequisites in any scientific pursuit. In science ultimately truth prevails, because science is nothing, but truth. There can be no better moral value of a subject than this virtue.

Considering the importance of science, the science curriculum must incorporate all the provisions to fulfill the position and importance of science in human life and living.

REFERENCE

Bhaskara Rao, D. (1994). *Scientific Aptitude*. New Delhi : Ashish Publishing House.

Bhaskara Rao, Digumarti and Pushpa Latha Digumarti (1995). *Achievement in Science*. New Delhi : Discovery Publishing House.

Karla, R. N. (1976). *Innovations in Science Teaching*. New Delhi : Oxford and IBH Publishing Co.

6

OBJECTIVES OF SCIENCE

The science curriculum will be designed according to the objectives of the course. Many commissions and individuals have proposed different objectives for science teaching.

Education Commission (1964-66) stated that Science education must become an integral part of school education; and ultimately some study of science should become a part of all courses in the humanities and social sciences. The quality of science teaching is to be developed considerably so as to achieve its proper objectives and purposes. *viz*., to understand basic principles; to develop problem-solving. Analytical skills and ability; to apply them to the problems of material environments and social living besides promoting the spirit of enquiry and experimentation. Science strengthens commitments of man to free enquiry and search for truth as its highest duty and obligation. By its emphasis on reason and free enquiry, it even helps to lesson ideological tensions.

Although science is largely occupied with the understanding of Nature of present, its development is tending more and more to help man to understand himself and his place in the world in such developments. The commission observes that the pursuit of mere material affluence and power would be subordinated to that of higher values and the fulfillment of the needs of individual. This concept of mingling of science and spirituality is of special significance of Indian Education.

It is commonly felt that a child's education cannot be complete unless he has some knowledge of science irrespective of the field of study he wishes to pursue in latter life. Today the great advances in science rendered it absolutely necessary that a fundamental knowledge of science should be the 'sine qua non' of any person who was educated and who wished to lead a life which combined in itself something of scientific aspects of existence.

Objectives in any areas of curriculum should be regarded as the directions of growth and not as the ultimate ends to be completely reached. In this respect, science is not different from other branches. It is important that objectives should be selected towards which the growth and development of the individual may be directed from a very practical point of view. Objectives need to be selected and stated in such a way that progress towards their attainment may be appraised (Heiss, Obourn and Hoffman, 1950).

A judicious formulation and selection of worthwhile objectives for any school subject goes a long way in enriching and shaping both the teaching and testing in that subject and such objectives should be evolved in relation to the needs of the individual in his society. The three main sources for the formulation of the objectives are—

(1) the needs and capabilities of the pupil;

(2) the specific demands of his social environment, and

(3) the nature of the subject matter.

Science teachers have long recognized the need for sound objectives in curriculum planning. In an examination of over 3,000 statements written from 1901 to 1950 by secondary school teachers, Paul Hurd (1954) noted that the objectives of science teaching were the teacher's first consideration in planning curriculum. Objective strongly influence the organization of the curriculum and at the same time they provide the guidelines on the selection of teaching techniques.

National society for the study of Education in its Yearbook (1947) published the objectives under these categories, *viz.*

(1) functional information of habits.

(2) functional concepts.

(3) functional understanding of principles.

(4) instrumental skills,

(5) problem solving skills,

(6) attitudes,

(7) appreciations, and

(8) interests.

Bloom. *et al.* (1959) classified the educational objectives under three domains, *viz.*, the cognitive, the effective, and the psychomotor. The cognitive domain includes those objectives which deal with the recall or recognition of knowledge and the development of intellectual abilities and skills. The affective domain includes objectives which describe changes in interests, attitudes, values, and the development of appreciations and adequate adjustment. The work done in that period on manipulative or motor-skill was very less which includes motor activities.

Rai (1975) in his report on school Science Teaching stated that the main objectives for teaching of science should be—

1. To arouse the curiosity of the student about the world we live in and to encourage him to understand the various natural phenomena.
2. To train to acquire that habit of making observation in a planned way.
3. To develop in him science attitude.
4. To give him an idea how a scientist works.

The aims and objectives of teaching general science according to All India Seminar on Teaching of Science (1963) should be—

1. To familiarize the pupil with the world in which he lives and make him understand the impact of science on society so as to enable him to adjust himself to his environment.
2. To acquaint him with the scientific method and enable him to develop scientific attitude.

3. To give the pupil a historical perspective, so that he may understand the evolution of scientific development.

The Directorate of Extension programmes for Secondary education, Government of India, in its brochure on 'Evaluation in General Science' sets some of the objectives of teaching general science in secondary schools as—

1. The pupils studying general science should acquire knowledge of the fundamentals of science useful to all in everyday life.
2. They should develop the ability to apply the knowledge in everyday life.
3. They should acquire experimental skills such as :
   (*a*) handing apparatus and instruments;
   (*b*) arranging apparatus for an experiment; and
   (*c*) preserving apparatus, chemicals, specimens, models, etc.
4. They should acquire constructional skills such as ;
   (*a*) improvising simple instruments and appliances, and
   (*b*) repairing certain instruments and appliances of everyday life.
5. They should develop drawing skills such as:
   (*a*) drawing and sketching certain objects, instrument sand arrangements; and
   (*b*) photography in certain objects and specimens.
6. They should be able to locate reliable and recent information from appropriate sources.
7. They should be able to interpret scientific data given in various forms such as tabular, graphical, scientific, etc.
8. They should develop the power of minute observation of their surroundings.
9. They should develop the power of oral expression in science to discuss, argue, describe and raise questions using scientific terminology

10. They should develop the scientific method in thinking and action.
11. They should adopt the scientific attitude in making statements, accepting information and forming beliefs.
12. They should develop interest in scientific reading and hobbies.
13. They should be able to appreciate the impact of science on life, bath personal and social, the struggle through which science has advanced, and the inspiring works of the scientists.

The following similar set of objectives was formulated by the principals of Delhi Higher Secondary Schools in the third summer camp organized by the extension department of the Central Institute of Education, Delhi.

1. To develop in the student a scientific attitude.
2. To develop in the student critical thinking.
3. To enable the student to acquire the fundamentals of scientific method.
4. To develop in the student skill in laboratory techniques.
5. To enable the student to be creative.
6. To develop in the student the ability to apply scientific knowledge and principles to problems of everyday life and new situations.
7. To enable the student to comprehend scientific terms, concepts, symbols, various tables and their uses.
8. To enable the student to construct and interpret graphs, diagrams and models.
9. To enable the student to collect and interpret data for the solution of problems.
10. To enable the student to be familiar with the natural resources of his environment and their uses.
11. To enable the student to be familiar with the trends in modern science.
12. To enable the student to appreciate the beauty and order in nature.

Approach paper on science and mathematics in General Education (1985) developed by NCERT thought of the possibility of fulfilling the following objectives for secondary level for enabling the students—

1. To study a few aspects of physical and life sciences in detail with a special emphasis on those areas of concern like food, shelter, health, energy, nutrition, and major components of environment;
2. To appreciate the need of quantification in the scientific students;
3. To develop in science and ability to put the interest into action;
4. To manipulate tools, equipment in a proper manner;
5. To identify the factors operating in the environment; and
6. To collect data, classify and draw reasonable inferences.

These objectives of secondary stage are to be fulfilled along with the objectives of primary and middle stages which include - collection of information; classification of objects, events, etc.; identification of cause and effect relationship; development of scientific attitudes; acquainting with natural phenomena; giving emphasis to the relevance of science to daily life, etc.

Bhaskara Rao (1989) stated that a teacher must formulate some definite objectives and specifications. . . . in order to achieve desirable behavioural changes among pupils. He emphasized on objectives such as knowledge, understanding, application, skill, interest, scientific attitudes, and appreciation.

The objectives of science explained by various individuals, commissions and conferences are concerned to biology also. Certain specific objectives are also developed only for biology. Let us observe then now.

First Asian Regional conference on school Biology (1966) held at Manila recommended the following aims and objectives of school biology teaching in Asia.

1. To develop and instil in student the scientific attitude of inquiry and experimentation.

2. To provide sufficient understanding of the concepts o biology to enable students to become worthy citizens o' the world.
3. To provide the opportunities for a practical understanding of the method of biologists which give them confidence to attempt the solution of problems which they have to face in their individual and social lives.
4. To give the student the incentive to pursue the study at higher levels of biology and related fields.
5. To encourage respect and feeling for living things.

And the latest national Policy on education—1986 states that 'Science Education will be strengthened so as to develop in the child well defined abilities and values such as the spirit of inquiry, creativity, objectivity, the courage to question, and on aesthetic sensibility.

All the above aims and objectives of science stress, directly or indirectly, the importance of scientific attitude, scientific aptitude, skills, abilities and interests. And also we can sense that a pupil of biology should be in a position to utilize his classroom learning in daily life through proper achievement and application.

REFERENCE

Bhaskara Rao, Digumarti and Digumarti Pushpa Latha (1995). Achievement in Science. New Delhi : Discovery Publishing House.

Bhaskara Rao, D. (1995). Jeevasashtra Bodhana (Teaching of Biology). Guntur : Creative Press.

Bhaskara Rao, D., editor (1996). National Policy on Education, 2 Vols. New Delhi : Anmol Publications Pvt. Ltd.

INSTRUCTIONAL OBJECTIVES

Objectives decide the teaching learning processes in a curriculum and they determine the place of a subject in the curriculum in shaping the content.

The objectives of teaching science should be formulated on a solid philosophical, psychological, sociological and scientific footing. The utility, appropriateness, practicability, and timeliness of the objectives should be considered. The main sources for the formulation of objectives are-the needs and capabilities of the learner, the needs of the society, the nature of the subject matter, the feasibility constraints, and the nature of the educational system.

The objectives thus formulated should be specific, useful, unambiguous, feasible and in accordance with the aim of education.

The objectives have been mainly divided into 3 domains, viz., cognitive, Affective, and Psychomotor, by Bloom and his associates. Here, the objectives and specifications developed by national council of Educational Research and Training, India are gives for Biology, Physics and Chemistry.

INSTRUCTIONAL OBJECTIVES OF BIOLOGY

1) The pupil acquires KNOWLEDGE of biological terms, facts, concepts, principles and processes.

Expected Learning Outcomes

The pupil

1. *recalls* biological facts, concepts, principles etc.
2. *recognizes* biological apparatus, specimen facts, concepts, principles etc.

2) The pupil develops UNDERSTANDING of biological terms, concepts, principles and processes.

Expected Learning Outcomes

The pupil

1) *translates* biological terms, symbols, formulae, data etc. from one form to the other.

2) *Cites illustrations* of biological principles, concepts, phenomena etc.

3) *identifies* relationship between various concepts, processes etc.

4) *detects* errors in biological experiments, processes etc

5) *compares* biological terms, concepts, principles etc.

6) *classifies* specimen., facts, concepts etc.

7) *interprets* biological concepts, data, graphs.

8) *explains* biological concepts, principles, processes and phenomena.

3) The pupil APPLIES knowledge and understanding of Biology in unfamiliar situations.

Expected Learning Outcomes

The pupil

1) *analyses* the given data or observed biological facts and phenomena to identify different components and their relationships.

2) *formulates* hypotheses on the basis of given data or observed facts and phenomena.
3) *suggests* appropriate and alternative experimental procedures, for a given purpose.
4) *gives* reason for certain causes and effects in biological phenomena.
5) *draws* conclusions, generalisations and inferences from the gives data.
6) *predicts* biological phenomena from the observed facts or given data.
7) *judges* the relevance, adequacy and consistency of biological concepts and principles in the given data, experimental procedures and other biological phenomena.

4) The pupil develops SKILL in

A. Drawing diagrams, charts, graphs, sketches etc.
B. manipulating apparatus and instruments.
C. collecting, mounting and preserving specimens.
D. observing biological specimens, phenomena structures, etc.
E. reporting biological information, evidence and results, using scientific terminology.

Expected Learning Outcomes

A. Drawing skills

The pupil

1) *draws* diagrams, charts etc. of observed or given specimens, material, apparatus and instruments *faithfully*.
2) *completes* the incomplete diagrams correctly.
3) *recognizes* the various structures in the sketches and diagrams concerned with various functions.
4) *labels* sketches and diagrams methodically and correctly.
5) *draws* sketches and diagrams neatly at a *reasonable* speed.

B. Manipulative skills

6) *arranges* the apparatus systematically.
7) *handles* the apparatus and instruments carefully.
8) *reads* the instruments and apparatus with precision.
9) *maintains* the apparatus and instruments in order.
10) *improvises* apparatus and models, using locally available materials.

C. Collecting, Mounting and Preserving Skills

11) *locates* the right habitual for a particular specimen.
12) *gathers* the required specimen during the appropriate seasons.
13) *handles* efficiently the appropriate equipment and instruments for collection of specimens.
14) *uses* the appropriate material economically to mount the specimens.
15) *selects* the right preservatives for different specimens.

D. Observing Skills

The pupil:

16) *notices* the relevant details in the given specimens and biological phenomena carefully.
17) *reads* the apparatus and instruments correctly.
18) *discriminates* between closely related structures, parts and specimens accurately.
19) *locates* the desired parts in a dissection or specimen exactly.
20) *detects* errors in experimental set-up and procedures.

E. Reporting Skills

The pupil:

21) *selects* the appropriate biological terminology in describing specimens and biological phenomena.
22) *uses* the appropriate terms in proper sequence and right context.

23) *puts* the ides in clear, precise and unambiguous terms.
24) *records* the evidence or data from various sources faithfully.
25) *tabulates* the data or evidence in appropriate form.
26) *presents* the biological information on a logical order.
27) *summarizes* the data and evidences in accordance with the desired pattern.

5) The pupil APPRECIATES the biological phenomena in nature and the role of Biology in human welfare.

Expected learning Outcomes

The pupil:

1) *recognizes* the unity of life in diversity of form.
2) *signifies* the inter-relationship among various types of organisms.
3) *develops* insight into the means and methods of biology used for exploiting nature for human welfare.
4) *understands* the role of tools and techniques of biology in the development of life sciences.
5) *realises* the struggle for existence among living organisms and the role of adaptation for adjustment.
6) *gets thrilled* at the beauty of nature and is convinced of the role of biology in developing aesthetic sense in human beings.
7) *feels* the importance of biology as inquiry in exploring the secrets of nature.
8) *visualizes* the impact of biology on Social behaviours.

6) The pupil develops INTEREST in the living world.

Expected Learning Outcomes

The pupil:

1) *enjoys* collecting, mounting, preserving and displaying biological, specimens.
2) *participates voluntarily* in biological club activities.

3) *frequently* writes biological articles in school and other magazines.
4) *visiti of his own* the botanical gardens, zoos and museums and other places of biological interest.
5) *undertakes* hobbies such as improvising biological models, gardening, and field-study *in his spare time.*
6) *reads* regularly the books and journals on the life and works of biologist *with pleasure.*

7) The pupil develops SCIENTIFIC ATTITUDE towards biological phenomena.

Expected learning Outcomes

The pupil

1) *becomes inquisitive* about the biological phenomena.
2) *is open minded* in accepting others' view points.
3) *believes* in cause and effect relationship.
4) *does not accept* things without proof of justification.
5) *suspends judgements* in the absence of adequate evidence.
6) *shows* perserverence in undertaking biological activities.
7) *manifests* intellectual honesty in reporting results of experiments.

INSTRUCTIONAL OBJECTIVES IN CHEMISTRY

1) The pupil acquires KNOWLEDGE of terms, concepts, processes, techniques and principles relating to chemistry.

Expected Learning Outcomes

The pupil

1) recalls the terms, facts, concepts, processes, principles etc.
2) recognizes the terms, facts, concepts, principles and processes.

2) The pupil develops UNDERSTANDING of terms, concepts, facts, theories, principles and techniques of chemistry.

Expected Learning Outcomes

The Pupil

1 translates symbolic statements into verbal statements and vice versa.

2 illustrates terms, concepts and principles by citing examples.

3. identifies relationships, between various concepts, reactions, chemicals, terms, etc.

4. compares between related terms, concepts, reactions, and other chemical phenomena.

5. uses appropriate units to express various quantities.

6. classifies substances, facts, concepts, reactions, phenomena etc.

7. locates an error in a known experimental set up, statements and apparatus, and rectifies it.

8. performs simple, chemical calculations by substituting the formulae.

9. extrapolates from known information.

10. explains chemical reaction, concepts, phenomena.

3) The pupils APPLIES knowledge of concepts and principles to new or unfamiliar situations pertaining to chemistry.

Expected Learning Outcomes

The pupil

1. analyses situation related to chemical data, phenomena etc.

2. formulates hypothesis on the basis of given or observed findings, facts, process data etc.

3. suggests procedure to test hypothesis using the underlying concepts, principles, laws etc.

4. establishes relationships, between causes and effects in the chemistry involved in the situations.

5. draws inference using concepts, principles, processes etc. in newer situation.
6. suggests new methods or alternative apparatus, chemical and procedures to test a hypothesis or to verify the inferences.
7. gives reasons for happenings, reactions etc. in unfamiliar cases.
8. predicts chemical changes on the basis of known facts and principles.
9. judges relevance, adequacy, consistency, fallacy etc. in the given data, observations, changes etc.

4) The pupil develop SKILLS required in chemistry such as manipulating skills, observational skills related to practical work.

A. Manipulative Skills

The pupil

1. arranges the apparatus systematically.
2. handles the apparatus and chemicals properly.
3. reads the instrument with correct procedure.
4. revises appropriate apparatus.
5. keeps the apparatus and chemicals in order.
6. improvises apparatus and uses alternatives efficiently.
7. prepares a sequential plan for observation.

B. Observational Skills

8. reads the instruments with precision and in sequential manner.
9. notices the relevant changes in chemical reactions using senses.
10. detects errors in experimental set ups and procedures.
11. discriminates between the closely related substances, reactions, phenomena etc.

C. Reporting Skills

12. arrives at concordant value, calculates and obtains correct results in the volumetric analysis.

13. infers correct results (e.g. group tests in qualitative analysis on the basis of observations).
14. uses proper formulae to communicate.
15. reports the results in a systematic manner.

5) The pupil APPRECIATES achievements in chemistry and its role in nature and society.

Expected Learning Outcomes

The Pupil

1. shows thrill and excitement at the discoveries in chemistry and chemical processes occurring in nature.
2. enjoys collection and exhibiting pictures of chemists' chemical activities and cuttings about developments in chemistry.
3. realises the role of various types of reactions introducing spectacular and colourful experiments such as colour changes, crystal development, chemical garden etc.
4. feels thrilled in clearing his own experimental achievements as well as those of others.
5. gets satisfaction in reading about the achievement and sacrifices of great chemists.

6) The pupil develops INTEREST in chemical pursuits.

Expected Learning Outcomes

The pupil

1. collects specimens of material such as minerals voluntarily.
2. reads with satisfaction extra literature from books and journals on allied topics in chemistry.
3. performs extra experiments in his spare time.
4. engages in chemical hobbies and science clubs activities.
5. visits places of chemical interest such as factories. Science clubs, museums, exhibitions and allied institutions to get additional information in chemistry.

6. takes part in debates, lectures, paper reading etc. on his own.
7. enjoys preparing models and charts and collects informations, from books and journals.
8. improvises apparatus for his experiments without any ones guidance.

7) The pupil develops scientific ATTITUDES toward chemical phenomena.

Expected Learning Outcomes

The pupil

1. does not accept or reject anything without valid reasons.
2. has a keen desire to know how and why of anything that happens.
3. is prepared to face hazards in his investigations.
4. admits his mistakes unhesitatingly.
5. suspends judgement till it is repeatedly confirmed.
6. is unbiased in his approach to problems.
7. does not ignore any detail even if it is of not direct relevance to the work in hand.
8. shows intellectual honesty in reporting data, procedure and results.

INSTRUCTIONAL OBJECTIVES IN PHYSICS

1) The pupil acquires KNOWLEDGE of terms, facts, concepts, definitions, fundamental laws, principles and processes in the filed of Physics.

Expected learning Outcomes

The pupil

1. recalls, terms, facts, concepts principles and processes related to Physics.
2. recognizes various terms, facts, concepts and principles of Physics.

2) The pupil develops UNDERSTANDING of terms, facts, concepts fundamental laws, principles and processes in the field of Physics.

Expected Learning Outcomes

The pupil

1. translates verbal statements into symbolic equation and vice versa.
2. gives illustrations of principles of Physics.
3. sees relationship between cause and effects of physical phenomena.
4. compares the various methods, concepts, principles etc.
5. detects errors in given statements, circuit, arrangements etc. and rectifies the same.
6. classifies as per criteria, the objects, facts, concepts etc.
7. gives explantation of physical phenomena, principles, concepts, etc.
8. reads and interprets graphs representing physical quantities and relationships.
9. solves numerical problems involving physical quantities principles, concepts, etc.
10. recognizes the significance and limitations of physical principles.

3) The pupil APPLIES his knowledge and understanding of Physics to unfamiliar situations.

Expected Learning Outcomes

The pupil

1. analyses the unfamiliar situations, statements, observations, evidences etc.
2. formulates hypotheses based on data, observation etc.
3. devises new experiments for verification of the hypotheses and for known laws and principles etc.
4. establishes relationship between cause and effect, the known and unknown.

5. selects the principles relevant to a phenomenon.
6. gives reasons to explain unfamiliar physical phenomena.
7. draws inferences and conclusions from the given data or observed phenomena.
8. makes predictions on the basis of data, evidence etc.
9. judges the relevance, adequacy and consistency in statements, data, evidences, etc.

4) The Pupil develops

A. Observing skills

B. Manipulating skills

C. Drawing skills

D. Reporting skills

A. Observing Skills

The pupil

1. reads instruments, measures physical quantities, accurately.
2. takes observations in a systematic and sequential manner.
3. takes the number of observations necessary.
4. reads graphs accurately.

B. Manipulating Skills

The pupil

5. selects appropriate apparatus, tools etc.
6. checks the tools, apparatus, equipment regarding its working
7. knows the limitation of the apparatus etc.
8. sets the apparatus in a proper way
9. performs the experiment with reasonable speed, accuracy, neatness.
10. makes correct substitution in formula (if any).
11. calculates the result accurately.

12. interprets data and draws conclusion.

C. Drawing Skills

13. daws neat, proportionate and correct diagrams.
14. labels the diagram correctly.
15. shows direction of force, say of current.
16. traces the circuit diagram correctly.
17. draws graph, selecting proper scale.

D. Reporting Skills

18. presents the observations in an appropriate manner/ sequence.
19. presents the calculations/results in proper sequence/ manner/units.
20. calculates (and compares) the percentage error etc. using appropriate symbols and formulae.
21. explains orally the procedures, precautions and limitations of the equipments, apparatus and experiments.

5) The pupil APPRECIATES the contribution of Physics to human happiness.

Expected learning Outcomes

The pupil

1. follows and adjusts to the impact of Physics on society and individual.
2. derives pleasure in understanding the scientific advances in inter-planetary travels, radio astronomy, electronics etc.
3. feels that more inventions and discoveries are possible.
4. shows respect and admiration for great scientists.
5. manifests a spirit of scientific enquiry.

6) The pupil develops INTEREST in the world of Physical science.

Expected Learning Outcomes

The pupil

2. reads scientific literature and biographies of prominent scientists with satisfaction.
3. takes up scientific hobbies in his spare time.
4. takes part in science talks and debates willingly.
5. visits places of scientific interest on his own.
6. organises and actively participates in science club activities.
7. contributes articles on topics of scientific interest frequently.
8. enjoys observing natural and man-made surroundings.

7) The pupil develops scientific ATTITUDE through the study of physical science.

Expected Learning Outcomes

The pupil

1. respects the teacher of physics.
2. records and interprets his observations honestly.
3. bases his judgements on verified facts and not on opinion.
4. willing to consider new ideas and discoveries.
5. is prepared to reconsider his own judgement.
6. develops independent thinking.
7. pursues his activities with precision and consistency undaunted by failures.
8. shows spirit of team work, self-help and self-reliance.
9. realises the danger in the misuse of scientific knowledge.

TRENDS IN ELEMENTARY SCHOOL SCIENCE

Teachers, principals, and supervisors need to study relevant trends in the science curriculum and thus update the objectives, learning activities, and evaluation procedures utilized presently in the elementary school science program. Which are selected relevant trends in elementary school science that could be implemented?

EXPERIMENTING IN THE SCIENCE CURRICULUM

Each unit of study should stress the importance of using related science experiments. In fact, experimentation should be a major way of obtaining concepts and generalizations for pupils in the curriculum area of science. This is true for the following reasons:

1. Scientists in a laboratory setting perform experiments as a means of gathering information.
2. Problem solving can be emphasized in ongoing units of study in science such as identifying a problem, gathering information pertaining to the problem, developing a hypothesis (or hypotheses), testing the hypothesis (or hypotheses), and

developing needed modifications and revisions of the stated hypothesis, if necessary. Problem solving needs to be stressed in all curriculum areas in the elementary school as well as in life.

3. Pupils must skills relating to critical thinking when content is evaluated pertaining to ultimately developing a hypothesis. Critical thinking is important in all curriculum areas in the elementary school as well as in life.
4. Pupils need to become careful observers in ongoing learning activities involving science. Too frequently, learners want to jump to hasty conclusions pertaining to the outcome or outcomes of a science experiment. Pupils, however, should carefully observe what is happening during an experiment and base their conclusions on what has been observed. In units of study in elementary school science and in the natural environment, pupils may be guided to observe facets of the following.
   (a) leaves, twigs, rocks and minerals, different kinds of soil, trees, grass, and clouds.
   (b) birds, fish, turtles, frogs, and diverse animals included in the category of mammals.
   (c) animals without backbones such as worms, grasshoppers, bees, oysters, crabs, spiders, and ants.
   (d) the effect of heating selected liquids, solids, and grass.
   (e) the hardness of different kinds of rocks and minerals.
   (f) objects and items attracted or repelled by magnets.
   (g) the effects of a grass covering on soil having a hilly contour.

READING CONTENT IN SCIENCE

Pupils gain much valuable content in ongoing units of study in science through reading of ideas. Reading sources in elementary school science may include the following.

1. elementary school science textbooks.
2. general encyclopedias as well as science encyclopedias.
3. library books containing science content.
4. content from basal readers obtaining information pertaining to science.

5. pamphlet, leaflets, and related sources containing content in the area of science.

When reading content in science, pupils need to read for a variety of purposes such as:

1. gaining relevant concepts, e.g. liquids, solids, gases, magnetism, electricity, electromagnets, electrons, protons, neutrons, compounds, and elements.
2. acquiring generalizations, e.g. liquids, solids, and gases basically expand when heated. There are exceptions, such as water, a liquid turning to ice, a solid.
3. gaining facts, e.g., stegosaurus, allosaurus, tyrannosaurus rex, and the brontosaurus were dinosaurs that lived during the Mesozoic era.
4. obtaining directions, e.g. reading directions to make science equipment in ongoing units of study, e.g. magnets, electromagnets, and develop a complete circuit through parallel and series wiring.
5. gaining sequential ideas, e.g. reading content to notice the order of relative durations of geological eras— Precambrian, Paleozoic, Mesozoic, and Cenozoic.
6. thinking critically about content read, e.g., noticing factual statements as contrasted with statements of opinion or accurate statements from those which are inaccurate.
7. thinking creatively pertaining to ideas gained from reading, e.g. stating a hypothesis pertaining to a problem area prior to conducting a related experiment. Thus, the learner presents a unique original hypothesis before a science experiment is performed relating to an ongoing unit of study.

CONDUCTING EXCURSIONS

Pupils with teacher guidance need to experience reality. Too frequently, the science curriculum has presented abstract learnings to pupils largely. It is important for pupils to experience reality for the following reasons;

1. Pupils may then gain accurate concepts, generalizations, and main ideas.
2. Learners desire a variety of learning activities rather than

sameness in experiences.

3. concrete situations, such as the taking of excursions, are a way of learning for pupils.
4. Pupils may be guided to sequence their own learnings in concrete situations.

Excursions should be taken under the following circumstances only:

1. The place to be visited is free from danger for learners.
2. No reasonable substitution can be made for the excursion in terms of other learning experiences.
3. Parental or guardian permission has been given in writing for taking the excursion. Duplicated forms can be developed readily for obtaining permission for pupils to go on excursions.
4. Adequate guide service is available to aid learners in achieving optimal development during the excursion.
5. The excursion helps pupils achieve relevant objectives in an ongoing science unit.
6. Pupils perceive purpose or reasons for taking the excursion.
7. Content presented during the excursion is meaningful and understandable to pupils.

There are many units of study in elementary school science in which related meaningful excursions may be appropriate for pupils:

1. If pupils are studying a unit on 'The Pond Community', they may actually visit a pond site with teacher guidance. Prior to visiting a pond community, the teacher should guide pupils to perceive purpose for the excursion. A set of pictures or a filmstrip presentation may set the stage for pupils participating in the excursion. From these learning experiences, pupils may be stimulated to ask questions such as:
   (a) What kind of life generally is in evidence in a pond?
   (b) What is the surrounding environment like adjacent to a specific pond?
   (c) How can pond communities be kept clean?
   (d) How does a contaminated pond affect human beings?

The identification of problem areas by pupils provides readiness activities prior to pupils visiting a pond community. The actual excursion can provide answers to pupils related to the identified problem areas.

2. If pupils are studying a unit of "Preventing Soil Erosion," they may visit an area where:
   (a) gully erosion or sheet erosion has occurred.
   (b) steps have been taken to prevent erosion, e.g., grass has been seeded, terraces have been build, strip-cropping is in evidence, and trees have been planted.

Observations made by pupils need to be discussed to reinforce and clarify learnings.

USING CONSTRUCTION ACTIVITIES

Pupils with teacher leadership should have ample opportunities to engage in construction activities in ongoing units of study in science. The following are selected values pupils may attain from participating in construction activities:

1. Eye-hand coordination may be developed by pupils. Thus, psychomotor skills (use of the finer or larger muscles) are being emphasized in units of study pertaining to science.
2. The actual making of science equipment can be psychologically sound for learners in that creativity is being emphasized in the science curriculum.
3. There needs to be balance between and among cognitive, psychomotor, and affective objectives since life itself consists of activities in these three domains.
4. Pupils can actually use science equipment made in ongoing units of study. Not all equipment used in science experiments should, of course, be commercially purchased. Active involvement rather than passive learning is involved when pupils plan, develop, and evaluate what has been constructed in terms of science equipment and materials. Feelings of participation on the part of pupils are important in the elementary curriculum.
5. Pupils participating in construction activities can open future doors to vocational and a vocational interests. Each pupil

should have opportunities to discover his/her interests and develop these talents to the maximum possible.

Ultimately, pupils should have some questions that need answering after experiencing appropriate readiness activities. The contents of the telecast may provide answers to these question.

1. Actual viewing of the telecast. The contents of the telecast, of course, will guide learners to attain the stated objectives in the guide. Also, the readiness activities prior to viewing the telecast should aid pupils to attach meaning to concepts and generalizations contained in the presentation.

During the time that pupils are viewing the telecast, the teacher should—

(a) supervise pupils so that maximum attention is given by learners to the telecast.

(b) have the television set properly adjusted so that clarity of ideas may be gained by learners.

(c) have pupils seated at appropriate places in order that all learners can acquire needed content from the television presentation.

2. Follow-up activities. After viewing the telecast, pupils need appropriate learning experiences to reinforce as well as develop acquired concepts and generalizations in greater depth. The teacher may guide pupils in follow-up learning activities such as:

(a) having pupils do research using a variety of reference sources to find out how igneous, sedimentary, and metamorphic rocks are formed.

(b) showing and discussing a filmstrip with leaners pertaining to how rocks are formed.

(c) taking learners on an excursion to notice how rocks are utilized in buildings and other human-made features in the environment.

(d) having pupils collect and develop a display of labeled rocks in the class setting.

(e) guiding pupils in completing drawings pertaining to selected igneous, metamorphic, and sedimentary rocks.

(f) having pupils predict future findings of rocks and future uses of rocks in the human-made part of the environment.

The teacher then must guide pupils to use what has been acquired from the actual viewing of a telecast.

USING FILMS, FILMSTRIPS, AND SLIDES

The teacher should made ample use of audio-visual aids such as films, filmstrips, and slides. Pupils can see movement and reality in motion picture film presentations. It is difficult, however, to stop a film presentation at a given point for discussion purposes. The use of slides and filmstrips, of course, provides ample opportunities to stop a presentation and discuss the contents when needed. In fact, it is highly recommended that pupils raise questions and present related ideas pertaining to any frame in a filmstrip or any one slide. Clarification of ideas is important in any learning experience. The following experiences are important for pupils prior to viewing an audio-visual presentation:

1. Introductory activities. Pupils must experience selected learning activities prior to the audio-visual presentation in order that interest, motivation, and purpose are developed and maintained. If pupils, for example, are to view an audio-visual presentation on "The Human Body", they may, as introductory activities, participate in—
   (a) discussing how to develop and maintain good health.
   (b) using a microscope to look at onion cells.
   (c) developing standards for safe living in the environment.
   (d) discussing foods to be eaten to maintain good health.
2. Follow-up activities. After the audio-visual presentation has been completed, pupils with teacher guidance may participate in—
   (a) doing research from a variety of reference sources on developing and maintaining good health. Pupils may divide into committees for this activity and report their findings to members of other committees.
   (b) drawing pictures of different kinds of cells, e.g., done, skin, and blood cells. Various reference sources need

investigation to provide background information.

(c) evaluating the home and school environment in terms of safety standards developed during the introductory activities.

(d) planning and serving a meal which would stress proper nutrition for pupils.

USING WRITING ACTIVITIES IN THE SCIENCE CURRICULUM

The language arts skills of writing should receive adequate emphasis in the elementary school science program. If pupils, for example, are studying a unit on "Plants, Animals, and the Seasons," they many engage in diverse kinds of writing experiences.

1. develop an outline. Each pupil with teacher direction may develop an outline pertaining to content that has been read relating to an ongoing unit of study. The outline should contain a title. Main divisions should include Roman numerals. Subdivisions may be presented with capital letters in sequence. Details may present the finer points of each subdivision. Hindu-Arabic numerals should represent each detail. The accuracy of an outline can be checked in terms of criteria such as the following:

   (a) Does the title cover the contents of the outline comprehensively?

   (b) Does each main division (represented by Roman numerals) relate directly to the title?

   (c) Does each item in the subdivision relate to the intended main division in the outline?

   (d) Do the details (represented by Hindu-Arabic numerals) relate directly to the intended subdivision?

A correctly developed outline should generally follow this format:

Title

1. Main Division

   A. Subdivision

   B. Subdivision

   C. Subdivision

1. Detail
2. Detail

II. Main Division

A. Subdivision

B. Subdivision

1. Detail
2. Detail

To have consistency in an outline, all parts should contain either sentences or phrases. Generally, if Roman numeral I is inherent in the outline, Roman numeral II must also be present. Additional main divisions may be added as needed. If subdivision A is utilized in the outline, subdivision B should also be inherent. Additional subdivisions may be added as needed. The same pattern would follow when utilizing details.

2. develop a written report. The content of the outline may be utilized to develop a written report. Written reports may deal with—

   (a) summaries of experiments conducted in ongoing units of study in science.

   (b) diary entries kept by pupils on a daily basis pertaining to understandings, skills, and attitudes acquired. Members on a committee should be rotated in writing these diary entries.

   (c) logs kept on a sequential basis relating directly to what pupils have achieved in an ongoing unit of study in science. Content in a log would pertain to learnings acquired during a longer period of time than on a daily basis, such as ideas recorded once a week.

   (d) content written on a particular topic chosen by a child or a committee of learners. Thus, in a unit on "Weather and How It Affects Us," reports may be written on the following areas:

   — what causes rain to fall.

   — different kinds of clouds, e.g., cumulus, cirrus, et.

al.

— weather forecasting.

— tornadoes, cyclones, and hail.

— sleet, snow, and frost.

— the monsoon climate, Mediterranean climate, desert areas, and jungle regions.

In developing written reports, the following concepts should be emphasized by pupils as readiness would permit:

— unity of ideas in a paragraph.

— appropriate sequence of paragraphs.

— thorough development of content within a paragraph.

— creative and critical thinking inherent in the written product.

— correct spelling of words.

— legible handwriting.

— proper capitalization, punctuation, and usage.

Ideas must come first in any written product. The mechanics of writing such as correct spelling of words, legible handwriting, and proper capitalization, punctuation, and usage are of secondary importance.

3. write poetry. Pupils can reveal previously gained learnings in science by writing poems. Thus, learners may reveal acquired understanding, skills, and attitudinal objective in ongoing units of study as a result of engaging in the writing of diverse kinds and forms of poetry. Creative thinking is emphasized thoroughly when pupils exhibit spontaneous, unique ideas as a result of writing selected poems. The following kinds of poems may be written by learners:

(a) Haiku poetry. Pupils should possess needed prerequisite learnings before participating in the writing of haiku poems, or any other kind of learning activity. Haiku poems contain three lines-five syllables, seven syllables, and five syllables in sequence. Generally, haiku poems contain content dealing with the natural environment. Selected units of study in elementary school science may then provide relevant content. Illustrations may be drawn by learners related to the written content.

The learning environment needs to be arranged so that pupils are intrinsically motivated in wanting to write haiku poetry. Content in selected slides, pictures, filmstrips, films, and the outdoor environment may aid in setting the stage for learners in desiring to write haiku poetry. If pupils, for example, are studying a unit on "Wildlife in Our Community," ultimately, from a rich learning environment, individual pupils may choose a topic to write about.

Cardinals

Happy Cardinals
Flying, hovering, gliding
Freshly out of sight.

This poem contains three lines following the five, seven, five sequence in terms of syllables per line. Pupils inductively may learn to distinguish haiku from other forms of creative writing. The teacher may read selected haiku poems to pupils. These poems may be printed on the chalkboard. Learners may then be guided in developing relevant generalizations pertaining to what a haiku poem is.

(b) free verse. Pupils do not need to have ending words rhyme when writing free verse. The lines may vary from each other as to length when free verse is written. Free verse then is a very open-ended approach in the writing of poetry. From a stimulating learning environment, pupils may select a title for writing verse following tenets of free verse. If pupils are studying a unit on "Proper Nutrition and diet," free verse may be written on—

Drinking Milk
Protein Foods
Carbohydrates
Starches
Staying Healthy.

Pupils voluntarily may wish to share their written products with others, thus noticing how content may vary from free verse to free verse.

(c) couplets, triplets, and quatrains. Pupils should have ample opportunities to engage in writing verse where diverse patterns of rhyme are inherent. Couplets contain two lines of rhymed verse, whereas triplets have three lines with all ending words rhyming. Quatrains contain four lines; the first and second lines as well as the third and fourth lines may rhyme. There may be other lines which rhyme in a quatrain such as lines one and three as well as lines two and four. The lines in a couplet, a triplet, and a quatrain should be somewhat uniform in length.

Pupils should be stimulated through a variety of learning experiences to write verse creatively. If pupils, for example, are studying a unit on "The Use of Simple Machines," the stage may be set for creative writing of verse by having pupils—

(a) Look at and discuss simple machines such as the lever, screw, wedge, pulley, wheel and axle, and the inclined plane.

(b) observe and evaluate pictures showing diverse simple machines.

(c) discuss the uses of simple machines observed in the surrounding environment of the school.

(d) read about and appraise the history of simple machines.

Ultimately, pupils may become stimulated to write creative verse. The following are examples of diverse kinds of rhyming verse:

(a) couplet

The man was working with a wedge.
Nearby was a fence containing hedge.

(b) triplet

He tried to use a lever.
The rock was moved, never.
Nonetheless, he moved objects ever.

4. Other forms of written work. There are many additional kinds of writing activities that pupils may participate in such as
   (a) writing plays, announcements, and notices.
   (b) wirting biographies of famous scientists.

ART WORK IN THE SCIENCE CURRICULUM

Learning activities involving art work can do much to enrich the elementary school science curriculum. Thus, the science teacher must provide a variety of learning experiences involving art in the science program.

1. **Developing murals.** Pupils in a committee with teacher guidance may plan and develop a mural pertaining to an ongoing unit of study in science. Thus, if pupils, for example are studying a unit on "animals with Backbones," they may decide upon scenes involving—
   (a) diverse kids of fish.
   (b) amphibians, e.g., toads and frogs.
   (c) reptiles, e.g., snakes, turtles.
   (d) various types of birds.
   (e) mammals, e.g., human beings, monkey, chimpanzees, gorillas.
2. **Developing friezes.** A series of pictures developed by a committee of pupils is inherent in cooperatively planning and implementing the frieze concept in art work. A variety of media should be available to pupils when working on a frieze. Thus, crayons, colored chalk, water colors, colored pencils, and finger paints should be readily accessible at the frieze center. If pupils, for example, are studying a unit on "Animals Without Backbones," they may develop a series of illustrations (a Frieze) on—
   (a) protozoans, e.g., the ameba, the paramecium, and the euglena.
   (b) porifera (sponges).
   (c) coelenteratas, e.g. hydras, jellyfish, coral, and sea anemones.
   (d) platyhelminths (flatworms), e.g., planarian, flukes, and tapeworms.

(e) aschelminthes (roundworms), e.g., hookworm, ascaris, and the trichinella.

(f) annelida (segmented worms), e.g., earthworm and sand-worm.

(g) echiondermata (spiny animals), e.g., starfish, the sea urchin, the sea cucumber, and the sand dollar.

(h) mollusca (shellfish), e.g., clams, scallops, mussels, oysters, slugs, and snails.

(i) arthropoda, e.g., shrimp, lobster, crayfish, and crabs.

Insects also are members of this phylum-praying mantis, grasshopper, walking stick, dragonflies, ladybugs, and potato bettles.

3. **Developing individual pictures.** To reveal what has been learned during and after the time a unit has been in progress, pupils individually may complete an illustration pertaining to a relevant concept or generalization. If learners for example, are studying a unit, "The Human Body and How it Works, " each pupil may select to develop an illustration pertaining to—

   (a) the digestive system, e.g. a carefully planned and prepared picture, using a variety of art media, may be developed on the stomach and digestion.

   (b) the muscular system, e.g., an illustration may be completed pertaining to the heart, an involuntary muscle, which cannot be controlled by the human body, or to voluntary muscles which can be controlled by the human being.

   (c) the circulatory system. The individual pupil may choose to complete a drawing on the heart, the blood vessels, and general circulation of the blood.

   (d) the respiratory system, e.g., the lungs, bronchial tubes, the throat, the voice box, the nose, nasal passages, and the windpipe.

DRAMATIZATIONS IN THE SCIENCE CURRICULUM

In selected units of study in science, pupils with teacher guidance may participate in dramatic activities. Thus, for example, in a unit entitled, "Biographies of Famous Scientists," pupils may engage in research from a variety of reference sources to plan, develop, and implement selected dramatizations. Ultimately, pupils may reveal obtained learnings by dramatizing specific scenes from, among others, the lives of:

(a) Louis Pasteur
(b) Edward Jenner
(c) Enrico fermi
(d) Albert Einstein
(e) Sir Isaac Newton
(f) Robert Oppenheimer

Creative dramatics would stress the use of words, spontaneously presented, as the need arises. This form of dramatic activity should follow the following standards:

1. The presentation should be accurate and reveal pupils' related understandings, skills, and attitudes.
2. the creative presentation should indicate comprehensiveness of content gained from research activities.
3. Each pupil must reveal that effort has gone into develoning the final presentation.
4. Learners individually need to reveal that meaning and understanding are attached to what has been learned.
5. Each pupil should develop feelings of belonging and participation in the ongoing dramatic activity.
6. Pupils individually and within the group must develop feelings of satisfaction and success from creative dramatics learning experiences.
7. Each learner should be encouraged to identify and recognize new problems and questions requiring additional needed research.

SCOPE AND SEQUENCE IN THE SCIENCE CURRICULUM

There are important questions that teachers, supervisors, and principals need to identify and solve in the area of elementary school science. The concept of scope pertains to "what" should be taught in diverse units of study in elementary school science. Thus, breadth of unit titles in a kindergarten through grade six continuum would pertain to the problem of "what" should be taught in the elementary school science curriculum.

Directly related to the problem of scope (what is to be taught) in the elementary science curriculum is the concept of sequence. The concept of sequence pertains to "when" specific units of study should be taught, such as on the kindergarten level, grade one, grade two, grade three, grade four, grade five, of grade six. The concept of sequence may be expanded to include generalizations pertaining to the order of units of study within any specific grade level.

When implementing desirable standards pertaining to the concepts of scope and sequence in the science curriculum, the following questions need ultimate solutions:

1. Which content in specific units of study is relevant for pupils to understand and attach meaning to in the elementary school science curriculum ?
2. Which skills and attitudes should pupils gain in ongoing units of study science ?
3. What is the best order (sequence) for learners to acquire these desired understandings, skills, and attitudes ?
4. What criteria may be utilized to select relevant units of study in elementary school science ?
5. What methods or approaches may be utilized to determine appropriate scope and sequence in diverse units of study in elementary school science ?

The following units of study in elementary school science, among others, are commonly taught on the kindergarten level through grade six:

1. Our Pets
2. Insects—How They Help and Hinder Us
3. Exploring Space
4. Uses of magnetism and Electricity
5. Machines—How They Help Us
6. Ecology and a Clean Environment
7. Living things and Prehistoric Life
8. Our solar System
9. Air, Weather, and How It Affects Us

10. Plants and Animals in Our Environment
11. The Seasons—How They Affect Us
12. The Changing Surface of the Earth
13. Stars, constellations, and the Universe
14. Chemical Changes, Molecules, and Atoms
15. How the Human Body Works
16. Uses of Sound and Light
17. Heat and Its many Uses

There are significant questions that require careful consideration pertaining to the above-named unit tiles:

1. Can well—developed criteria be formulated to determine on which grade level or grade levels each of the above units should be taught?
2. What are appropriate standards to utilize in determining the best order or sequence of these units of study within each grade level?
3. Should the scope of the science curriculum (Breadth of unit titles) be broadened to incorporate more content from mathematics, social studies, language arts, and health?
4. Who should be involved in determining appropriate scope and sequence of units of instruction in elementary school science?

IN SUMMARY

A variety of interesting, purposeful, and meaningful learning experiences need to be provided for elementary school pupils in the science curriculum. The following learning activities are important for pupils in the science curriculum:

1. experimentation
2. reading
3. excursions
4. construction activities
5. educational television

6. films, filmstrips, and slides
7. written work
8. art work
9. dramatizations

Teachers, principals, and supervisors must give careful considerations to scope (what is taught in science) and sequence (when pupils are to develop appropriate understandings, skills, and attitudes) in determining relevant units of study in elementary school science.

REFERENCES

Herman, Jerry J. *Developing an Effective Elementary Science Curriculum.* West Nyack, New York: Parker Publishing Company, 1969.

Lewis, June E., and Irene C. Potter. *The Teaching of Science in the Elementary School.* Englewood Cliffs, New Jersey: Prentice—Hall, Inc., 1990.

Renner, John W., et. al. *Teaching Science in the elementary School.* Second Edition. New York: Harper and Row Publishers, Inc., 1973.

Rowe, Mary Budd. *Teaching Science as continuous Inquiry.* New York: McGraw-Hill Book Company, 1993.

Victor, Edward. *Science for the Elementary School.* Fourth Edition. New York: The Macmillan Company, 1985. Chapters 6A and 6B.

SCIENCE EDUCATION IN SECONDARY SCHOOLS

Many policies, committees and commissions, seminars and symposia have formulated a good number of objectives for science education. Some of the important objectives are—

— Pupils have to gain knowledge and understand the principles and formulae, processes and products, dates and events, facts and relationships, etc.

— Pupils are expected to develop scientific attitudes, creative faculties, independent thinking, decision making and problem solving.

— Pupils have to acquire skills such as drawing, observation, experimentation, manipulation, improvisation, collection and preservation, recording and reporting.

— Pupils have to observe the environment and enrich their experiences in observation, communication, measurement, formulation and testing of hypotheses.

— pupils are supposed to apply the acquired knowledge in familiar and unfamiliar situations.

— Pupils have to appreciate the contributions of science and scientists to human welfare.

— Pupils have to develop socially desirable habits, like honesty, truth, tolerance, self-reliance, etc.

Let us explain some of the inadequacies prevailing in our school science education. Among them, the most important drawbacks are the curriculum, the teacher and the school which are woven in and around the children. If we carefully examine the above mentioned drawbacks, we can confidently question—

IS OUR CURRICULUM A SUITABLE ONE?

Highlighting the role of curriculum, Cunningham says that "curriculum is the tool in the hands of the artist (the teacher) to mould his material (the pupils) according to his ideals (aims and objectives) in his studies (in school)" It means that the curriculum is the chief source of all school activities. Because of this, *first of all we have to decide why, what, when and how should we teach science?* Without keeping these questions in our mind, whatever in formation we dump in the classrooms may result in the wastage of manual and material resources.

If we critically examine our present science curriculum, we can find that the drawbacks out-number the merits. To quote—

— Curriculum is not in conformity with the aims and objectives of science teaching.

— Subject-entered, rigid and examination ridden.

— Bookish, theoretical and devoid of activities.

— Cut of from real life and no scope for vocational training.

If this is the conditions for our curriculum, then—

Who are Teaching Science in our Schools ?

Science is made a compulsory subject up to 10+level due to its multifarious advantages. To teach such a useful subject lively and meaningfully, we need efficient and effective science teachers. The quality of science teaching mainly depends on the quality of its teacher, but neither on the facilities available nor on the richness of the content. Unfortunately, many of our school are equipped with the science teachers who lack in—

— necessary teaching and manipulative skills.

— scientific attitudes, creativity and originality.

— interest either in teaching or in the future of children and the state.

— adequate knowledge in subject and the latest happenings around the world.

— appropriate pre-service or in-service training.

— the idea of allowing children to grow in physical and mental capacities spontaneously.

We do not, of course, blame the teachers alone. Our school children too will also not cooperate in effective teaching-learning process. In this occasion too, *the teachers have a role to play in moulding their clientele according to their requirements.*

What types of schools do we have ?

The schools in our country are, mostly, without having necessary furnished buildings, well equipped laboratories; adequate library facilities; and required number of qualified and efficient teachers.

These are some of the important drawbacks which are standing as obstacles in the path of achieving a better science education.

What changes we have to bring?

Continuous efforts are being carried out by the science educators and experts to improve the quality of science education and teacher training in the light of the changing needs of the child and society and the changing nature of the subject mater, but it has not gained momentum. Even after these strenuous efforts to improve the quality of science education and training, we have to do a lot.

In this context, it will be worthwhile if some ideas are placed before the educationists for open discussion to improve the quality of science education in secondary schools.

— The curriculum must be need-based.

— Curriculum should develop scientific attitudes and decision making power.

— Content organisation must consider the contemporary scientific knowledge.

— Curriculum should consider various age-groups, sex and I.Q.

levels,

— Curriculum must bring certain learning (productive) outcomes in its pursuers in the domains cognitive, affective and psychomotor in order to find a place in the world of work.

— Emphasis should be given to the acquisition of abilities in affective and psychomotor fields.

— Emphasis must be given to learning of concepts rather than to acquisition of information.

— Curriculum should be child-centered.

— Curriculum should encourage interdisciplinary approach.

— Environmental resources should be utilised.

— Curriculum must bring awareness in the thrust area like health, nutrition, shelter, environment, agriculture, energy, wild life, social forestry, industry, human welfare, ecological balance, etc.

— Learning outcomes must be property evaluated.

— Provision must be made for practical work.

— Schools should be adequately equipped with library, laboratory and physical facilities.

— Schools should acquire the necessary audio visual materials either professionally made or improvised, but they should not sacrifice the accuracy of science in the name of zero-cost or low-cost aids.

— The teachers, as earlier stated, are the only instruments to impart quality education, hence, their pre-service and in-service training must be strengthened.

— Teacher should be made aware of the concept of scientific literacy.

— Teachers must be enriched in content and methodology.

— Children should be involved intensively in learning.

— Science education must reach the out of school children through non-formal agencies.

— Teacher educators have to find out the thrust area, identify the drawbacks, develop feasible procedures to practice them in both training colleges and schools.

— Teacher educators, the key agents of change, can easily mould their student clientele up to the mark, in turn the products will put into practice the advantageous teaching techniques and ideas to upgrade the children's consciousness of science, its importance and its impact on day-to-day life.

IN CONCLUSION

Let us concludes, hopefully, with the words of the NEW EDUCATION POLICY, 1986 which read as "Science programmes will be designed to enable the learner acquire problem solving and decision making skills and to discover the relationship of science with health, agriculture, Industry and other aspects of daily life. Every effort will be made to extend science education to the vast numbers who have remained outside the pale of formal education".

DESIGNING SCIENCE UNITS OF STUDY

To design the curriculum area of science, careful attention needs to be given to the structure of unit planning. The objectives for students to attain may be stated in measurable terms. To achieve balance in the curriculum, cognite, affective, and psychomotor ends need to be stated with precision. Each domain of objectives is salient for student attainment. After instruction, it is impossible to measure if a learner has or has not achieved the measurably stated objective.

Toward the other end of the continuum, general objectives may be stated and implemented in ongoing units of study. To stress balance among general objectives, understandings, skills, and attitudinal goals should be emphasized in teaching-learning situations. With general objectives, it is not possible to measure if a student has or has not achieved the chosen end. However, flexibility in curriculum development may be emphasized, such as student-teacher planning.

The measurably stated objectives vs. general objectives debate represents differences in assumptions and beliefs in education. The measurable objective movement stresses:

1. what has been learned is observable and measurable.
2. certainty needs to be in evidence in terms of what a teacher is to teach and students are to learn. Uncertainty of which cognitive, affective, and psychomotor objectives (specificity of ends) to stress in lessons and units represents teachers who waver and are uncertain of themselves.
3. the importance of learning routes or activities which must harmonize directly with the chosen ends.
4. validity in testing. Items on a test must match the objectives emphasized in teaching-learning situations.

General objectives advocates believe

1 important learnings, be it subject matter, skills, or attitudes cannot be measured with precision.
2. an adequate number of goals should come from teacher-student planning of the curriculum.
3. individual students may well pursue goals different from other learners. Common goals for all the attain then is not possible.
4. an open ended curriculum needs to be in evidence which meets students' interests, purposes, and needs. General objectives can make provisions for individual difference among leaners.

The debate between measurably stated and general objectives might be harmonized in utilizing the former where feasible and possible and the letter whereby students with teacher assistance develop goals, learning opportunities, and appraisal procedures.

The writers recommends the following for science teachers in the measurably stated versus general objectives debate:

1. teachers individually need to be highly knowledgeable pertaining to assumptions involved in each of the two kinds of objectives.
2. both measurable and general objectives need to be implemented in the science curriculum.
3. science teachers need to appraise how specific and general objectives affect student progress in ongoing lessons and units.

4. each teachers needs to analyze the quality of teaching being emphasized when contrasting the utilization of measurable stated versus general objectives. Under which conditions does the teacher of science believe that learners can achieve in a more optimal·manner?
5. curriculum constraints need to be taken into developing the science curriculum. Does a state mandate Criterion Referenced Tests (CRT'S) with the utilization of measurably stated ends to ascertain learner progress in science?
6. the ultimate statement in the teaching of science pertains to helping each student achieve as much as possible in each lesson and unit of study.

PHILOSOPHIES OF SCIENCE EDUCATION

Diverse philosophical schools of thought in science are in evidence to develop and implement lessons and units in science.

Experimentalism emphasizes the use of problem solving experiences for students. Flexible steps in problem solving involve

1. identifying the problem.
2. gathering data to solve the identified problem.
3. developing a hypothesis, directly based on the obtained data and in answer to the problem.
4. testing the hypothesis.
5. revising the hypothesis, if evidence warrants.

Experimentalism emphasizes that real live problems be identified by students. The problem then come from society. In society, earthquakes, hurricanes, tornadoes, volcanic eruptions, among many other natural phenomena, occur. Out of these scenes and situations, problems arise and are identified, such as "What makes for the happening of earthquakes?" Information then needs to be gathered to answer the problem or question. An answer, tentative in nature, is then developed. The answer, a hypothesis, is then checked against further content, secured from a variety of reference sources. Modification of the original answer or hypothesis may then be needed.

Idealism, as a philosophy of education, emphasizes an idea centered curriculum. Science then becomes a part of the general education program. A subject centered, not an activity centered philosophy, is then in evidence. Diverse academic disciplines, such as geology, botany, physics, astronomy, biology, chemistry, and geology provide subject matter for ongoing units of study. Textbooks, workbooks, worksheets, and a few selected audio-visual aids provide content to students. Universal ideas or generalizations in science units needs to be achieved by students. The teacher needs to be a true academician and scholar to stimulate student learning.

Realism, as a third philosophy of education, advocates the utilization of precise, measurable objectives. Realists believe that the real world of science can be known in whole or part as it truly is. What students achieve in each science unit can be measured. The real world of natural phenomena can then be stated in precise, measurable objectives. A variety of concrete learning activities, in particular, should be provided for students to attain the specific ends. Semi-concrete as well as abstract activities also should be in the offing. After instruction, it is observable and measurable if an objective has been achieved by students.

Existentialism, as a fourth philosophy of education, emphasizes the learner, himself or herself, being heavily involved in deciding *what* (the objectives) to learn, as well as the *means* (learning activities) in ongoing science units of study. Thus, as learning centers philosophy may be emphasized. More centers and tasks for learners to pursue are in evidence than what can be completed. Each students may then sequentially choose which tasks to complete, as well as which to omit. Students individually are involved in making these decisions. The teacher develops the centers for learner interaction. Better yet, student-teacher planning may be used to develop the centers and their inherent tasks.

When looking at the diverse philosophies of education and their implementation for the science curriculum, we recommend the following:

1. each teacher needs to become thoroughly familiar with each philosophical school of thought.
2. each philosophy needs to be implemented on a trial basis in ongoing lessons and units.
3. the affect of the diverse philosophies needs to be observed in terms of students progress in science.

4. the science teachers needs to appraise the self as to how each philosophical strand affects one's own teaching style.
5. teachers individually need to develop their very own philosophy of teaching science. The adopted philosophy must harmonize with students learning styles and one's own beliefs about learners.and the actual act of teaching.

PROCESSES VERSUS PRODUCTS

Science educators tend to disagree as to which is more significant in the curriculum - the processes or the products of learning. The American Association for the Advancement of Science (AAAS) in Science, A Process Approach (SAPA) emphasizes in the program of units of instruction that students achieve the following processes:

1. Observing
2. Recognizing and using number relations
3. Measuring
4. Recognizing and using space-time relations
5. Classifying
6. Communicating
7. Inferring
8. Predicting
9. Defining operationally
10. Formulating hypotheses
11. Interpreting data
12. Controlling variables
13. Experimenting

The above named processes can be utilized in any academic discipline in science. With quality processes emphasized in teaching-learning situations, students in science lessons and units should attain vital, relevant subject matter. However, emphasis in the AAAS SAPA program processes are more important than products, that is subject matter learnings acquired by learners.

Other science educators advocate products (vital facts, concepts, and generalizations) as being the major outcomes of teaching-learning situations. Thus, from the academic disciplines involving zoology, botany, biology, astronomy, chemistry, physics, and geology, students should acquire structural ideas, as well as significant concepts, and facts.

The writers recommend that

1. processes and products receive equivalent emphasis. With quality processes stressed in science, worthwhile facts, concepts and generalizations should follow as end results.
2. each teacher should be highly knowledgeable about diverse process and product goals in teaching science.
3. objectives in the science curriculum reflect an adequate number of processes, as well as products.
4. learning opportunities to guide students to attain process ends as well as product goals should be inherent in each ongoing lesson and unit.
5. evaluation procedures need to emphasize processes and products in the science curriculum. A variety of appraisal procedures should be utilized, such as teacher observation, student self-evaluation, teacher written tests, as well as standardizes tests.

A LOGICAL VERSUS A PSYCHOLOGICAL CURRICULUM

Who should sequence or order objectives and learning experiences for students to pursue? The science teacher, a team of teachers, and/or state mandated Criterion Referenced Tests (CRT) may determine sequence in attaining objectives in science. These educators then base order of learning for students on logic or rational thought.

Toward the other end of the continuum is a psychological science curriculum. A learning centers psychology may be well be emphasized here. An adequate number of centers to be in evidence. At each center, five or six different tasks should be available. Enough centers and tasks should prevail so that students may truly select what to pursue and complete, as well as what to omit. Interest, purpose, and meaning need to be in evidence for each learning activity pursued. The teacher develops the centers and tasks. Teacher-student planning can also be in evidence at the diverse centers with its inherent tasks. In a psychological science curriculum, each student selects sequential tasks within a flexible framework.

In viewing the logical versus psychological science curriculum, we recommend that

1. each student needs to achieve optimally regardless of which psychology is utilized.
2. the best order or sequence in learning needs to be in evidence for students individually.
3. new ways of developing sequence need to be sought and tested in actual teaching-learning situations.
4. experimental studies need to be conducted to determine under which sequential plan - a logical, a psychological, or a combination of the two approaches - is best for guiding students on an individual basis to achieve as much as possible.
5. teachers should focus on the concept of *sequence* when implementing ongoing lessons and units.

SCOPE IN THE SCIENCE CURRICULUM

What should be the breadth of knowledge, abilities, or attitudes emphasized in science instruction ? Each of the categories of objectives should receive adequate attention. Numerous ways are in evidence to determine scope.

First of all, problem solving can be emphasized in a quality science curriculum. The problems should be real and life-like. Students need to perceive purpose and meaning within the problems identified. Thus, from events items, the following come up repeatedly:

1. What causes rain, dew, frost, snow, and hail to occur?
2. What causes mountains to form?

A variety of reference sources need utilization to secure reliable information in answer to the identified problems. Testing and revising of answers is a definite possibility. A quality science curriculum in stressing *scope* might then emphasize problem solving.

A second approach in achieving *scope* would be to utilize basal textbooks, single or multiple series, together with workbooks and worksheets. The table of contents of the basal series will indicate *which* units are to be emphasized. The writer would thoroughly recommend if textbook contents determine scope in the science curriculum that an adequate number of audio-visual materials be utilized to clarify ideas presented from the reading materials.

A third approach in determining scope in the science curriculum is to emphasize teacher-student planning. Within each science unit, teacher can stimulate students to plan definite goals, learning opportunities, and appraisal procedures. Students are encouraged, not hindered, to participate in developing the science curriculum.

A fourth method of scope emphasizes project methods of instruction. The late William Heard Kilpatrick, (1871-1964) professor at Columbia University in New York City, advocated flexible steps to follow in the project method. In the project method, Dr. Kilpatrick recommended open ended flexible procedures. First of all the student needs to perceive purpose or reasons for the project. Next, the learner with the teacher plan the project, as established in the purpose. After the planning has been completed, the student guided by the teacher carries out the plan. Once the project has been completed, its quality needs to be evaluated in terms of desirable standards. The total number of projects, successfully completed by students, would pertain to the *scope* of the science curriculum.

There are numerous approaches available in determining scope in the curriculum. When using problem solving procedures, the textbook method, student-teacher planing, and/or the project method, provision needs to be made for fast, average, and slow learners. The writers recommend the following in achieving a desirable scope in the curriculum:

1. use diverse, not a single procedure. Students like variety of methodology in teaching and learning.
2. determine under which conditions, students achieve more optimally. A carefully developed research design could emphasize quality practical research in the curriculum.

3. study other methods of determining scope in science. Scope should not remain static, but be subject to modification and change to provide more adequately for each individual student.
4. use the carefully selected basal textbook as the core in determining scope. Have problem solving, student-teacher planning, and the project method elaborate on textbook subject matter.

IN SUMMARY

The writers have identified numerous issues in teaching science. These issues include

1. specific versus general objectives in teaching.
2. diverse schools of thought in the philosophy of education.
3. process versus product ends of instruction.
4. a logical versus a psychological sequence.
5. numerous different means in determining scope in the science curriculum.

Methods of teaching science need to incorporate ways to resolve the above identified issues. The ultimate goal of teaching science is to assist each student to attain as much as possible in the science curriculum.

REFERENCES

Abruscato, Joseph. *Teaching Children Science*. Englewood Cliffs, New Jersey: Prentice Hall, Inc., 1982.

Beane, James A., et. al. *Curriculum Planning and Development*. Boston: Allyn and Bacon, Inc., 1986.

Carin, Arthur, and Robert B. Sund. *Teaching Science Through Discovery*. Columbus, Ohio: Charles E. Merrill Publishing Company 1985.

Gega, Peter, C., *Science in Elementary Education*. Fifth edition. New York: Macmillan Publishing Company, 1986.

Henson, Kenneth T., and Delmar Janke. *Elementary Science Methods*. New York: McGraw-Hill Book Company. 1984.

Jacobson, Willard, J., and Abby Barry Bergmain. *Science for Children, a Book for Teachers*. Englewood Cliffs, New Jersey: Prentice-Hall, Inc., 1980.

Moore, W. Edgar, et. al. *Creative and Critical Thinking*. Boston: Houghton Mifflin Company, 1985.

Trojacak, Doris A. *Science With Children*. New York: McGraw Hill Book Company, 1979.

Victor, Edward, *Science for the Elementary School*. Fifth edition. New York: Macmillan Publishing Company, 1985.

PROBLEM SOLVING

The science curriculum should emphasize problem solving activities for students as a major goal. To engage in flexible steps of problem solving, a creative mind is needed. Thus concepts of uniqueness, novelty, originality, and curiosity need to be in emphasis. The creative being perceives gaps in knowledge. These gaps become problems to solve. Each problem needs to be meaningful and clear. Clarity of problem identification in science is salient. Only with an adequately delimited problem students may gather relater need information. Science experiments, basal science textbooks, library books, videotapes, video-discs, films, models, filmstrips, slides, and transparencies, among other materials, provide vital information directly related to the identified problem. In sequence, an answer from the acquired information, is developed. The answer can be called a hypothesis. The hypothesis is tentative and subject to testing.

In a science experiment, the developed hypothesis may be tested. By performing the actual experiment, the hypothesis is than tested. The result is to accept, modify, or refute the hypothesis.

Throughout the problem solving activity in science, students, need to develop attitudes of being objective. With reading and audio-visual materials, facts, concepts, and generalization developed by students need to be appraised in terms of accuracy, and comprehensiveness. Subject matter attained by students is not an end in and of itself, but is utilized to solve problems in science.

Problem solving methods in science may well be compared with other psychologies of teaching.

BEHAVIORISM AND THE TEACHING OF SCIENCE

Behaviorism, as a psychology of teaching, emphasizes the utilization of measurably stated objectives. The objectives are precise. Either students do or do not attain the objectives as a result of teaching. Student achievement in science is then measured against the precise ends. These precise ends may be developed on the state level. The state then mandates the objectives for all school districts within their borders. Instructional Management Systems (IMS) also emphasizes the utilization of behaviorally stated objectives. IMS can be developed on the state or district level. The objectives are written prior to their implementation in the science curriculum.

Science teachers select learning opportunities for students to attain the objectives. The learning opportunities need to match up and align with the objectives. Concrete (experiments, demonstrations, models, excursions, objects, and science equipment), semi-concrete (video-tapes, video-discs, films, slides, transparencies, pictures and study prints), and abstract (reading, writing, listening, and speaking) activities, may be utilized as teaching-learning activities in science.

Evaluation techniques utilized as appraisal procedures emphasize testing and measuring. Evaluation techniques align with the objectives. Validity and reliability of appraisal instruments are important to determine student progress in science.

Behaviorism, as a psychology of learning, does not stress:

1. student-teacher planning of objectives, learning opportunities, and appraisal procedures.
2. the use of learning centers in which students select and sequence their own tasks.
3. contract systems whereby heavy involvement of students is inherent in choosing activities and experiences to complete in

science.

4. decision-making by students in developing the science curriculum. Behaviorism stresses a logical curriculum in which state mandated objectives, IMS, or the science teacher sequences objectives for student attainment.

HUMANISM AND THE SCIENCE CURRICULUM

Humanists believe in a psychological, not a logical science curriculum. Openness and open-endness are key concepts in teaching science to learners. The student the must be heavily involved in determining purposes, activities, and evaluation procedures in science. A humanistic science curriculum emphasizes humanness in science lessons and units taught. Thus, each students needs to have input into ongoing activities and experiences.

Learning centers approaches harmonize with advocates of humanism, as a psychology of teaching and learning. Here, an ample number of centers needs to be in evidence in the classroom. Each center needs to have several tasks on cards. This makes it so that a learners may choose which tasks sequentially to pursue, as well as which to omit. The student is the selector of which tasks to pursue and in which order.

A second method in emphasizing humanism, as a psychology of learning, stresses teacher-student planning. Thus, the objectives, activities and experiences, as well as appraisal procedures may be planned cooperatively in ongoing lessons and units in science. Student input into the ends, means, and evaluation procedures in science is necessary if humanism is too prevail. With student input, the learner is better able to perceive sequence in learning. A psychological, rather than logical science curriculum, is then in evidence. Students achieve at a higher rate if they are involved in lesson and unit development.

A third approach in emphasizing humanism in science is through a contract system. The learner with teacher guidance plans what to learn in science and this is written into a contract. The learning opportunities in science listed in the contract need to have a due date for their completion. The order of completing each activity is the choice of the student.

Humanism, as psychology of learning, does not advocate:

1. predetermined objectives in science developed as state mandated, IMS or written individually by the teacher.
2. the science teacher solely selecting learning activities and appraisal procedures.
3. science curricula developed exclusively by teachers, supervisors, and administrators.
4. passive learners reacting to an adult determined science curriculum.

THE STRUCTURE OF KNOWLEDGE AND THE SCIENCE CURRICULUM

Advocates of the structure of knowledge believe that academicians should determine vital, key ideas for science teachers to utilize in teaching students. Thus, university professors in their specific academic areas of speciality select salient, non trivial, content for objectives in the science curriculum. Each academic discipline in science such as astronomy biology, chemistry, zoology, geology, botany, and physics, among others has salient ideas for students to attain.

The key ideas identified by academicians are available to science teachers. Science teachers then assist students to attain the key ideas inductively. Inductive learning emphasizes inquiry as well as critical and creative thinking. Teachers of science need to be proficient in leading students to use inductive or learning by discovery means in securing structural ideas.

The science teacher also needs to have students utilize methods of inquiry as advocated by academicians their academic areas of specialty. For example, a student in ongoing lessons and units in astronomy would utilize approaches in securing structural ideas, as advocated by astronomers. A variety of materials need to be available to students to utilize methods as advocated by the academician in their academic area of specialty.

Structure of knowledge advocates do not believe in:

1. student-teacher planning of objectives for the former to attain. Rather, academicians select key concepts and generalizations for science teachers to emphasize in teacher students

2. deductive methods of teaching science. Instead learning by discovery or finding out on their own is stressed when students acquire the structure of knowledge in science.
3. the use of behavioral stated objectives. These objectives are too restrictive when students learn and acquire knowledge inductively.

STIMULUS-RESPONSE LEARNING IN SCIENCE

Edwin C., Gutheria (1884-1959), among others, emphasized a strict stimulus-response (S->R) theory of learning. S->R theory emphasizes that students are exposed to a stimulus. Thus, in a science unit on "Prehistoric Life", students are exposed to a single stimulus in a picture, such as short forelegs on the Tyrannosaurus Rex dinosaur. The response in S->R theory is that students identify from pictures short forelegs (the Tyrannosaurus Rex) as compared to those with long forelegs (the diplodocus and the brontosaurus). A single stimulus is presented so that students make a single response. Simple contiguity is then emphasized as a psychology of learning in ongoing lessons and units. Next, as a single stimulus, students can be shown, using audiovisual aids, serrated teeth on the Tyranosaurus Rex Dinosaur, where as in picture form, students may learn about the smooth teeth of the diplodocus and the brontosaurus. Again students are taught to associate the stimulus with the response. As much as possible a single stimulus is followed by a single response. Simple contiguity is then in evidence.

How do learnings acquired in one situations transfer to another in S->R theory? The answer is that identical elements transfer, rather than broad generalizations, from one situation to another. Thus, a specific response to a stimulus will transfer to a new situation if the identical knowledge or skill learned is required in a new situation in science.

S->R theorists in psychology do not emphasize:

1. the use of general objectives in teaching science.
2. student-teacher planning of objectives, learning activities, and evaluation procedures in ongoing science lessons and units.
3. internal learnings such as attitudes, interests and purposes of students in science as being important. Rather,

that which is observable and measurable in science learnings remain significant only.

IN CLOSING

Comparisons were made among the following models in teaching science:

1. problem solving by students with teacher guidance.
2. behaviorism with its predetermined precise objectives for student attainment.
3. humanism and its emphasis upon students selecting sequential activities from among alternatives.
4. the structure of knowledge with key concepts and generalizations identified by academicians in their respective academic areas of specialization. Science teachers assist students to achieve these structural ideas inductively using methods and procedures of scientists in a laboratory setting.
5. stimulus-response learning of students in which a specific response is associated with a precise stimulus.

The writers advocate a problem solving approach be utilized in teaching science. From a stimulating learning environment in science, students with teacher guidance identify and solve vital problems. Problems solving skills are useful in all academic areas, as well as in the societal arena. Behaviorism, humanism, the structure of knowledge, and stimulus-response learning may be emphasized within the framework of problem solving situations. Subject matter is acquired by students in each of the above named approaches in teaching science. Subject matter in science may then be utilized in the problem solving science curriculum.

PRACTICAL WORK

Practical work is a part of science curriculum. Practical work as well as practical examinations in science are far from satisfactory. There is over emphasis on measurement of product of performance while the processes of performance are quite often relegated to the background. The validity and reliability of the practical work and examinations are being affected by disproportionate weightages to different types of practical skills, inadequate number of laboratory exercises, lack of uniform instructions to the experts and examiners, inappropriate marking schemes, etc. The following details on practical work and examinations are the outcome of the Seminar on Practical Examinations and Workshop on Practical Examinations organised by Dr. Pritam Singh of National Council of Educational Research and Training (NCERT), India.

I. OBJECTIVES OF PRACTICAL WORK

It is needless to say that the purpose of science teaching is not only to acquaint the students with the knowledge of scientific facts, concepts and principles, but also to develop practical skills and scientific attitudes in the students, pertaining to these subjects. Science theory contributes a lot to the substantive structure of the subject, more emphasis is given to the development of scientific concepts while the syntactical structure of the subject is relegated to the background. It is only through various mode of inquiry that all scientific concepts and generalisations are arrived at. It is this aspect of science which refers to the development of practical skills. Development of practical skills in science subjects not only leads to learning of scientific concepts but also is instrumental in developing scientific attitudes among the students besides reinforcement of learning. It is, therefore, necessary that while formulating instructional objectives, care may be taken that proper weightage is given to the psycho-motor skills as also to objectives in the affective domain which relate to appreciations, interests and attitudes. Psycho-motor skills include manipulative skills, dissectional skills, observational skills, drawing skills reporting skills, etc. All these skills must be taken care of while teaching the science subjects. There is need to define each of these skills into their component skills so that the nature and scope of practical work is properly delineated.

For the realisation of the stated objectives various types of activities are to be selected and organised. The teachers would select them according to the objectives of the discipline. Practical work, in any case, will play a major role in this respect. It will be based on the knowledge already gained and as such it will reinforce it. Doing with one's own hand leads to better understanding about the processes of science and will enable pupils to apply them to familiar as well as unfamiliar situations. A well organised programme for practical work will develop interest among students and appreciation of environments. Unlike objective in the cognitive domain psycho-motor skills can be developed only by doing practical work. Therefore, development of skills is the most predominant objective of practical work in sciences.

There are various types of skills like those of drawing skills, observational skills, manipulative skills, dissectional skills, collecting, mounting and preserving skills. But in each of these skills we can identify and delimit two aspects of performance. These are:

(a) Process of performance/performance in progress

(b) Product of performance/resultant outcomes

Both these aspects are equally important in teaching and testing. It will be very desirable to specify them in terms of specific tasks envisaged under each aspect. This specification will help both the teachers and testers. Each branches of science will have slightly different specifications and will have to be separately defined to make them useful to teachers and evaluators.

As an illustration, the specifications of Process of Performance and Product of Performance in Physics are defined as under:

A. Process of Performance

Specifications

The pupil:

1. Selects appropriate apparatus, tools, instruments, etc.
2. checks equipment, apparatus, tools regarding their working.
3. detects errors and limitations in the fitting up of apparatus.
4. rectifies errors;. If possible, under laboratory situations.
5. sets up apparatus, tools, etc., for an experiment.
6. prepares a systematic and sequential plan for taking observations.
7. records observations in accordance with the design of the experiment.
8. states the principles, formulae and the symbols needs to report results in an experiment.
9. handles apparatus, tools and instruments with care while performing the experiments.
10. measures quantities and reads instruments, apparatus, etc. accurately.
11. takes necessary precautions in handing instruments, chemicals, and materials.
12. makes accurate observations of part, processes, etc.
13. draws graphs relevant to the experimental data whenever necessary.
14. calculates accurately the relationships to draw inferences or conclusions.
15. performs experiments with reasonable speed.

16. performs experiments with reasonable accuracy and precision.
17. performs experiments with neatness and in an orderly manner.
18. adapts himself with somewhat new and different apparatus in setting novel experiments.
19. explains orally the sketches of a given arrangement of apparatus or experimental set-up.
20. dismantles and cleans the apparatus, wherever necessary.
21. arranges the apparatus, substances, etc. at their appropriate places at the end of the work.

B. Product of performance

Specifications

The Pupil:

1. records the observed data in terms of objectives of the experiment in verbal, graphical or numerical form.
2. interprets the data or recorded observations to finalize the results.
3. draws conclusions from the recorded data or observations.
4. identifies the given specimen, apparatus, materials, substances, etc.
5. summarizes the findings to reject or accept a hypothesis.
6. reports the results in a systematic manner using technical terminology, graphs, sketches, etc.

The above list of specification is by no means exhaustive but only suggestive. Each science subject has it own skills and can be defined separately in terms of processes and products of performance. Specification of drawing, observational, manipulative, dissectional skills, etc., are indicated in skill objectives given under instructional objectives of each subject.

Major purpose of such operational definitions is to enable the teacher to appreciate the hierarchy in development of skills and the sequence needed in development of these skills. It is through continuous evaluation at the various stages of skill development, like imitation, patterning, mastering, applying and improvising, that can help in diagnosing the inadequacies and proficiency in performance on the basis of which remedial programme can be taken up. Moreover, it is this specification of skills in terms of performance in progress or product of performance that provides the basis for instruction and evaluation of skills. It is on the basis of adequate coverage of these skills that a framework or design is worked out for setting question paper on practical examinations in science subjects, the technique of which is discussed in the next chapter.

II. IMPLICATIONS FOR TEACHING AND TESTING

Improved pattern of practical examinations discussed in the last few pages will be practicable only if only procedures are properly followed not only in the external examinations but also in school evaluation. Whereas the theoretical work in science is expected to promote pupils' growth mainly in cognitive domain, the practical work does not only promote pupils' growth in the psycho-motor domain but also helps to develop wholesome interests in the subject and scientific attitudes. Thus practical work in science is of great significance in all-around development of the pupils. However, for effective conduct of practical work and improvement of practical examinations the co-operation of different agencies and their special efforts would be required. The improved pattern of practical examinations envisages a number of implications for taking necessary steps by different agencies concerned with the improvement programme. The important agencies are schools, teachers, paper scatters, examiners, departments of education. Unless certain conditions are fulfilled it will not be possible to implement the improved pattern of practical examinations. The implications relevant to each to these agencies are listed below:-

A. Schools

1. School laboratories will have to be properly maintained by providing adequate number of sets of the apparatus to provide opportunity to every student to undertake practical work.
2. Schools will have to reduce the rigidity of the time table thus

enabling the science teacher and pupils to work with freedom in the organisation of various activities such as demonstrations, laboratory work etc.

3. More initiative on the individual teacher and pupils will be needed in conducting such activities related to practical work. Teachers may be encouraged to undertake some projects to study different aspects of these improved procedures.
4. The practical examinations in the school will have to be carried out on the same pattern as recommended for Board Examinations.
5. The results of practical examinations will have to be used for improvement of instructional strategies to develop practical skills among students.

B. Teachers

1. The science teachers will have to change to present outlook towards practical work as merely an activity for verifying or just repeating what is done in the past. The tendency of mechanical repetition of some standard experiments will have to be discouraged. They will realise that this work is meant to develop experimental skills in a systematic manner. They will, therefore, organize the practical work in such as manner so as to realize the above objective of developing various psychomotor skills among students. They may equip themselves by receiving training in this field. For this they may take advantage of the various training courses and workshops and the literature produced in this field.
2. They should encourage the pupils to take initiative in undertaking small projects of practical nature, involving all the types of skills designated in the courses of study or the design provided by the examining agency.
3. They will have to organise the exercises in such a manner that the students get maximum opportunities in acquiring simple skills leading to more complex skills which can be attained as get more and more training and experience in undertaking practical work.
4. The practical exercises should be repeated in order to reinforce the desire skills. It is implied that these exercises will be

in conformity with the objectives laid down for practical work.

5. It should always be kept in mind that the practical and theoretical work go hand in hand for effective teaching and learning, and to get better results in terms of proficiency in skills.
6. The teachers will prepare in advance the practical assignments on each expertise for students to make necessary preparation on the basis of which pupils can be allowed to undertake practical work. This is to be followed by practical work in the Laboratory with necessary briefing by the teacher.
7. Special emphasis to inculcate the habit of cleanliness and orderliness during practical work in the laboratory will have to be laid by the teachers.

C. Paper Setters

1. Paper setters of practical examinations will take cognizance of the objectives of practical work. They will set practical exercises to ensure adequate coverage of objectives and content as far as possible by giving short as well as long exercises. They will give weightage to different aspects as stipulated by the design supplied by the examining agency.
2. Whenever alternative experiments are to be given the paper setters should ensure that these are comparable in respect of skill tested, difficulty level and time requirements.
3. The paper should frame the exercise in a manner that the tasks are clear to the examinees in terms of expected performance.
4. The paper setters will review their papers by preparing an exercise-wise analysis to check whether the requirements of the given design are fulfilled.
5. They will develop a detailed marking scheme as per requirements of the design. The marks will be distributed over various aspects of skill covering all the intended process of performance and products of performance. This detailed marking scheme will be sent to each examiner so that they could follow in during the conduct of practical examination.
6. They will issue necessary instructions which help in proper conduct of practicals and help to minimize the subjectivity in

assessment of students and scoring of scripts.

7. They will use the performa provided by the board for reporting significant details about the performance of pupils or develop one if not provided. Necessary entries regarding pupils' performance, laboratory conditions, services, record etc. are made. Consolidated reports of various examiners can reflect on practical work and suggestions for improvement can be made. This report will act as very useful evidence for schools as a feedback device for improvement of practical work in the institutions.

D. Examiners

1. Examiners will be very watchful throughout the time students are performing their experiments in order to observe the performance in progress and product of performance of the candidates and record them systematically in the scoring sheet provided by the paper setter or the board.
2. They will follow the instructions received by them regarding conduct of examination and scoring of scripts or evaluation of students.
3. If they find a candidate to proceed for want of specific information they should help them by supplying the necessary information. While scoring the performance of such candidates the marks reserved for related understanding only, may be deducted and credit for showing proficiency in desired skills may be given.
4. If an alternative exercise is to given instead of original exercise for want of equipment the examiners will see that such an exercise is comparable in respect of the specific skills being tested, time requirement and difficulty level of the exercise.
5. They will prepare a very detailed report of their observations and findings about the performance of candidates and sent it to the examining agency in the prescribed reporting proforma. The examining agency will analyse these reports school-wise and send the same to respective institutions for necessary improvement in school practices. These reports will also be useful for the examining agencies for improving the testing procedures related to practical examinations.

E. Examination agencies and Education Departments

1. School laboratories will have to be better equipped so that they may provide for all the experiments prescribed.
2. Practical syllabi, may be reviewed in terms of objectives of practical work and provision be made to include larger variety of experiments to provide for development of all needed skills.
3. Flexible time-table will have to be permitted so that the students may perform experiments in their spare periods and teachers concerned could organise practical work accordingly.
4. Better inspection and guidance programme will have to be ensured for proper instruction and evaluation of practical work.
5. Only qualified paper setters and examiners with training in paper setting and evaluation will have to be selected for practical examinations.
6. Examinations' reports will have to scrutinized and findings reported to schools for necessary action regarding improvement of instructional strategies to develop experimental skills among the students.

III. RECOMMENDATIONS

In order to implement the improved pattern of practical examinations following suggestions are made:-

A. Syllabus

1. Instructional objectives as stated in the syllabi of science subjects at present are not clearly defined in terms of pupils' behaviour and this creates difficulty in planning appropriate learning experiences for attaining the desired objectives. It is, therefore, absolutely essential that the syllabi in the subjects may be clearly stated and specified for providing proper guidelines for instruction and evaluation.
2. Present syllabi contain only the lists of the experiments to be performed but they do not indicate as to the various processes and products of performance to be emphasized. It is, therefore, felt that unless the various experiments as listed in the

the prescribed syllabi indicate the various types of skills to be developed as a result of practical work, it would be difficult to develop and assess the practical skills in a proper manner. For this some more practical experiments emphasizing different processes and more should be introduced for adequate coverage of skills, keeping in view the physical facilities available in the schools.

3. Demonstrations by teachers are pre-requisite for guiding theory and practical work. To help the teacher in planning and execution of demonstrations it is felt that the syllabi should contain a list of demonstrations to be shown to the pupils before the pupils themselves perform the experiments in the laboratory.
4. In the recent past through scientific talent search and other agencies our educationists have encouraged independent projects by pupils. A list of projects could be incorporated in the syllabi with hints for planning and execution of the same for guidance of the teachers.
5. In order to develop spirit of inquiry among the pupils a suggested list of open ended experiments may be included in the list of experiments. Such as list could be prepared with the help of experienced teachers and lecturers.
6. For healthy competition among the students and proper record of pupils' practical work together the grading of their performance by the teacher on each experiment, a progress chart/performa may be devised by the board and circulated to the schools for use of teachers conducting practical work.
7. As improved practical examinations viz-a-viz instruction presupposes adequate laboratory equipment and material, it is recommended that the concerned departments should supply the necessary apparatus and materials well in time.
8. In order to prepare the students for practical examination at the higher secondary stage it may be quite useful to introduce practical examination in science subjects at the end of secondary school stage also. Unless sufficient practice is given in developing fundamental skills it may be difficult to expect good performance from the pupils.

B. Laboratory

1. It is also recommended that one qualified laboratory assistant in each of the science subject should be appointed.
2. Provision should also be made for training of the laboratory personnel in up-keep of laboratory and in assisting the teaching staff for conduct of practical work.
3. For proper conduct of practical work, essential services in the form of electricity, gas water, fume-cupboards, exhaust fans etc. should be provided in the laboratory.
4. Equipment, furniture, fittings, fixtures storage cabinets etc. should be so designed and arranged that it facilitates the use of laboratory chemicals, apparatus and materials besides ensuring safety measures.

C. Mechanics of Examination

1. Analysis of question papers in practical examination revealed that there is no set pattern of emphasizing different skills or the coverage of content. It is, therefore, essential that a design of question papers for practical examinations may be got prepared with the help of subject experts and supply the same to the paper setters as well as to the schools. This would help sampling of skills for evaluation purpose besides proportionate coverage of various subjects areas
2. Minimum pass mark in practical examinations should be 40%. This would help to emphasize practical work more in the instruction of science subjects.
3. As the improvement pattern of practical examinations entails a lot of work and time in evaluating students' performance, it is desirable that the examiner-examinee ratio should be at the maximum 1 to 15.
4. On the lines of the sample proforma worked out by the group for reporting pupils' performance in practical examinations the examining agency should get the reporting proforma prepared for science subjects and supply them to the examiners. Such as proforma would be very useful for consolidation and use of pupils' performance besides providing useful information for feedback to the schools. This would go long

way in improving the instructional programme in science subjects.

5. In order to emphasize the importance of practical work and its place in teaching of science subject it is necessary that passing in practical examinations should be made obligatory.
6. Present number of exercises specially in the subjects of Physics and Chemistry appears to be inadequate and it is not possible to have good coverage of skills and different content areas. Therefore, it is felt that the number of exercises may be increased by replacing one or more major exercises by short exercises requiring less time and testing different skills. This would ensure better validity of the practical examinations.
7. In Biology it is felt that viva-voce may be dropped as it is mostly based on theory that can tested better through written examinations. Moreover, it takes away a lot of time which can be used more profitably for observing students' performance. However if it has to be continued it should test only functional understanding related to the practical work in hand during the process of performance.
8. The paper setters should be selected only from among those who have received training in practical examination through seminars or workshops conducted examining agencies.
9. The paper setters should prepare a scoring sheet for use of the examiners giving all the necessary details of the allocation of marks and the criteria for evaluation. Such a sheet should be prepared in a manner that it facilitates scoring and minimize the time for recording.

D. Paper Setting

1. Design of question paper must be supplied by the board of school education.
2. Looking to the total volume of the work of paper setting in the new pattern it is considered desirable that there should be a panel of paper setters consisting of not less than two members. Out of these, one should be from the university/college and the other from experienced school teachers.
3. The panel should prepare the question paper/papers according to the requirements laid down in the design supplied by the

Board.

4. It will be necessary for the paper setters to prepare instructions for the examiners along with the detailed marking scheme for each exercise. This will ensure uniformity in assessment which is highly necessary in public examinations.
5. It is suggested that there should be an internal examiner along with external and he should be suitable remunerated. In Biology, out of the two examiners one may be of Botany and the other of Zoology.
6. The load of work of paper setters and examiners will be much increased than what it is today. Therefore, it is suggested that their remuneration be suitably enhanced.

E. Production of Literature.

1. In order to orient the teachers and the students about the new pattern of practical examinations, there is a great need for developing suitable literature. It is, therefore, recommended that a brochure explaining the framework of the new pattern of practical examination and giving some sample materials illustrating the pattern should be produced by each board and supplied to all the schools.
2. It will also be desirable to produce laboratory manuals and teachers' guides in addition to the above-mentioned brochure.
3. Since different sets of question papers are needed every year for setting question papers, the need for variety of exercises cannot be over-emphasized. It is, therefore, suggested that examining agencies may develop pool of practical exercises in each of the Science subjects. Such a pool can be used by external and internal examiners for developing and evaluating students for practical skills.

F. Orientation of Personnel

1. For effective implementation of the new pattern of practical examinations it is desirable that the paper setters and examiners be oriented to this approach. It is, therefore, suggested that the examining agencies should organise such orientation programmes for their present and prospective paper setters and examiners.

2. In order to make this programme a success the teachers should also be made conversant with this new pattern of teaching and testing in practical work, so that they could prepare their students more efficiently for improved pattern of practical examinations. It is, therefore, desirable that in addition to the supply of suitable literature to the teachers, tailor-made training programmes should also be organised for teachers of science.

REFERENCE

Singh, Pritam (1983). *A Monograph on Improving Practical Examinations in Science.* New Delhi : National Council of Educational Research and Training.

13

NATURE STUDY

Education is the apprenticeship of life. It is constant inquiring. The moment we stop to inquire, we stop to educate ourselves as well as others. Hence education should conform to the natural processes of growth and mental development, it should engage the spontaneous self-activity of the learner, it should be a pleasurable activity as well of the mind of the learner. For this one should be in touch with the real world i.e. material world which is nature. Luther Burback says that there is no other door to knowledge than the door Nature opens; there is no truth except the truths we discover in Nature. Nature is real, propelled, by her own laws whereas the natural laws are unchangeable and the whole universe is governed by them. Nature alone contains the normal and the final answer to all the problems on hand.

The scientific knowledge is of highest value and utmost worth, so the scientific knowledge must be in context of living. The knowledge that is gained through observation is of greatest value. Values are the residents in the nature. One has to live in harmony with nature to realise the values which mostly govern the life. The values are created in terms of specific needs and purposes which are the outcomes of the conditions of life. As the man is an off-spring of the nature he should study nature thoroughly and make maximum use of it.

Through nature study we know the various aspects like, facts and truths of nature. If we come in close contact with nature we get a rich, varied and realistic experience rather than oral or bookish. It develops appreciation and intelligent outlook on the phenomenon of the nature among the learners. It is the study of both inmate and un-inmate beings who develop curiosity in the hearts of the learners and help to go ahead to achieve high goals. According to Ravidranath Tagore, traditional pattern of schooling is colourless, lifeless and devoid of natural beauty. Nature study gives freedom to the learner and with this free atmosphere the learner finds proper and suitable opportunities for his spontaneous growth and development.

We can say that there is nothing to be learned in the University of Education without nature. Victor Hugo once observed that nature, like a kind and smiling mother, lends herself to our dreams and cherishes our fancies. It develops the habit of careful observation and clear thinking which are required for man to develop. Darwin and Lamark said that life is dynamic, ever changing and ever-developing and needs constant adjustment on the part of the organism.

Nature study is intended to develop the learner's sensitiveness and to make him feel at home with nature, because it brings the individuals close to the environment. This nature study brings the coordination of various sense organs which are helpful for a successful life and these sense organs are the gateways of knowledge.

The "School of Naturalism" came into existence basing on the preceding principles. The naturalists say education as a natural necessity. It encourages, formulates and applies natural laws to the educative process and education is a process of development of the natural life. The most prominent naturalists are Bacon, Pestalozzi, Froebal, Rausseau, spencer, Lamark, Ravindranath Tagore, Sir T P. Nunn, Bernard Shaw etc.

The subject matter should not be object based and rigid, as far as possible, but it should be of interest to the learners. It should be based upon the Psychology and age of the learner. It should be broad-based and should include animal life, plant life and the role played by the non-living things in this vast universe. T. H. Huxley prefers literary and aesthetic culture to be the main points, Rousseau suggests that the learner should learn through direct experience in the lap of the nature and was against verbalism and text-books. The subject matter should not be traditionalised, but it should develop initiative and ingenuity of the learners. John Brown opines that the aim of-course should be to teach the children to make observations, take and write about what they observe, to acquaint them with the wonder and beauty of nature".

To involve the learner in the nature study all rigid, uniform, traditional and stereo-typed techniques of teaching should be discarded. The learner should be allowed to grow according to his own nature. Rousseau says, that give your scholar no verbal lesson, he should be taught by experience alone. Dr. Premnath and Freobel have recommended the Play Way Method as a valuable technique of teaching because through play the learner acquires various skills and the Kindergarten and Montessori methods are based upon this principle. Heuristic, question-answer, learning-by-doing methods are also advisable. Mass instructions or collective instructions will not be very useful in nature study. The learners should be encouraged for individual efforts. W. A. F. Hopper says that the most effective teaching-learning strategy would be peer group learning.

To study the nature in many aspects, it is better to leave the portals of the educational institutions and observe nature by way of excursions, field trips etc. There the learners should collect and preserve the material that should be discussed in the class. Seasons should be followed for these trips in order to learn more. St. Bernard says that "what I know of the divine sciences and holy scripture : I learnt in woods and fields. I have had no other master than beaches and the parks."

Teacher has to play an effective role in nature study and can play that role if he himself has interest in nature study. Tagore opines that to teach a child, a teacher ought to have and realise child in himself. He should provide suitable atmosphere to create interest and curiosity in nature study. He should act as a protector of the learner from any repression and mental disorder of any kind. He should observe and understand the learner and in no way interfere with his spontaneous growth and development. Rousseau and Fichte are in favour of non-intervention, because they believe that the child's nature is essentially good. Montessori also considers the teacher's interference as harmful. A teacher does not use force against a child, as followed in A. S. Neill's school. Summerhill, True sincerity is needed on the part of the teacher.

In conclusion, nature study gives first hand experience to the learners and the learners will learn various skills. There is nothing beyond nature, behind nature and other than nature to learn. I think that it is not advisable to completely depend on the nature study due to its advantages neglecting the other school subjects, but the nature study should be included in the curriculum as one of the school subjects as well as a compulsory subject.

CREATIVITY

Creative endeavours are needed for students. Unique content coming from students emphasizes the learner and the curriculum being integrated, not separate entities. Science curriculum can then make integrated, not separate entities. Science curriculum can then make many contributions in guiding creative development for students. Pertaining to students making discoveries, Lipman, Sharp, and Oscanyan[1] wrote:

> So it is with Children. The meaning they hunger for cannot be dispensed to them the way wafers are dealt out to communicants at a mass; they must seek them out for themselves, by their own involvement in dialogue and inquiry. Nor is that the end of the matter, for meanings, once found, must be cared for and nurtured, as one might care for one's house plants, pets, or other living and precious treasures. But the children who cannot make sense of their own experience, who find the world alien, fragmentary, and baffling, are likely to cast about for short-cuts to total experiences, and eventually may experiment with drugs or succumb to psychoses. Possibly we could teach children before they reach out for such desperate remedies by helping them find the meanings so lacking in their lives.

PROBLEM SOLVING, CREATIVE BEHAVIOUR AND SCIENCE

Students in the science curriculum need to receive quality activities and experiences to achieve the broad goal of revealing creativity in the school and class settng. Creative being are very much needed in school and in society. Thus problems need identification and novel solutions. The tried and true, as well as the traditional, too frequently do not work in solving vital problems. Which learning opportunities might then assist students in science to achieve the overall goal of developing the creative being ?

From an on-going science experiment, students might be encouraged to identify questions and problems. Each should be recorded on the chalk-board or transparency. Value judgements should not be made as the questions/problems are selected. Rather, generating of ideas is salient. From the listing, students individually or in committees may select an area to pursue. Students then, with science teacher's guidance, may choose that which is perceived as important. For example, if the performed science experiment pertains to changing selected solids to liquids, students in the on-going unit could raise questions such as the following :

1. Why do these solids (diverse kinds should be in evidence) change to liquids at different temperature readings ?
2. What happens when solids change to liquids ?

Questions raised will depend upon the developmental level of the involved student. The above are given as examples. For each question raised, answers need to be sought using diverse reference sources. Students may work individually or in committees to find needed information. With student-teacher planning, the former may have much input into seeking and selecting the reference sources. Experimentation and demonstrations, among other activities, may as learning activities, guide students to find needed answers to identified questions. An open-ended approach is in evidence for students to select reference materials.

From the data gathered, students may brainstrom hypotheses or answers to identified problems. Selected hypotheses may be tested to notice their quality and objectivity. If the hypotheses needs revising, a discussion may follow to make modifications and changes.

Pertaining to experimentalism as a philosophy of education Ozmon and Craver[2] wrote :

> According to the pragmatists, education should be an experimental enterprise as well as something that assists in social

renewal. It should promote a humanistic spirit in people, as well as the desire to explore and find new answers to our present-day problems in economics, politics, and other social life. Education should promote our true individualism that will result in a diminishing of our reliance upon custom and tradition in the solving of our problems, and cause us to rely more upon intelligence to achieve our goals and interests.

Dewey point out that a "philosophy of eudcation" is not the application of readymade ideas to every problem but rather the formation of right mental and moral attitudes to use in attacking contemporary problems. Philosophy itself is "the theory of education in its most general phases." When changes occur in social life, we must reconstruct our educational programme to meet these challenges. Thus, our ideas will have a pragmatic function. Learning helps us to meet environmental changes and affects our character as well. In this way, education has a moral influence and should play a vital part in helping us to become the kind of moral persons who are interested not only in promoting our own growth, but also in promoting the growth of others.

POETRY, CREATIVITY AND SCIENCE

Enjoying and writing of poems can certainly emphasize creative endeavours for students. The science teacher may read orally selected poems to learners relating to the unit being taught. Poems need to be chosen on the basis of the following criteria:

1. Will each poem capture leaner interests ?
2. Will students attach meaning to the poem ?
3. Will individual differences be adequately provided for ?

The science teacher should also introduce selected poems in a stimulating manner to encourage students to read the content on their own. A bulletin board display of poems, attractively arranged, may well encourage students to do more reading of poetry related to the on-going science unit.

Readiness experiences for poetry writing may come from experimentation, audio-visual presentations, and/or reading activities in the science curriculum. Types of poems which students may write include :

1. couplets—two lines with ending words rhyming.
2. triplets—three lines with rhyme in all words at the end of each line.
3. quatrains—four lines with diverse patterns of rhyme, such as lines one and two, as well as lines three and four rhyming.
4. limericks with rhyme in lines one, two, and five, as well as in lines three and four.

The above named poems contain rhyme. Free verse contains no rhyme and does not adhere to any specific number of lines needed within the poem. Also, students with science teacher assistance need to be introduced to writing poems emphasizing syllabication when readiness is in evidence. The following poems may then be read to and written by learners in on-going science units :

1. haiku with its five, seven, five syllables for each of three lines of verse.
2. tanka with its five, seven, five, seven, and seven syllables for each line of poetry.
3. cinquain with its two, four, six, eight, and two syllables respectively per line in a poem five lines in length.

To emphasize enthusiasm in the writing of poems in the science curriculum, students should experience

1. onomatopoeia or echoic sounding words in the written product.
2. alliteration, another poetic device, emphasizing two or more sequential words starting with the same phenome or sound.
3. imagery in which creative comparisons are made such as "the moon looks like a smiling face." Here *moon* is creatively compared with a *smiling face*. The word *like* connects the two above italics words. If the words "like" or "as" make the connections, a simile is in evidence. Otherwise, the creative comparison is a metaphor, e.g. the moon is a smiling face above.

Creativity as an objective might well be achieved by students' writing poetry directly related to facts, concepts, and generalizations achieved in an on-going science unit.

PROSE, CREATIVITY AND SCIENCE

Students should experience prose from selected library books directly related to the present science unit being taught. An interesting type of prose for teachers to introduce and read to learners is tall tales. Readiness activities are then being provided students to read tall tales.

Inductively, students can generalize as to what makes for a tall tale. The following are its characteristics :

1. a superhuman being is necessary. Paul Bunyan and Pecos Bill in American tall tales exemplify the superhuman concept.
2. the superhuman gets into one or more difficult situations.
3. the superhuman being is able to get out of the prescribed difficulties.

Students could take a famous scientist and develop a related tall tale. Students need to be imaginative, possess openness to new content, like being playful with ideas, exhibit tendencies of fluency of thought, as well as pursue a poem to its completion in writing.

Writing tall tales presents opportunities to the students to relate the science curriculum to a truly open-ended kind/type of creative endeavour.

ART WORK IN SCIENCE

Creative experiences may certainly be emphasized in correlating science and art. The writer when supervising a student teacher in the public schools observed a well done mural or prehistoric lifc, a science unit. The student teacher developed, planned, and implemented the unit in science. One activity emphasized a committee of sixth grade pupils developing the pre-historic life mural utilizing a variety of art media. In the mural, students portrayed the following sciences :

1. a tyrannosaurus rex dinosaur attacking a stegosaurus.
2. a brontosaurus situated in a body of water eating plants.

3. an archeoepteraux flying overhead.
4. fern plants growing in abundance.

Pupils with student teacher guidance evaluated the mural in terms of :

1. effort put forth by each learner.
2. input from all committee members in developing and completing the mural.
3. new ways of presenting subject matter in art form.

Prior to developing the mural on pre-historic life, the science teacher:

1. showed and discussed a related filmstrip.
2. presented and appraised illustrations.
3. provided readiness for students to read from their basal science textbooks. Facts, concepts, and generalizations secured by learners were discussed with teacher leadership.

Additional art project develop by committees in the unit on prehistoric life were the following :

1. papier maché models on the diplodocus and the anklasaurus.
2. clay models of duch billed dinosaurs.
3. a diorama containing a three dimensional scene, in an enclosed box with the front open, showing diverse dinosaurs with a natural environment for its day in prehistoric times.

Students need encouragement and re-inforcement to develop feelings of creativity and spontaneity.

CREATIVE DRAMATICS AND SCIENCE

Numerous opportunities are available for learners to participate in creative dramatics in on-going science units. In a unit on "Famous Scientists," the science teacher needs to guide students to secure background information pertaining to famous scientists being studied. Reading and audio-visual activities should provide readiness experiences for learners.

Students may then be divided into committees. Each committee needs to plan roles for members to paly as famous scientists being studied in the on-going science unit. Famous scientists to be included in the unit and from which students individually will have parts for the creative dramatics presentation could include:

1. Louis Pasteur.
2. Anton Leuwenhoek.
3. Joseph Lister.
4. Sabin and Salk
5. Pierre and Madame Curie.

The above named scientists are given as examples. Goals need to be clear for students to achieve in creative dramatics. Background subject matter obtained and the creative dramatics presentation in and of itself need to be appraised in terms of stated goals. Students should be involved in self-evaluation endeavours. Creativity is the major goal for students to achieve in the dramatic activity. At the same time, relevant subject matter needs to be achieved by students.

CONSTRUCTION ACTIVITIES IN SCIENCE

Students might as well reveal creative behaviour through constructing items and objects in the science curriculum. Individual or committee endeavours may be emphasized here. Each project constructed needs to show a carefully thought through purpose. Thus, a student perceives reasons for the construction activity. Then the purpose or goal needs to be planned by students with science teacher guidance. Here, a psychological sequence is involved in developing the plans for constructing and making. The learner does the sequencing in a psychological science curriculum when planning to attain the inherent purpose.

After planning, the actual carrying out of the plans is involved. Each ordered sequential step needs to be implemented. Application is involved when the planning is carried out to completion. The final process is to appraise the project utilizing quality standards. Input from the student is needed to appraise the worth or value of what has been constructed.

Depending upon the science unit taught, many construction activities can be completed by learners on their present level of readiness. The following, among others, in a unit on "Our Changing Weather" could be appropriate:

1. hygrometers
2. thermometers
3. rainfall guages
4. barometers
5. wind vanes
6. anemometers

IN CLOSING

There are many learning opportunities in science curriculum which emphasize creativity. Among others, the following might well be salient :

1. problem solving experiences.
2. poetry reading and writing.
3. prose and its applications in creative endeavours.
4. art work as creativity in science.
5. creative dramatics and famous biographies of individuals in the world of science.
6. construction experiences to achieve objectives of students creativity in science curriculum.

Pertaining to creative writing and utilization of trade books, Gega[3] wrote:

> Here are some ideas for creative writing that you can use repeatedly with different trade books.
>
> Diary. Write an entry from an event in the life of George Washington Carver, Marie Curie, and so on ("February 18, 1897. Is it impossible ? I have now tried dozens of ways to—")
>
> Letter to a famous scientist from the past or present ("Dear Dr. Einstein:")
>
> Interview with a famous person ("What was it like being an astronaut, Mr. Glenn ?" "It had its ups and downs, Sally," he said with a grin.)
>
> Future autobiography ("An exciting page from your life in the

field of—!")

TV or radio script : "You Are There !" (Re-enactment and report on the first moon landing, first colony on the moon, development of the first human clone, first successful brain transplant, peaceful visit to earth by creatures from another planet, discovery by junior scientists from room 6 of the languages used by dolphins, chimps, dogs, and so on, and what they have been waiting so long to "tell" us.)

REFERENCES

1. Lipman, Mathew, Sarp, Ann Margaret, and Oscanyan, Frederick S. *Philosophy in the Classroom*. Second edition. Philadelphia: Temple University Press, 1980, page 7.
2. Ozmon, Howard and Craver, Samuel, *Philosophical Foundations of Education*. Fourth edition. Columbus, Ohio: Merrill Publishing Company, 1990, pages 139–140.
3. Gega, Peter C. *Science in Elementary Education*. Sixth edition. New York: Macmillan Publishing Company, 1990, page 106.

COMMUNITY RESOURCES

The school, in the past, has kept itself aloof from Social realities. When the rate of social change could be measured in generations, the failure of change for the school to adjust itself was not noticeable. Today, the rapidity of change demands that school shall keep in close touch with contemporary social process.

The educationists have come to realize that the immediate community is a wonderful curriculum laboratory which can provide extremely dynamic, interesting and real life opportunities for learning. The community provides concrete data on cultural, industrial, political, geographical and scientific facts and relationships. These data are tangible, visible and describable. Robertson rightly says that 'a child cannot be adequately educated until and unless he often comes out of four walls of class room'. We all also know that the instruction can end when students leave the portals of educational institutions, but education goes on throughout life.

There are, chiefly, two methods of utilizing the community resources. Taking the school to the community by the way of Field Trips, Community surveys, School Camping, community service projects etc. The other one is by bringing the community to the school by the way of Inviting Resource Persons, Parent-Teacher Associations, Social Service Activities, Festivals and Days, Arranging talks on National and International Problems. Financial Aids by the community members and providing apprenticeship experiences to the students by local traders.

According to E. D. Heiss, O' Bourn and C.W. Hoffman (1961) the community resources can be utilized for the purposes of

(i) to serve as a preview of a particular lesson and for gathering instructional materials;

(ii) to create teaching situation for cultivating observation, keenness, discovery, to encourage children to see and know about things;

(iii) to serve as a means of arousing specific interests;

(iv) to supplement classroom instruction, to secure definite information for a lesson;

(v) to verify previous information; and

(vi) to provide additional information other than in the curriculum.

The real practitioners of the curriculum should make use of the community resources to achieve the goals of education in an intelligent way. K. Freeman, T. I. Dowling, N. Lacy and J.S. Tippet expressed the following reasons for the use of community resources:

(i) there is a wealth of material readily accessible;

(ii) rich, direct experience supply verification and enrichment for vicarious experiences;

(iii) the use of community resources provides a variety of approaches to learning which avoids mystifying the dull and boring the bright with an exclusive diet of 'canned' verbal learning;

(iv) children learn most readily from first hand experiences which give them sensory impressions of feeling, smelling, seeing and hearing;

(v) abstractions may be made concrete and real;

(vi) information purely local in nature or for any other reasons not accessible in school sources may be obtained in the community;

(vii) powers of problem-solving and keen observation in the out-of-school environment may be developed;

(viii) the use of results from contacts which are made to develop good school and community relations;

(ix) the use of scientific discovery in improving community living is copiously illustrated; and

(x) Science is; thus, identified as being everywhere in our daily living, instead of being a mystic laboratory abstraction.

Prof. Narendra Vaidya (1976) states that through regular and repeated visits to the community or reproducing part of the community at school, both schools and students gain much. Students

(i) encounter scientific phenomena first-hand in natural settings;

(ii) develop functional vocabularies and understanding:

(iii) gain in problem-solving abilities

(iv) familiarize themselves with scientific skills of the community (thus exposure to standards) and lastly;

(v) their abilities to gather scientific data objectively get a short in the arm.

Teachers on the other hand,

(i) try hard to close the gap between the school and the community;

(ii) that is blend school life with the outside world putting pupils in direct touch under learning situations, with things, persons, movements, relationships, environments, occupations, tendencies, trends and functionings;

(iii) promote intelligent interest in their immediate environment (man made and natural)

(iv) provide immense opportunities for individual and group work;

(v) help students in organising and vitalizing their knowledge;

(vi) enable students to see the real world of work in which they will enter sooner or later (educational and vocational guidance);

(vii) create learning situations internationally with a view to familiarize them (students) with the various aspects of the scientific attitude as well as the unity of knowledge (correlating loose ends of the various branches of science and knowledge in general) and lastly (viii) effect a genuine socialisation of school procedure.

The latest slogan in education is "Let us study the community, use the community serve the community and involve the community". So the school must enrich with community resources. Let us build bridges between the two, so that the two-way traffic is not only possible but useful and pleasant also. In this regard the teacher should be careful in developing the right attitudes towards the community for better understanding of science.

MICROCOMPUTERS

There are a variety of learning activities available to guide students in attaining relevant objectives. Audio visual aids (slides, filmstrips, films, illustrations, and transparencies), excursions, and reading materials (single or multiple series of textbooks, library books, pamphlets, and brochures), may be utilized in providing significant activities and experiences for learners.

A rather recent innovation-software and the microcomputer also needs adequate emphasis in a modern school science curriculum. Numerous quality programs are available in guiding learners to achieve stated goals.

CRITERIA IN SELECTING SOFTWARE

Teachers need to have appropriate standards in mind when choosing and utilizing quality software in ongoing lessons and units in science. Which guidelines are vital to utilize?

1. Programs used should relate directly to ongoing lessons and units. Knowledge that is related should be retained for a longer period of time compared to that which is unrelated. Thus, learning opportunities used in the classroom, including microcomputers, should challenge learners to make progress in achieving objectives in lessons and units.

2. Appropriate sequence within a program needs to be in evidence. A sequential learning that is too complex may make for a lack of progress in achievement. Toward the other end of the continuum, an order that lacks challenge may make for feelings of boredom. Quality programs, before wide usage, should be field tested in pilot studies. Improved, modified sequence within the programme should be a viable end result. If the content between frame one and frame two is too difficult, an intermediate step of learning should come between the two steps. Or, if the level with the order needs increasing.
3. Debugging needs to receive high priority. Inaccurate content, erroneous spelling, and errors in punctuation in programs need to be eliminated prior to student use and interaction. Defective models on the screen should not be emulated by the involved learner. Rater, inadequate content and mechanics in writing need elimination.
4. Textbook content, workbook exercises, worksheets, and audiovisual materials (slides, filmstrips, films, experiments, and demonstrations) should provide learnings in addition to microcomputer experiences. A variety of activities should assist in providing for individual differences among pupils in a class.
5. Objectives for each software program should be clear and meaningful to teachers as well as learners. Vague, hazy goals do not aid in helping students decide what is to be learned. Specific and general objectives are useful here.
6. Content in software should motivate students to achieve. Graphics, color, and sound as peripherals should stimulate learners achievement. The learner then has a desire to learn if motivation is in evidence. Intrinsic motivation or learning is its own reward is an ideal in microcomputer usage. However, extrinsic motivation provides external rewards for encouraging selected students to learn. Thus, smiley faces or statements of "that's excellent" appearing on the screen after a correct response by a pupil can be motivating. Or a pleasant sound or musical chime after a right answer provided by a pupil can be stimulating to the learner to progress continuously.

USES OF MICROCOMPUTERS AND SOFTWARE

There are numerous purposes involved in utilizing microcomputers in science. One use is tutorial. New subject matter is acquired by the student when software stresses the concept of tutorial instruction. Adequate emphasis in tutorial software includes students interaction. Thus, the learner should not merely read content on the screen or monitor. Opportunities need to be ample in which a learner acquires subject matter with provisions to make responses of multiple choice, true-false, completion, essay, or matching item. After typing in a response on the terminal, the pupil frequently needs to receive feedback in terms of correctness or incorrectness as to his/her answers. A student then does not practice what is incorrect but first receives corrective information as to rightness or wrongness of responses made.

Drill and practice is a second purpose involved in utilizing software and the microcomputer. There are selected facts, concepts, and generalizations that students need to review in science. Vital subject matter only, should be emphasized within the framework of drill and practice. With an increased emphasis upon the explosion of knowledge in science, it behooves software developers to select what is significant and not transitory. Thus, to increase retention of worthwhile content, students need ample opportunities to review that which has been acquired previously.

Quality sequences emphasizing drill and practice activities need to be in evidence on the monitor or screen. Appeal and interest is also important. Too frequently, drill and practice content is boring and lacks stimulation.

Computer services may be utilized to score tests in the science curriculum. Test results may be stored and retrieved when necessary. Comparisons should be made of earlier as compared to more recent test results of each student. The concept of diagnosis may be emphasized in the specific errors of a learner may be noticed by the teacher and the involved pupil. Remediation work should then be provided. Pupils individually need to receive assistance in overcoming deficiencies in learning in the science curriculum.

From a printout, the teacher may notice which test items have been marked incorrectly by students. Item analysis data from the ıntout provides the teacher needed information to arrange test items from easiest to those which are increasingly more complex.

Simulation experiences are significant in the science curriculum. There are selected quality programs in the area of simulation. Attempts are made to have students experience the real world in a simulated environment. The real world, however, has been simplified as a model. No threatening experiences make it so that pupils freely can engage in choosing and deciding. Feedback to the involved student comes after each choice or decision has been made.

Generally, simulation utilization is quite motivating to the learner. Reality based content and information received immediately as to the wisdom of each choice seemingly provides its own motivation for students. Learners do need to possess readiness factors and background information in order to benefit from the simulation. Simulations differ from tutorials in that the later does not stress decision making in the real world. Also, simulated experiences differ from drill and practice in that the former does not emphasize the concept of repetition or review. The concepts of diagnosis and remediation seemingly have no role in simulated programs. The former stresses pinpointing specific weaknesses and overcoming the deficiencies. Simulations pursue answers to sequential problems. A miniature society is then emphasized in problem solving. School and society tend to become increasingly integrated as simulations are utilized in the curriculum.

Wright and Forcier[1] list the criteria to evaluate drill and practice, tutorial, and simulation, and tool learning software: (see table on page 153).

Games can provide valuable microcomputer experiences for students. Software emphasizing gaming must be challenging and yet not overwhelming. Games should emphasize the development of wholesome learner attitudes even though competition between players or teams is in evidence.

One of the writers has observed games which teachers have made to encourage pupil progress. Thus, a spinner is flipped by the student covering the separate spaces of one through five. If a student, for example, spins the spinner and it shows "three", he/she can move forward three spaces on the same board if a question is answered correctly. The cards, each containing a question, are

Drill and Practice	Tutorial
1. Personalized (relates to user).	1. Introduction of material complete and understandable.
2. Reinforces/rewards user.	2. Pretest for placement.
3. Student-controlled pace.	3. Frequent testing.
4. Interest maintained.	4. Limited number of retries on error.
5. Level of difficuluty. —Student choice. —Continuum (easy/hard).	5. Reteach when established number of errors accumulated.
6. Comulative score presented.	6. Properly sequenced tasks.
	7. Program can branch.
Simulation	**Tool Learning**
1. Directions clear.	1. Help commands on page.
2. Interest maintained.	2. Flexible entry and retrival.
3. Realistic.	3. Adequate storage.
4. Graphics: —Present. —Appropriate.	4. Security measures adequate.
	5. User prompts given.
5. Level of difficulty. —Student choice. —Continuum (easy/hard).	6. Performance speed.
	7. Flexible report formatting.

placed face down. The opposing player turns face up the top card and reads the question contained thereon to the learner who spun the value of three. The student must answer the question correctly to advance three spaces on the game board. If he/she cannot respond with the correct answer, the opposing player spins the spinner, attempts to answer the question correctly on the card turned right side up by the opposing player. The person who reaches the finish space first on the game board was the winner.

Similar principles of learning may be stressed in gaming using software and the computer.

MICROCOMPUTER LITERACY IN THE CURRICULUM

Each person needs to achieve objectives involving computer literacy. Why? Computers are commonly used in the business world as well as home use. School and society should not be separated from each other. Rather, what is emphasized in society that is deemed worthwhile also has significance in developing the school curriculum. Which goals then become salient for teachers and students to achieve in the computer area?

Objectives need to be carefully selected. With the explosion of knowledge in school and in society, relevant goals need to be chosen. Trivia must be omitted. Learners need to perceive purpose or reasons for achieving desired understandings, skills, and attitudinal goals.

Certainly, students need to experience quality sequence in learning. Thus, software for computers needs to be evaluated carefully using quality criteria. If learnings are not sequential for students, a lack of feelings of success in achievement might well be an end result. Each new learning acquired needs to be related to previous content mastered. Poorly developed sequence in software contains subject matter either too complex or too easy for students. Quality software assists students to progress toward mastering increasingly complex items with sequential success, Reinforcement in learning is in evidence.

Relevant subject mater needs to be in evidence in computer software. Thus, computer programs must guide learners to achieve vital goals. Teachers and administrators need to appraise software in terms of containing significant content. Merely utilizing computers in the curriculum does not answer problems in guiding students to achieve optimally. Software accepted by educators in the school curriculum must meet criteria pertaining to being salient. Irrelevant learnings for students need to be minimized or omitted. Useful learnings that have transfer value must be emphasized in selecting vital software components.

A third problem area in utilizing microcomputers involves its integration with other worthwhile experiences for students. A variety of activities need to be experienced by learners to provide for individual optimal progress. Each student has preferred learning styles which need implementation in the curriculum. Thus, slides, films, filmstrips, cassettes, educational television, transparencies, excursions, illustrations, drawings and resource personnel need to be utilized in addition to micro-computers to provide quality learning experiences for students. The influence of technology certainly is being felt in the curriculum due to heavy computer use in society. With the utilization of computers in teaching learning situations, hopefully, each learner will achieve more optimally in the curriculum.

IN CLOSING

Microcomputer and software utilization needs to be emphasized as learning opportunities to assist pupils to achieve relevant objectives. Appropriate principles of learning should be followed in selecting and developing software. Thus, pupils individually need to experience interest, purpose, and meaning in the science curriculum.

REFERENCE

1. Edward C. Wright and Richard C. Forcier, *The Computer: A Tool for the Teacher*. Belmont, California; Wadsworth Publishing Company, 1985, page 159.

READING

Reading in science is one avenue of learning in this vital curriculum area. There are numerous kinds of subject matter for learners to read. Factual as well as fictional content then can be read by pupils in ongoing science units of study. Both should provide for enjoyment and encouragement to attain objectives in this science curriculum. Objectives emphasizing knowledge, skills, and altitudes need to be in the offing. Individual differences must be provided for so that fast, average, and slow learners might well attain optimally.

INDIVIDUALIZED READING

We recommend strongly that each pupil has adequate time to select and read trade books on an individual basis. Library books related directly to the science unit being taught need to be located at a learning center. The books should be on a variety of achievement levels so that each pupil can choose a book that is his/her reading level. It is frustrating for the learner if a library book is too complex to read. Should the chosen book be too easy to read in terms of content, boredom may set in and be an end result. Each pupil must experience challenge and interest in reading a self selected library book.

To further provide for individual differences, library books should be on diverse topics, but definitely related to the unit in science being taught presently. Thus, if pupils are studying a unit on "The changing surface of the Earth," they need to be able to select books on a variety of titles such as those pertaining to volcanic eruptions, mountain formation, erosion, climate, and earth quakes. With different topics being covered in library books, each pupil may choose what is of most personal interest. Interest is a powerful factor in motivating pupil achievement. Pupils when selecting their own library books to read follow their very own purposes. Possessing perceived purpose also is a motivational force in guiding optimal progress in science achievement. We believe pupils tend to perceive increased purpose or reasons due to reading when self selection of materials is involved rather than the teacher choosing what learners are to read. The content acquired by pupils from reading should be discussed within the unit title emphasized in a contextual setting, not in isolation from other experiences in the current unit being studied in science. For example, if pupils are discussing the causes of earthquakes, what has been read from library books on that topic may be applied in problem solving situations. Or, if learners are studying the causes of volcanic eruptions, reading of subject matter from library books may confirm or modify what occurred in a related science experiment. Interest, purpose, and relating of content acquired are powerful days of having pupils achieve, learn, and grow in the science curriculum. This is also true when pupils read or experience other kinds of learning opportunities in science. Each pupil reveals different characteristics from others in the classroom and needs personal attention to these individual factors and traits.

With self selection of reading materials directly related to the present science unit being taught, individual differences in interests and reading levels can be provided for.

HIGHER LEVELS OF COGNITION

The science teacher needs to guide pupils to attain well in higher levels of cognitive domain objectives. Thus in reading science content, learners must learn to read for different reasons or purposes. Too frequently, pupils have read subject matter to acquire facts. Relevant facts can be salient and important for learner acquisition. Pupils should have ample opportunities to reflect upon factual content read. Thus if pupils have read how sedimentary rocks are formed, they should think about the involved facts. Merely memorizing what has been read makes for a lack of meaning. Questions raised by the teacher and involved pupils about facts read can stimulate thought. Perhaps, the acquired facts can reveal comprehension by using these ideas in new situations. Facts gained then about the formation of sedimentary rocks can be applied to the uses made of this kind of rock in society, such as in building barbecue pits or natural rock walkways and fences. When pupils read, they should be able to apply or use what has been learned.

When pupils read critically, as an even higher level of cognition, they separate one category of information from another, facts from opinions, fantasy from reality, and accurate form inaccurate content. Thus when learners read about rock formation. They should be able to distinguish the forming of sedimentary from igneous rock, or sedimentary from metamorphic rock. Clarity of ideas is vital when learners categorize knowledge. There are numerous opinions that individuals have about science phenomenon. However, science and its content prizes accuracy of subject matter content acquired. Objectivity is a key concept in studying scientific information. An independent environment outside of the observer's perception is in evidence. Thus content in science is objective regardless of who does the observing. To be might well be to be perceived by someone, but there is an independent reality which does not require an observer. Subjectivity in subject matter knowledge is then not a part of the knowledge and skills in science. It is true that our knowledge of science changes, such as the ringlets now accepted as being true in the planet Saturn, not the solid core of rings around this planet. However, with modern techniques of acquiring more information in the world of science new facts change ideas about scientific knowledge due to improved scientific methods of securing information, not due to changes in the rings around the planet Saturn, unless the changes are due to scientific (objective) data. For example, the surface of the planet earth changes due to volcanic eruptions, earthquakes, and erosion, among other factors. So too, many other planets change in time, such as Saturn.

Creative reading is another salient kind of comprehension in science. Creativity here stresses a desire by the learner to fill gaps in information in the ongoing science unit of study being emphasized. A gap represents what the pupil does not know and would like to fill in the necessary content. Reading is one approach of doing this. Curious learners who lack information at a given point may do more reading to fulfil that gap. The science teacher should assist learners to identify what they do not understand. Learning opportunities guide pupils to fill the gap or the unknown. A creative mind can lead to the next kind of reading comprehension and that being to emphasize problem solving. Pupils should be assisted by the teacher to identify problem areas. These problem areas become broad questions, framed so they allow pupils to secure needed content for answers. A variety of learning opportunities may be used to obtain answers. Reading, experimentation, demonstrations, audiovisual materials, excursions, and discussions are and can be used as learning opportunities to secure information in answer to identified problem areas. Pupils with teacher guidance may select problem areas well as resources to use to obtain answers. Next in problem solving, pupils should develop a hypothesis or answer to the problem. We recommend a brain storming approach here. No value judgments should be made as each pupil provides a hypothesis. The hypotheses may be printed on the chalk board as presented to avoid duplication of answers given by learners. The purpose of brain storming is to generate answers. Hypotheses can be tested through experimentation, further reading, use of audio-visual aids, and presentations by qualified resource persons, among other worthwhile procedures. Hypotheses may then need to be revised, if evidence warrants.

There are additional purposes for pupils in reading science content. Thus reading to follow directions can be salient. Individuals in ongoing units of study and in society read directions. These directions must be understood so that they can be followed correctly. Scanning of content is another important purpose in reading content in science. With scanning, the pupil quickly secures an overview of a page or chapter to notice if it contains the necessary information being looked for to solve problems. If so, the pupil may wish to read the rest of the printed ideas. It does save time when a pupil can scan materials to notice if the rest of the ideas need to be read so that relevant ideas are secured.

Reading for facts is another salient purpose for comprehending science materials. There are vital facts for pupils to read which assist in understanding content better in an ongoing lesson or unit of study. We find that reading selected facts on our part is done for sheer interest in many cases. The desire to know is a powerful factor in learning. Not always is subject matter, such as reading to obtain factual information, done to attain further ends such as to solve problems, but is done for its on sake. Hopefully, there will be a concrete use for these ideas at a later time. Anyway when pupils read to secure a main idea or a generalization, facts will support or refute the accuracy of these broad statements. Thus reading to secure a main idea or generalization is vital. One reason being that facts are relatively easy to forget whereas the broader statements (main ideas or generalizations) are much easier to recall generally since they are fewer in number.

USE OF BASAL TEXT BOOK IN SCIENCE

Basal textbooks, carefully selected, related directly to ongoing units of study can assist pupils to obtain necessary information. The textbook used should be on the reading level of the involved learner so that he/she attaches meaning to what is being read. If the text is too difficult to read orally or silently, the pupil will not understand the contents read. If the text is too easy, boredom may set in for learning on the part of the pupil. The science teacher must to observe each pupil to determine if the latter is learning and achieving from the reading experience. Most pupils reveal comprehension from reading if they can answer questions during a discussion covering content of what has been read. However, a few pupils may be shy and not participate in the discussion even though the can read its contents with understanding. Here the teacher needs to encourage all in the classroom to participate. Each pupil needs to attain optimally from reading.

Readiness for reading is important. There is much the science teacher can do to guide pupils to achieve well when reading, even though the content may be slightly difficult for the reader. The teacher then should print in neat manuscript letters words that might cause problems in identification for pupils when reading. These words can be printed in isolation or within a contextual situation in sentences. In the latter case, each possible new world needs to be underlined or highlighted. The teacher should then guide pupils to pronounce each new world correctly as listed on the chalkboard. Learners should also understand the meaning of each word either though a brief definition or through use in a sentence. The Glossary located in back of the basal can assist pupils in securing definitions for new words. Pupils need to posses adequate background information in order to attach meaning to what will be read in the reading assignment. If pupils are to read abut volcanic eruptions, they should have the needed prerequisite content to understand what is being read. A purpose or reason for reading needs to be stressed. The purpose can be in question form from the teacher and better yet from learners themselves. Pupils should then be ready to read so that information in answer to these questions can be gathered

The follow up to the actual reading activity is a must. Interest in reading and the follow up is extremely important. The following are suggested as follow up experiences for learners:

1. discussing what has been read such as answering the questions in the purpose.
2. outlining selected ideas from the reading selection.
3. summarizing major subject mater read by listing main ideas.
4. drawing a series of illustrations to reveal understandings gained.
5. dramatizing ideas acquired.
6. using attained ideas to solve problems or check hypotheses from ongoing science experiments.
7. doing experiments based on content read.
8. reading from other reference sources to confirm or modify subject mater contained in the basal.
9. researching related data by using reputable sources of information.
10. engaging in a homework activity by identifying and solving a relevant problem.

Using a basal science textbook can truly become a good learning activity if pupils understand and can apply information obtained. Subject mater should make sense to the pupil and not be trivialized. The pupil needs to reflect upon its meaning, think critically and creatively about its contents, and make use of ideas to solve problems. Providing readiness for pupils prior to reading is time well spent for the science teacher. A relevant science curriculum will have as one of its learning opportunities the skill of reading; other kinds of materials to use in teaching-learning situations will include the semi concrete and concrete means of learning. Reading stresses the use of abstract materials in the science curriculum. Additional abstract experiences include listening. Speaking, and writing. The latter three kinds of abstract learning activities need elaboration so that related reading skills might be increased for each learner.

LISTENING IN THE SCIENCE CURRICULUM

Listening well assists pupils to achieve more optimally since we learn much from listening to others. In small and large group discussions within a science unit, pupils should develop skill to grasp ideas readily. It might be that any spoken idea is said one time only. If a pupil did not secure the idea, he/she has not learned as much as possible. The too, what one fails to secure as a results of listening may also hinder from obtaining other information due to its contextual setting. There are numerous purposes or reasons for quality listening in the science curriculum. Among others, these include listening to

1. a discussion of an ongoing science experiment such as problem selection, possible solutions to the problem, data gathering, and appraisal of the solutions offered previously.
2. an evaluation of ideas presented in a science demonstration. Content therein should be appraised and evaluated.
3. a book report on a relevant issue in science.
4. acquiring information from a committee project when elaborated upon by its members.
5. a creative or formal dramatization pertaining to the life and times of a scientist.
6. poetry written pertaining to an ongoing science unit.
7. showing and explaining a mural developed by volunteers in an ongoing science unit of study.
8. a cassette recording related to lesson presentation.
9. a video-tape on a selected topic in science.
10. creative prose written by learners such as tall tales, myths, legends, and others, relating to interests of pupils in science.

To provide for individual differences, pupils need to experience a variety of activities in science. Each pupil needs to learn as much as possible. Learners differ form each other in learning styles possessed. This means that different activities should be available for learner interaction.

SPEAKING ACTIVITIES IN SCIENCE

A variety of rich speaking experience should be available to pupils so that quality communication in science is achieved by each. The teacher needs to guide the concept of excellence in oral communication. Scientists tend to be strong in oral communication skills. Pupils too should be assisted to truly communicate well with others. What might pupils learn to communicate in science well so that evidence?

1. the development of and results of a science experiment.
2. the completed reading of ideas contained in a textbook, library book, journal, or other printed materials related directly to an ongoing science unit.
3. oral reports given pertaining to content read inherent in a lesson.
4. main ideas circulating within a committee setting.
5. brain storming to solve a problem within the class as a whole.
6. dramatic endeavors to communicate selected content to peers.
7. reader's theater to present specific subject matter to listeners.
8. purposes involved in planning, developing, and evaluating a project in science.
9. pupil demonstration and explanation of a phenomena being studied in science.
10. committee exploration of methods of solving an identified problem area in science.

The science teacher must have as a major goal in the science curriculum to assist pupils to be able to communicate well as that more optimal attainment for each learner is an end result.

WRITING IN SCIENCE

Writing can be a difficult skill to achieve when proficiency is involved. Abstractions are stressed here such as symbols representing content in science. The symbols pertain to a code that must be broken to read and understand subject matter. When writing, the situation is reversed, the writer encodes so that a reader can ascertain the inherent ideas. The encoding with letters to represent words and larger units such as sentences, paragraphs, and entire selections must be accurate and complete. Vagueness and a lack of coherence must be eliminated in writing. What pupils learn in language arts can then be transferred to the area of writing in science. The following salient writing purposes need to be stressed in science.

1. the plan and results of a science experiment.
2. notes taken over content read from the basal text.
3. outlines written covering a relevant selection.
4. business letters written to order vital materials pertaining to a unit of study.
5. friendly letters written to pen pals to share ideas about what is presently being studied.
6. diary entries written pertaining to subject matter acquired on successive days of learning.
7. log entries recording coverage of content covering a week or for the entire unit of study.
8. journal writing reflecting upon the learner's achievements for and in learning.
9. written book reports telling a few major ideas acquired from reading.
10. a formal dramatization in which play parts are written for the life and times of a famous scientist.

A variety of writing activities should be in the offing so that pupil proficiency is developed when communicating ideas. Individual differences in writing achievement need to be considered by the science teacher. The pupil and teacher need to appraise what the former has attained previously in order to ascertain if improvement in writing has occurred in the preset completed sample of written work. A folder for each pupil's written work needs to be kept so that earlier written work can be compared with later products to notice progress of the learner in writing for a variety of purposes.

IN CONCLUSION

Reading of subject matter in science is a salient activity along with other kinds of experiences involving the concrete and the semi concrete. The science teacher needs to be certain that pupils are ready for reading content prior to the actual reading activity. This is especially true of reading from the basal text. Thus the teacher should have pupils see and attach meaning to the new words in the text prior to reading. Learners also need adequate background information of what will be read, prior to reading. A reason or purpose for reading will increase reading comprehension. Thus pupils have a framework or questions to answer in reading for ideas, facts, concepts, and generalizations.

There should be a follow up of experiences after pupils have completed reading a given selection so that comprehension and retention of content is in evidence.

Complementing the reading activity are listening, speaking, and writing activities. Divers kinds of activities are in evidence here to encourage pupils to communicate ideas through speaking and writing, as well as acquire subject matter through reading and listening. Pupils individually need to achieve as much as possible in ongoing lessons and units of study in science.

WRITING

Pupils need to become quality communicators of content in writing. Why ? Scientists in a laboratory setting must be able to write their findings in an accurate, objective approach so that effective communication among experts, as well as others, is in evidence. Not being able to communicate effectively in writing would greatly hinders scientific achievement in sequence on a continuing basis. Thus, in poorly developed written communication, scientists could not benefit from each other's research and findings. It behooves the teacher to encourage, assist, and motivate each pupil to do as well as possible in writing in on-going science units of study.

WRITING AND THE PUPIL

The science teacher needs to determine where each pupil is presently in achievement in writing. At this starting point, the teacher must guide learners on an individual basis to attain optimally and in a sequential manner.

A. Writing Experience Charts in Science

Early primary grade pupils tend to enjoy writing experience charts. A cooperative teacher who supervised a student teacher of mine taught a unit on *Animals in Our Lives*. She had three goldfish in an aquarium, tadpoles in a jar, a frog in a terrarium, a small garter snake in a different terrarium, and a pet canary in a bird cage. Pupils observed the goldfish carefully as they swam in the aquarium. Pupils were then asked to present ideas on what they saw to the teacher who in return recorded in writing observations presented. The following sentences, among others, were given in which first grade learners could see talk written down and experience writing:

1. The gold fish swam rapidly.
2. The bright colors mixed with the sunlight.
3. Water in the aquarium has bubbles inside of it.
4. Fish come up to breathe air.
5. It is fun to watch the fish being fed.

The numerals were then removed from the above experience chart and pupils read the content with teacher guidance. The teacher pointed to the words as the young learners orally read the content together with the teacher. There were numerous pupils to do so as the teacher patiently pronounced the words sequentially in the group exercise using the experience chart. The experience chart was saved and posted on the wall. Pupils could then view the chart as the need arose. A week later, the teacher again read the contents of the chart with the children involved. Several asked to read it individually to the entire class. This developed considerable enthusiasm. The teacher announced to the class that anyone wishing to read the contents off the chart to her (the teacher) should do so at any time. At this point and stage of achievement, most of these first grade pupils read the subject matter on the chart, making very few errors. This chart and later ones developed were saved for learners to re-read at their own convenience.

With the use of the experience chart approach in teaching writing, pupils can see talk written down. Thus what is said orally can be printed with the use of abstract symbols in grapheme-phoneme relationships. The experience chart concept of teaching reading is based upon learners having a personal experience. In this situation, the experience was to look at goldfish. Later experience charts would be based upon pupils seeing tadpoles, frogs, a snake, and a canary. This brought to the attention of pupils, fish, amphibians, reptiles, and birds as sequential classification of animals with backbones. Still later, the teacher brought her pet cat to class to show a mammal.

With concrete experiences of viewing life-like, real animals, pupils began to use language to describe what was viewed. The use of oral communication was then inherent. Pupils listened to the ideas presented by others. The content that resulted was printed in neat, manuscript letters by the teacher. Learners then read the content orally with teacher guidance as the latter pointed to the words and phrases within each sentence. Thus oral communication, listening, writing, and reading were experienced by each learner. The four language arts areas then become an inherent part of the science unit currently being studied.

When pupils are ready, they should write their own experience charts. This activity can be appropriate on any grade level.

B. Outlining Content in Science

Outlining content read from the basal or other reference source might well assist pupils to be able to organize information better in terms of sequence. A quality outline should possess the following parts:

1. The title
2. Roman numerals to show the main ideas or divisions
3. Capital letters under each main idea to show the relationship of these sub-divisions with the main idea.
4. Details with ordered numerals under each sub-division to show relationships between the sub-division and the related details.

In outlining content, such as from the basal textbook in science, pupils may perceive the relationship of subordinate ideas to the main idea, the details to the subordinate idea, and the general sequence of subject matter. A pupil that focuses too much upon isolated facts tends to forget content sooner as compared to those who perceive that broader ideas exist such as subordinate and main ideas. Then too, broader ideas tend to become a part of the general repertoire of the learner sooner as compared to the acquisition of isolated facts. Thus, there is a structure of knowledge in science for the learner when he/she perceives that key ideas can be selected and subordinate content and details can be related rather readily to the main ideas. We recommend that when pupils are ready, not before, they experience practice in outlining subject matter, not for the sake of doing so, but to perceive knowledge as being related.

A quality outline on a purposeful topic provides the learner with an excellent tool to present on oral report to others in the classroom setting. The pupil should never read ideas from an outline, but use the ideas therein to present well organised subject matter to listeners. Thus, if the learner forgets sequential content in the report, he/she may then refer to the outline. Quality organisation of content assists the listener to acquire what is being presented. If an oral report contains randomly presented ideas, the chances are that comprehension by listeners will be difficult.

Pupils may receive practice in reading content in science that is poorly organised and re-arrange the sentences so that coherence is in evidence. Noticing the differences between the two is important.

C. Writing Science Experiments

A very useful writing experience for pupils is to write up science experiments that have been or will be performed in on-going units of study. We believe that a plan developed by the teacher with pupil involvement will aid in writing that which is clear and distinct. First of all, the experiment needs to have a title which is meaningful to readers. If pupils are studying a unit or partial unit on water erosion of soil, a science experiment that is salient might well be entitled "Water and Soil Erosion". A problem then needs to be stated. The problem should be written clearly so that related information may be located as solutions. Hazy problem areas do not lend themselves to finding needed answers. A clearly worded problem might be the following : How does rainfall affect the soil in our school-yard ? Learners might then brainstorm answers to this question. No value judgement should be made to contributions of individual pupils. Respect for the thinking of others is necessary to generate ideas. The answers proposed in brainstorming should be recorded on the chalk-board to avoid unnecessary duplications. Higher levels of cognition are involved when pupils continue to offer answers. Initially, it probably is relatively easy to offer answers to the identified problem or question. After brain-storming, pupils need to ascertain which answers are acceptable and which are not.

Science experiments should be performed in the classroom to determine the affects of water upon soil as well as observing in the out-of-doors what happens to soil with different levels of intensity of falling rain. As many variables as possible must be observed too, such as the slope of the land, the covering (grass) of the soil, and the kind of soil (clay, sandy, loam, among others). Inside the classroom, two boxes of equivalent soil with equal slope may be used initially. A similar amount of water should be poured over each box containing the soil. The only variable tested here is that one box has a grass covering over the soil whereas the other box does not. The amount of run-off of the solid for each box may be determined with a small container as broad as each box at the base to catch the eroded soil. Other variables to test for include different cover crops, different kinds of soil, as well as different amounts of water with variable intensity poured over each box.

These activities can also be used in testing the different answers given in brainstorming:

1. reading from diverse sources which shed light on water erosion of soil.
2. viewing audio-visual aids on causes and prevention of erosion of soil.
3. listening to qualified resource persons.
4. doing additional experiments and observing demonstrations.
5. making models of soil preservation including terracing, strip cropping, and trees/vegetative coverings to prevent erosion in its diverse forms.

Answers to questions should be viewed as tentative with chances of making necessary modifications as the need arises. Each step discussed above should be written with clarity and precision. Thus the problem or question, the brain-stormed ideas, the data gathering, and needed modifications sections should be written with meaning and comprehension. Quality writing assists in communicating ideas more effectively.

D. Writing Book Reports

Summarizing what has been read from a library book directly related to an on-going science unit can be highly educational for pupils. The learner should have had the opportunity to choose his/her own book to read, from among others, at a reading center. There are several kinds of writing activities that can be implemented here. The pupil needs to select which procedure to use when writing about subject matter read from a library book. Thus, the pupils may choose from among the following:

1. writing a certain number of main ideas covered in the chosen book.
2. writing what was perceived to be the most interesting content contained in the reading material.
3. writing one or more paragraphs pertaining to the central idea contained in the library book.
4. writing questions that remain unanswered pertaining to the content.
5. writing a different beginning or ending if the contents of the library book are highly creative, such as the book *Miss Pickerel on Mars*.

Writing summaries pertaining to content read from library books should encourage, not destroy interest, in reading and writing. The teacher should evaluate achievement here and in all writing experiences based on the following criteria:

1. use standards that assist the learner to notice that which needs to be improved upon.
2. have reasonable standards for each pupil, not excessively difficult nor at too low a level of achievement.
3. do not emphasize too many corrections for any one pupil to make, lest the involved child is overwhelmed with corrections that need to be made.
4. focus upon ideas in the written product, not exclusively upon the mechanics of writing such as spelling, punctuation, and grammar.
5. emphasize clarity of ideas expressed, not quantity in content written.

It is important for teachers to have conferences with pupils, one on one, too assist learners to improve over previous attempts at written work. The conference should stress caring for the pupil in becoming a better writer. Negative criticism must be avoided in the conference setting. A positive attitude toward the learner and his/her ability to improve in writing in all school endeavours is a must.

E. Journal Writing in Science

Pupils need to be given time to engage in journal writing. This provides opportunities for learners to reflect upon what has been learned in on-going science units and lessons. Journal entries may be dated. What is written in the journal is up to the pupil. A pupil may then write what transpired in a science experiment or demonstration. The learner may wish to focus upon salient ideas discussed in a committee setting. With reflection, the involved learner will remember better what has been learned due to thinking upon key ideas or concepts stressed in science. The pupil might desire to write about attitudes and interests developed in science as a result of teaching and learning experiences.

Should the teacher appraise the quality of these journal entries ? If not, how does a teacher know if the time devoted to journal writing is worthwhile and assists the learner to attain relevant objectives ? If the teacher appraises the quality of journal writing, should the contents be graded ? These and other vital questions need careful consideration.

We would suggest that teachers encourage pupils to share their writings. This can be done by sharing content written with the teacher on a voluntary basis. Pupils might also meet in committees to share what has been written. It is best if pupils are not coerced to show what was written in the journal. However, a pupils may waste time and pretend he/she is writing, but is day dreaming or writing irrelevant content. We believe the teacher can and must observe pupils to notice that achievement is taking place in all learning opportunities. A general overview in observing learner achievement may suffice in appraising pupil progress in writing journal entries. The teacher needs to be a good observer and use quality criteria to appraise pupil progress. A listing of criteria may assist the teacher to make justifiable decisions pertaining to pupil journal writing. Among others, these include the following :

1. time on task is vital.
2. conscientious and judicious statements are a must.

3. proper order of written subject matter is salient.
4. clarity of content is necessary.
5. accurate mechanics in writing are needed to the degree it makes the written content more meaningful.

There should be a variety of kinds of learning opportunities in writing so that pupils feel that written work is utilitarian and purposeful.

F. Writing Diary Entries

Pupils individually or in committees need to have ample opportunities to write on a day to day basis what was learned in a science lesson. Each entry should be dated. By writing what was learned on a daily basis in science, writers review previously acquired information. With review, subject matter learned will be retained for a longer period of time than would otherwise be the case. Pupils should participate on a rotating basis in writing these diary entries. The following are examples of diary entries written by a committee of learners:

October One. The teacher explained to us the differences between sheet and gulley erosion. Emphasis was also placed upon the amount of top soil lost each year due to erosion. Farm crop yields decrease when rich top soil is not available for the growing of wheat, soybeans, and corn, among other grains. Marginal and tilled hilly land, in particular, are subject to increased erosion.

October Two. We went outdoors to notice gulley erosion beginnings on our playground. We leveled the soil and seeded grass to avoid erosion. We then came into the classroom to watch a videotape on "Preventing Soil Erosion." Before observing the video, we hypothesized on ways to prevent soil erosion. During the video, we were asked to list and describe different ways to prevent or minimize soil erosion as presented in the video. These ways include using terraces, seeding grass and planting trees, as well as emphasizing strip cropping, among others.

The teacher may discuss with the entire class what might be added to each diary entry. These entries should be kept so that pupils might use these for review Individual or committee members' names may appear on each page of diary entries and bound for future reference. Hopefully, the learning opportunity will increase learner interest, purpose, and meaning for writing in science.

G. Writing Log Entries

Pupils may review and combine the diary entries so that a log may be written. A log covers a longer period of time in terms of lessons content as compared to diary entries. Thus a log may pertain to recording what was learned within a week. The diary entries then become a part of the log. Individuals and committees who record the log entries must read carefully each entry so that broader generalizations may be written such as in a log. Log entries should be bound together with the diary entries so that pupils might review and rehearse what had been learned previously. Log entries provide a good basis in reviewing for an oncoming test.

Standards to follow in writing log entries include the following:

1. ideas should be specific enough so that misinterpretation is not possible.
2. quality human relations need to be stressed in any committee endeavors.
3. appropriate order of content is necessary so that sequence is in evidence.
4. correct spelling of words, punctuation, indentation of paragraphs, and grammar should be in evidence in order to communicate effectively. However, the focal point is on ideas in the logs, not the mechanics of writing.
5. log writing must encourage an increased desire to write rather than writing being perceived as a chore.

If pupils are to become good writers, writing should be emphasized across the curriculum. The curriculum area of science provides its many opportunities for pupils to become good writers. There are numerous purposes in writing in science. The author here recommends that pupils participate actively and fully in written work in ongoing lessons and units of study in science.

Using Word Processors

One of the greatest boon to writing has been the use of the word processor. The word processor indeed eliminates much drudgery attached to writing. The mistakes made in typing can quickly be corrected on the monitor before a final copy is sent through the printer. One can secure the desired copy, reading it on the monitor, before printing occurs. A perfect copy may then result even if a person's typing is not the best. A spell check program eliminates spelling errors in a hurry without retyping any part of the document. There are limitations here in that the computer does not catch errors in homonyms nor in selected other kinds of errors such as in punctuation or capitalization. The user of the word processor still needs to be able to proof read typed content carefully and oh so carefully. However, spelling errors can all be taken care of in a very short time indeed with a spell check program. Typing errors can be taken care of quickly be looking to see what is on the monitor and making needed revisions when proofing. I find it enjoyable to use a word processor in typing manuscript content each day. One can make much headway in typing with a personal computer that is very user friendly. A person who can type using the old typewriter can learn very quickly to use a word processor and be amazed at its capabilities!

Pupils who use word processors when ready, feel ownership of the tasks involved thereon. The pupil with teacher assistance determines the content to be put into the computer. He/she sequences the content to be typed. Revisions are made in terms of the writer's goals. When changes need to be made such as rearrangement of ideas in the typing, this can be done quickly. No longer does a writer need to start all over in typing a page if a single error has been made. Whiteout does not need to be used in making corrections as was true of typewriter use. The writing curriculum must be updated so that each learner can benefit from modern technology and its applications. With word processors, the following conclusion may well be emphasized:

1. writing tends to be more enjoyable since errors made can quickly and conveniently be corrected with user friendly technology.
2. the rearrangement of ideas for quality sequence can be quickly implemented, making it unnecessary to start over again in the typing process.
3. pupils may feel that what is done using the word processor is completely in their hands. The pupil gives

the commands to the computer and completely controls what will follow in terms of content and the mechanics of writing.

4. content typed can involve diverse purposes such as formal and creative writing. Each of the purposes discussed throughout this manuscript pertaining to writing may be emphasized using the word processor.
5. pupils individually or in dyads may write using the word processor depending upon goals stressed in writing in science. Goals may stress individual as well as group or committee endeavors in the curriculum.

IN CLOSING

The science teacher needs to provide a variety of writing activities for pupils. This is necessary to provide for individual differences. Pupils should be guided to become increasingly proficient in writing. One cannot expect a pupil to blossom immediately into becoming a good writer. Rather, sequentially, each pupil can build a repertoire of writing skills. By comparing a pupil's past written product with his preset written work, the teacher can notice the degree to which a learner is achieving more fully. Writing is a basic in the curriculum. The science teacher should incorporate writing experiences when it assists pupils to acquire more subject matter content. Acquisition of facts, concepts, generalizations, principles, and laws of science are vital. So too must skills objectives be emphasized in teaching-learning situations. Thus writing for a variety of purposes in science is salient. The science teacher needs to notice if quality attitudes are a by-product of subject matter and skills stressed in the science curriculum. Each pupil is unique in achievement and needs adequate provision so that continuous progress is possible in science.

EFFECTIVE COMMUNICATION

Communication is the process through which two or more persons come to exchange ideas, opinions feelings and motions and understanding among themselves. It means sharing of ideas and feelings in a mood of mutuality till it becomes common possession. Effective communication is a two-way process including interaction and feedback. The range of communication is from face to face to the mass.

Communication is derived from the Latin word 'Communis' meaning 'common', hence communication is having common experiences with people. Koontz and O'donnel explain "communication is an intercourse by words, letters, symbols or messages and is a way that one organisation member shares meaning and understanding with another'. Allen Louis A. Writes, "Communication is the sum of all the things one person does when he wants to create understanding in the mind of another. If involves a systematic and continuous process of telling, listening and understanding".

Newman and Summer feel, 'Communication is an exchange of facts, ideas, opinions or emotions by two or more persons'.

In the communication process, the source must have correct information and transmit accurately at optimum speed. The message may be designed for a single person or a group of people. It may be conveyed by expressions, gestures, spoken or written symbols or by hand-drawn or photographic pictures. Every medium exerts its influence and its peculiarities on the message and is this sense becomes a part of the message. The receiver must understand the message or in other words, must decode it or interpret it and must produce a desired response, or react which must be received by the sender.

The communication process is a continuous and dynamic interaction both affecting and being affected by many variables. The communication cycle can be represented as follows:

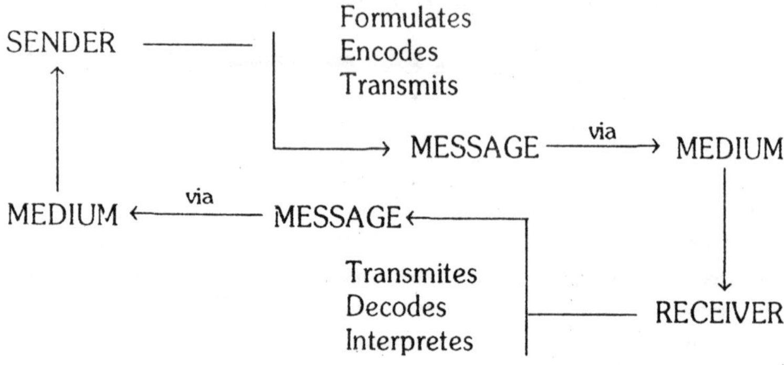

In the above diagram, SENDER is a person who intends to make contact with the objective of passing message to other persons; MESSAGE is the subject matter of communication, this might be an opinion, attitude, feeling, view, order, suggestion etc.; since the subject matter of communication is abstract and intangible, its transmissing requires the use of certain symbols such as words, actions, pictures etc., conversion of this subject matter into these symbols is the process of ENCODING; these symbols are transmitted to the receiver through certain MEDIUM or CHANNEL; converting the symbols the receiver received from the sender to give him the meaning of the message is DECODING; and the FEEDBACK is the process of ensuring that the receiver has received the message and understood in the same sense as the sender meant it.

There are, mainly, three types of communication. In the 'SPEAKING-LISTENING" type of communication, interaction is face to face as in the case of listening to a lecture. The listener can also share the feelings of the source in the same way as in the case of eye to eye contact. Listening to the radio programs is an example for it. In the "VISUALIZING-OBSERVING" type of communication, the observer is physically separated from its producer and yet is able to feel the impact of the message conveyed as in television or motion films. Communication can also take place more effectively by face to face contact with the source as in the case of dramatization when facial expression and gestures produce a greater impact than in the earlier case. In the third type of communication "WRITING-READING", the decoder is physically separated from the encoder all the time and yet the decoder is able to enjoy and appreciate the feelings of the author.

The information given either in written or by oral form should be followed by others easily. Clear information provided to others ensures getting the job done properly. Effective communicating is a skill that every individual must learn. For effective communication the mechanics are:

Shortness,

Simplicity,

Strength,

Sincerity.

FOR SHORTNESS :

Don't add needless information,
be word-stingy.
check unnecessary qualifies,
avoid repetition, unless for emphasis.

FOR SIMPLICITY :

Think clearly,
know your subject well,
prefer plain language,
avoid jargon and circumlocution,
use short words, often more apt,
write small sentences.
make compact paragraphs.

FOR STRENGTH:

rely more on active voice,
use picture verbs,
avoid hesitating language,
choose concrete, specific and strong words;
don't hedge or generalize, don't be hiding behind words;
make sure the punctuation or pause, or lack of it, has not changed your meaning;
keep the objective in mind and focus it;
the sharper the focus of your message, the greater its impact.

FOR SINCERITY :

avoid out-dated and stereo-typed words or phrases,
acknowledge mistakes, if any, in earlier communica tions;
speak or write in human terms;
read to yourself, and listen for the tone.

Communication in the teaching is to a considerable extent carried on through language-spoken and written; the former plays a greater role than mere communication. It is not enough if the pupil merely repeats the same word as conveyed, but the teacher's concern is that the pupil should recognise the word, understand the meaning and use it appropriately with correct spelling on future occasions. True learning is achieved only when the act of communication succeeds in making a permanent and meaningful addition to the pupil's communication skills. Class-room communication is not mere one-sided presentation of facts, but it requires inter-communication between the pupil and the teacher. There should be reaction and interaction with constant reciprocal feedback.

The teachers should know clearly about communication. Hence class-rooms are set up not for dictating teacher's ideas on the pupils but for the purpose of communicating which is a compulsory requirement for any successful individual. The teachers should provide ways and means of developing and improving the skills, because the pupils will constantly come under the influence of various communication media.

The teacher has to make use of modern communication

devices in is teaching in order to impart the latest knowledge. For this, modern technology has provided tapes, films, radio, television and other such mass media besides the old graphic aids, display boards and three dimensional aids. The audiovisual aids will minimize the problems of the teachers as communicators.

In the end we would like to suggest that the teachers must become good communicators by acquiring communicating skills. The greater the degree of understanding present in the communication, the more likelihood that the teaching will proceed in the direction of accomplishing the goals of teaching. The curriculum must also follow the communication techniques.

LEARNING DIFFICULTIES

There are few professions which demand such a range of skills and roles as teaching. The combination of technical, organisational and interpersonal roles, so often taken for granted by those outside the profession mean that teachers have to be exceptional people.

If a teacher finds that a student is not making any progress, or underachieving in a science classroom, he will obviously ask the student why he think this is happening. The teacher will not always get an answer which enables to help the student. Now what can a teacher do ? You, as a teacher, have to attend the following considerations and questions.

PRACTICAL CONSIDERATIONS

Does the student understand the given task ?

Ask the student to repeat what he believes the task to be. If the student repeats your own statements, check that the message is really understood. Make it easy for the student to admit misunderstandings or ignorance without loss of face.

Does the student have the correct tools for the task ?

If you have to ask students to 'make do' or improvise because you cannot supply specialist equipment, check that this improvisation is practical for unskilled students.

Is the environment suitable for the task ?

For instance, have you asked a student to lead a planning session in a noisy room ? Or is the role-play being conducted in a room which can be seen by people who are not involved, to the embarrassment of those who are involved ? Is the room so inconvenient that the student is not able to do dextrous enough for the task ?

Does the student have physical impairments ?

Partial deafness or uncorrected poor sight can go undiagnosed for years and seriously undermine the performance of your students.

Did you allow long enough for the task ?

Do not measure by your own performance the length of time needed for student tasks. Allow time for explorations, mistakes and reflection. Review learning schedules in the light of individual student performance, not standard expectations.

Is the task simply too difficult for the student at this stage ?

Can it be simplified or amended to better suit the student's capabilities ? Can the student be paired with someone who has complementary skills so that between the two of them they can successfully tackle the task ?

SOCIAL AND INTER-PERSONAL CONSIDERATIONS

Have you put together in a group who inhibit each other's peformance ?

This may be a question of antipathy or it may be a question of the quick learners making the slow learners redundant all the time.

Have you asked the student to tackle something which is alien to or forbidden in his culture ?

Do not assume that students will have the confidence to tell you about the cultural difficulties you are posing for them. It is upto you to check cultural patterns. Apparently innocuous assignments may pose enormous difficulties for some students.

Is the student afraid of failure in front of peers ?

The student may be unwilling to ask for supplementary informatioin because it will result in loss of face. Similar worries may inhibit experimentation, communication of ideas, and inventiveness. Some students will respond by deliberately and visibly under-achieving. Others will be torn between contradictory impulses to have a go or to refuse to participate. Their progress will also be haphazard. A variation on this pattern is the student who is afraid to succeed because the ethos of the peer group is to under-achieve. Many students will go to great lengths to avoid being labelled as the teacher's favourite. To overcome this pattern you have got to change totally the criteria for success and failure and thereby change the ehtose of the group. By setting individual targets, stressing process rather than outcomes, and helping students to develop co-operative skills, you may be able to create an environment in which students are supportive of each other's endeavours.

Are you the problem ?

Sometimes the student dislikes you or is afraid of you. Perhaps you taught an older brother or sister and a biased in your earlier stage in his school career and have not adjusted to the student's maturity. Students and teachers have to review and revise their attitudes to one another.

Does the course have sufficient status in the overall framework of your institution ?

It is not unnatural for students to underachieve, or behave diffidently, if they feel that they are engaged in an enterprise which carries a stigma or is undervalued.

INTERNAL CONSIDERATIONS: THOUGHTS, FEELINGS AND STATES OF MIND

Is the student worried or upset ?

There may be something preying on the student's mind which is making concentration difficult. It may be a crisis, such as a bereavement, or it may be an apparently trivial incident, such as a quarrel, or being sacked from a part-time job. The impact may be equally distracting. Before learning can be improved the student may have to talk about the worry and work through emotional difficulties.

Is the student physically unwell?

Students who have a long-term illness may have ways of coping with it most of the time but lapse occasionally. Students who are generally fit may find even a mild disease radically affects their ability to learn.

Is the student tired?

This may be due to the student's private social behaviour. But it is worth checking that you have arranged sufficient rest. Students have different recuperative needs. Some students hate tea breaks, but they want to see things through to a point where they feel happy to leave them. Others simply have to rest after a concentrated effort whatever stage the task is at. It may be difficult, but it is worth trying to find compromises which cater to some extent for this variety of needs.

Is the student bored? Does the incentive system you are using work for this student?

For some students the mere abstract notion of excellence is enough to motivate them. Others need more tangible incentives. Try to create staging posts which work for each students, so that they feel they are getting somewhere.

Is the student a perfectionist?

This is a very unfortunate state of anxiety which is sometimes talked about as if it were a virtue. The perfectionist, in extreme form, is a non-performer. He sets performance targets so high that he cannot begin the task because he knows he will not attain them. A rather nastier way of putting it is that he sets a high standard so that he does not have to start. This type of student needs to be helped to realise that the process of doing a task is important, as well as the outcome, and that making mistakes is natural and sometimes useful.

Is the student caught in a trap of overestimating his ability?

This type of student fails to make progress because he is so focussed on his prowess that he does not see what is out there in the discussion group or in the instrument. He misses important clues and does not adapt to changing circumstances. Get the student to slow down. do less. and think more. Try to foster the idea that the task has rewarding aspects which the student is missing. Resist the temptation to confront the student aggressively with his own unrecognised inadequacy. Underneath all arrogant students are insecurities. It is hard to believe at the time but the swaggerer needs to be made to feel safer so that he can dare to admit the mistakes and areas of ignorance

Is the student caught in a trap ?

'Either you are kind to people and let them insult you—or you are unkind and let them know what sods they are.' This student needs a course in lateral thinking. The gradations and subtleties of life are passing him by. There is no third thing. The student does not look at the full range of possibilities and thus keeps missing the solution and makes little progress.

Is the student thinking too much ?

Over-intellectualisation can freeze students. They overcome it by tricks which make it impossible for the student to think fast enough or accurately enough to cope. When person gives up trying to think out something he can often make progress not previously believed possible. You will have to devise your own tricks but your aim is to get this student to think about the task in advance and then get in there and act without any more pondering.

Has the student got such a low opinion of him that he cannot tackle the task?

You may be dealing with social class, race, or childhood trauma. Somewhere in the student's life the message got through that he was no good at something, or perhaps everything. You have got to stand shoulder to shoulder with this student and fight that message. Correct faults very carefully in the context or things achieved. If the low esteem is related to a specific task, try getting the student to tackle a related but different task. Build a bridge from success in one task to success in the feared task. There are the two secrets of fighting low-self image: lots of encouragement and positive feedback; plus bridges from success in one arena into success in the arena which causes difficulty.

Does the student have a basic skill deficiency. which is hampering progress in more general tasks ?

It may be necessary to arrange for special tuition or coaching but do not under-estimate the emotional and social difficulties associated with basic skill deficiencies of the students.

If all else fails......

You are supposed to make alternate arrangements. It is better to encourage the student to leave the present course to select most suitable course or vocation. Try to identify their interests. abilities. attitudes. skills and successes before suggesting a new alternative and appropriate position.

— The authors thank a gentleman for his original ideas presented in his book.

PROFESSIONAL SCIENCE TEACHER

The teaching science needs to be viewed as trained, educated beings within a profession. A teacher is a decision maker. Teachers make judgements pertaining to objectives, learning activities, evaluation procedures, as well as quality of the classroom environment. To be a teacher means to be a decision maker. Within an open-ended arena, problems arise and solutions need to be found.

Shepberd and Ragan[1] wrote :

> The present age is one of spectacular changes brought about by humans through science and technology. The past twenty years have witnessed more scientific and technological discoveries than had been witnessed in all previous recorded time. The achievement of many of our national goals, at home and abroad, depends upon a strong and growing science and technology. New insights into the processes of investigation, new knowledge in the various areas of science, a new information concerning what pupils at given levesl of development can learn, all require a rethinking of the objectives of science in the elementary school. Science is included in the elementary school curriculum for the contributions it can make to the intellectual,

social, and emotional development of children, and for the contributions it can make to the achievement of our national goals. It can interest some pupils in the excitement and satisfaction of a career in science; it can help all children to comprehend the kind of world in which they live, and to participate effectively in an increasing number of local and national decisions which require an understanding of science.

PROFESSIONALIZATION OF TEACHING SCIENCE

Classroom teachers need ample opportunities to grow, develop, mature, and change. Staying in the classroom continuously, experiencing the routine each day, feeling lack of challenge, having few opportunities to interact with other professionals, attending few or no professional meetings at home or away, and lacking motivation does not encourage meaning and interest in teaching. How then might the teaching of science truly become a profession?

1. Engage in doing research

Classroom teachers of science should actively be involved in conducting research. In conducting research, the teacher with the guidance of a research specialist, needs to identify an experimental group as well as a control group. Each group ideally should be selected at random. Instrumentation used in the study should have the necessary criteria pertaining to validity and reliability. The halo effect must be greatly minimized. If randomization was not utilized, analysis of co-variance should be used to equate the experimental and control groups, based on pretest results. Other variables that need to be taken into consideration are maturation, reactive measures, regression towards the mean, and history of study. Practical research should be emphasized generally by the teacher. However selected teachers may be interested in theoretical studies. With theoretical studies, the researcher attempts to attain a theory which explains or predicts what might happen under selected conditions. The theory is not a fact nor is it a generalization. Theory is hypothesis to be tested in a practical situation. B. F. Skinner, Jerome Burner, and David Ausubel, among others, developed valuable theories.

2. Do Professional Reading in Science

Each puplic school should have a professional library for

teachers. The library needs to house teacher education textbooks, educational journals, audio-visual aids, pamphlets, and other materials on the teaching of science. These should be available to assist teachers to improve the curriculum. Teachers should be given special time during the school day to read and reflect upon what has been read. Ample opportunities need to be given to teachers to discuss content read.

3. Attend Professional Meetings

The National Science Teacher's Association (NSTA) and state affiliates have quality conventions and meetings for teachers to attend. Money and time off from teaching are needed to attend. The local school district should provide the necessary financing as well as substitute teachers. Here the school district is investing in in-service education. An end result should be improved teaching performance in science. Teachers should have ample time to discuss ideas acquired with other professionals.

4. Participate in Faculty Meetings

Administrators and supervisors must schedule an adequate number of faculty meetings during a school year. Each faculty meeting needs to pin-point selected problems identified by teachers. Solving the problems would guide teachers to do a better job of teaching. These problems could deal with such items as discipline in the classroom, providing for individual differences in science, individualised programs of instruction, individually guided instruction, affective goals in the science curriculum, and peer mediated instruction, among others. An agenda should be in the hands of participants of the faculty meeting two days before it is held. Faculty members should have much input in developing the agenda. Leadership for conducting each faculty meeting should come from administrators, supervisors, and teachers themselves.

5. Take University Courses

Teachers must be encouraged to continue professional education beyond the baccalaureate degree. Opportunities to continue professional education need to be available to all science teachers. Incentives and motivation should be inherent to encourage teachers to pursue a master's degree or higher. The graduate degree program should place heavy emphasis upon content, subject matter, and methods of teaching science. Additional stress in the graduate degree program needs to emphasize the philosophy of education, the psychology of learning, field experiences in the public school setting, methods of conducting educational research, the sociological foundations of education, and current issues in teaching science. The graduate degree program should be challenging and meaningful to improve the quality of teaching science in the public schools.

6. Departmental Meetings

Teachers need to participate in scheduled meetings for their own grade levels taught in the elementary school or academic areas taught in a departmentalized plan of instruction. The sessions should emphasize problems experienced by teachers in teaching science. Related solutions need to be sought. Each meeting needs to be planned in terms of objectives, approaches to attain each objective, as well as means to appraise progress in goal attainment. Teachers should feel free to suggest items to discuss for each departmental meeting. Salient problems in teaching science need identification and discussion.

7. Plan an in-service education program.

Each teacher should plan a program of growth and development. The ultimate objective for in-service education should emphasize curriculum improvement in the teaching of science. Plans for in-service education need to stress means of assisting students to achieve more optimally. The following are given as examples to indicate what a teacher might plan with supervisory guidance :

a) how to motivate student achievement in science.

b) how to achieve self-discipline among learners.

c) how to guide students to increase problem solving skills in science.

d) how to assist learners to stay on task.

The teacher needs to do research to secure information pertaining to the above named topics. The in-service project could have a due date and signed by both the teacher and supervisor. The in-service project could count as credit in moving to a higher level on the salary schedule. Results from the in-service project should be shared with others in the school setting.

8. Workshop Involvement

Teachers need to be involved in professional growth endeavours. Participating in workshops might well be an opportunity to develop well professionally. A workshop must have a theme. The theme should emphasize purpose and meaning for teacher participants. The first level of participation in the workshop is the general session. Here teachers and supervisors identify and choose problems to solve. Each problem needs careful consideration. Instructional problems should receive primary attention. The suggestions of each participants in the workshop must be respected.

The second level of the workshop emphasizes committee work. Teachers and supervisors need to select a committee which has an identified problem possessing perceived purpose. Thus the selected problem to be solved within the committee is worthwhile in terms of effort and time put forth.

A third level of the workshop is individualized study. Each science teacher and supervisor may well have relevant topics to pursue. The topic is vital to the participant and provides for in-service growth. A better prepared teacher or supervisor to improve the curriculum for students needs to be an end result. Gathering information on the topic should assist in implementing a quality science curriculum for students.

Problem solving in computer use might well be a suggested theme for a workshop. Flake, McClintock, and Turner[2] wrote :

> Problem solving is probably the major factor in successful computer use; therefore, teaching problem solving is a major goal of computer education. Writing an original program is problem solving; the planning that leads to a program is problem solving. In fact, from one point of view, the problem must be solved before the program is written. Creative uses of computers require problem-solving processes.
>
> In general, problem solving is likely to become more central to education as society becomes more complex. Advanced technology requires sophisticated problem solving; at the same time, it provides the tools for sophisticated problem solving. The rapid alterations in today's world suggest that the form and the goals of education are changing. Some skills that used to be drilled for considerable

periods are now replaced by the skills of an inexpensive calculator. Rather than being memorized, some facts can be called from a computer's database. In modern society, knowing only facts, formulas, and specific solutions is not enough, because those can quickly become obsolete. Knowledge of how to approach and solve new problems, on the other hand, always will be applicable. Learning how to learn may become the focus of educational programs designed for changing societal needs. Problem solving as a way of learning is not likely to become obsolete.

9. School Newsletter

Teachers and supervisors should keep abreast of current trends in teaching science by sharing teaching suggestions with each other by way of a newsletter. Each educator in the school setting should share ideas with other professionals on ways to improve learning opportunities in science for students.

The newsletter should be available to teachers and supervisors weekly. The purpose of the newsletter should stimulate thought and energy to develop the best objectives, learning activities, as well as appraisal techniques for students. Teachers should report back to other prefessionals how well each teaching suggestion worked in the classroom that came from the newsletter.

10. Self-evaluation

Each teacher should have ample opportunities to cassette record, or better yet, video tape his/her own teaching. Peer evaluation, using quality criteria, should be utilized to appraise teaching. Lessons may be retaught following evaluation. The ultimate goal here is to improve the science curriculum.

To secure feedback from pupil achievement in science, Ediger[3] wrote:

> The teacher of elementary school science must use a variety of appraisal techniques to evaluate pupil progress. Thus, assessment procedures such as the following may be utilized to evaluate learner achievement :
>
> 1. observation by the teacher of pupil progress.
> 2. pupil participation in discussions.
> 3. written work of learners.

4. pupil's art products.
5. Information conferences conducted with pupils.
6. pupils evaluating their own achievement.
7. teacher-developed tests.
8. use of standardized tests.

No appraisal technique is a perfect device to assess achievement. Thus several techniques should be utilized collectively to evaluate total growth of learners in—

1. intellectual growth.
2. social development.
3. emotional growth.
4. physical development.
5. moral achievement.

IN CLOSING

Ten approaches were presented to assist science teachers in in-service education. These were the following:

1. engaging in research.
2. doing professional reading.
3. attending professioinal meetings.
4. conducting faculty meetings.
5. taking university courses.
6. being involved in departmental meetings.
7. planning an in-service educational program.
8. participating in workshops.
9. developing a school newsletter.
10. doing self-evaluation to improve the quality of instruction in science.

Gega[4] wrote:

> Three compelling influences shape elementary science teaching: science as a discipline, society's needs, and the characteristics of children. Understanding these imperatives enables us to judge what is basic, useful, and learnable.

Science is an organised search for patterns or regularities. Scientists construct generalizations to explain the patterns they observe and, when possible, to predict and control objects and events within the patterns. Non-scientists do this also but usually with far less precision and reliability. Evidence in science is acceptable only when it is collected and processed under objective rules generally agreed to be the scientific community. To conduct scientific investigations requires an integrated knowledge of process and content in the topic of study.

REFERENCES

1. Shepherd, Gene D., and William B. Ragan. *Modern Elementary Curriculum*. Sixth edition. New York: CBS College Publishing, 1982, p. 327.
2. Flake, Janice L., McClintock, C. Edwin, and Sandra Turner. *Fundamentals of Computer Education*. Second edition. Belmont, CA: Wadsworth Publishing Company, 1990, p. 111.
3. Ediger, Marlow. *The Elementary Curriculum*. Second edition. Kirksville, MO: Simpson Printing and Publishing Co., 1988, p. 185.
4. Gega, Peter C. *Science in Elementary Education*. Sixth edition. New York: Macmillan Publishing Company, 1990, p. 18.

MENTOR TEACHERS

Mentor teachers have an important role in inducting beginning teachers into the profession. They must possess good physical and mental health so that adequate time may be given to guide the new teacher into doing a good job of teaching.

QUALITIES OF MENTORS

Mentor teachers must be highly accepting of new teachers. They need to be able to work with teachers possessing a wide variety of personalities and purposes. These mentors understand the concept of culture and realize its relevance for and in working with other people. Mentors who are aware of the concept of culture realize that people may differ from each other in many ways. And yet, the mentor is able to work harmoniously with beginning teachers regardless of personal beliefs held by the latter. Thus a good working relationship is a must in guiding the new teacher in truly becoming a professional teacher.

CAREFUL SELECTION OF MENTORS

Mentor teachers must be chosen carefully. Ganser (1995) wrote the following:

It is useful to have a pool of mentors in advance of the need. This can prevent an experienced teacher in an awkward position that a mentor described to me. Shortly before the start of the fall semester, he was outside painting his house. Seeing him, the principal stopped his car and asked, "Could you be a mentor for a new teacher? I really need someone." The teacher felt obligated to say 'yes' even though he did not fully understand the responsibilities and time commitment involved in serving as a mentor. If a pool of prospective mentors is established, picking out a mentor to work with a beginner is greatly facilitated.

Before acceptance, the prospective mentor should have ample time to study and learn about the role of being a mentor. Otherwise, a prospective mentor has little or no time to become highly knowledgeable about mentorship responsibilities. A mentor must have demonstrated quality teaching skills and abilities prior to being chosen for the task. He/she needs to demonstrate quality human relationship abilities in order to work well with others. Without good human relations, a mentor teacher cannot be effective.

METHODS OF TEACHING

The mentor should be highly knowledgeable about methods of teaching that might be used to provide for individual differences among pupils. Reinforcement theory of learning has received much attention in the educational literature. With reinforcement, the teacher rewards pupils who do well on a specific activity. Thus verbal praise or physical prizes may to given only in situations where pupils are not able to achieve other wise. The ideal is to have pupils attain intrinsically due to an inward desire to learn. However, reinforcement theory is an acceptable way of having pupils learn.

Pupils being involved in choosing what to learn with teacher guidance has also received much acclaim in education. These advocates believe that pupils have inward interests and needs that should become a part of the curriculum. Teacher-pupil planning of objectives, learning opportunities, and evaluation techniques are important where learner input into the curriculum is desired.

Mentors need to be thoroughly familiar with different psychologies of learning such as using behaviorally stated objectives, cooperative learning, quality, scope and sequence (logical and psychological sequence) in the curriculum humanism as a psychology of teaching, multimedia approaches of instruction, and emphasis placed upon diverse styles of learning for pupils.

KNOWLEDGEABLE ABOUT PHILOSOPHIES OF TEACHING

A mentor teacher is able to use diverse philosophies of teaching to guide learners to attain more optimally. These must be something that provides direction for the mentor teacher in decision making and that something may be acceptable philosophies of instruction. The mentor teacher then needs to guide the beginning teacher to stress a problem-solving approach in teaching. Thus a beginning teacher is assisted by the mentor in adding pupils to identify relevant problems, gather data, develop hypotheses, as well as evaluate each hypothesis.

In addition to problem solving, the mentor is able to guide the new teacher in using a subject-centered philosophy of teaching. Vital subject matter to be taught is chosen for pupil acquisition. The subject matter has values in and of itself. Cognitive objectives pervade when subject matter is taught to learners. Vital facts, concepts, and generalizations need to be taught by beginning teachers to pupils.

Third, decision making skills need to be emphasized by the mentor and the beginning teacher. Here it is salient for the pupil with teacher guidance to plan objectives, learning opportunities, and evaluation procedures. Individual as well as grouped endeavors may be chosen to participate in as indicated by pupil choice with teacher guidance.

A fourth philosophy of teaching stresses the mentor and beginning teacher understanding and implementing predetermined objective in measurable terms for pupil achievement. The teacher then chooses learning opportunities for pupils so that objectives may be attained. This is followed by the teacher appraising the pupil to see if the objectives (s) have been attained.

A chosen mentor teacher then must be highly knowledgeable of diverse philosophies of teaching so that pupils individually may achieve as much as possible.

There are selected principles of learning from the psychology of learning which mentor teachers need to model and implement.

These agreed upon principles from educational psychology might well provide a broad framework for beginning teachers to emulate. These are the following which pupils should experience in the classroom:

1. meaningful lessons and units of study. With meaning, pupils understand and comprehend that which was contained in ongoing learning opportunities.
2. interesting content and skills in the curriculum. With interest, the pupil and the curriculum, become on, not separate entities. Pupils attend from ongoing lessons and units of study.
3. purpose in learning. With purpose for learning, pupils accept reasons for acquiring relevant facts, concepts, and generalizations presented. Purpose developed by the teacher may take little time indeed. With deduction, the teacher explains clearly and concisely why pupils should achieve the objectives to be stressed. With inductive approaches, the teacher raises a few questions about the new lesson whereby the pupil responds and perceives purpose and reasons for achieving. Extrinsic rewards can be emphasized. Here, the teacher announces prizes and awards that pupils can secure if they attain the objectives of the lesson, pupils need to know precisely what is to be learned to obtain the rewards.
4. sequence in learning. With quality sequence, pupils relate newly acquired content with that previously achieved. Pupils need guidance to perceive relationship of knowledge in teaching-learning situations.
5. balance among objectives stressed. Thus knowledge, skills, and attitudes—three kinds of objectives need to be achieved by students. These objectives interact and are not in isolation from each other. For example if pupils possess positive attitudes, they should achieve needed knowledge and skills more readily (Ediger, 1994).

Mentor teachers need to possess knowledge and skills pertaining to assisting all pupils to achieve well. Hilliard (1991) advocates that public schools involve parents in the educational process. Parents should be involved pertaining to decisions about the curriculum and about school policy. Teachers should be involved in ongoing inservice educational programs. The curriculum needs to be sensitive to different cultures and appropriate for the pupil's stage of development. Health and safety standards need to be emphasized. Administrators in schools should monitor the school environment to assist each pupil to achieve optimally. A variety of assessment procedures need to be used to appraise the effectiveness of the school. Mentor teachers then have a variety of responsibilities to mentees in the school and classroom setting. Schools are a part of the larger society and need to become integrated, not separate entities.

Huling-Austin (1990) advocates that mentors have enthusiasm for serving and desiring to assist new teachers in developing the latter's capabilities. Hopefully the enthusiasm will reflect within the mentee in becoming a quality teacher of pupils. Mentors should fulfil necessary roles in achieving objectives of the mentoring program. They need to be creative individuals who discover new ways of meeting role responsibilities. Mentors should have an inward desire to improve the mentoring process. These mentors are able to work effectively with others in the educational arena. Mentors should have a planned program of inservice education to improve their own personal skills and abilities. Positive attitudes toward others in interpersonal relations are musts. Furtwengler (1993) emphasizes the importance of having quality mentor service so that beginning teachers may develop well professionally. A school system should not wait to provide inservice education and professional assistance to teachers, but provide guidance as soon as the new teacher enters school in teaching pupils.

Ganser (1995) lists background experiences that potential mentors should possess. These background experiences might well provide assistance in choosing mentors who have had quality teaching experiences. Letters of nomination, written statements about beliefs pertaining to teaching, induction activities, vitae, portfolios, videotapes of actual teaching, and interviews provide additional information pertaining to securing prospective mentors. Mentors need to be chosen carefully in terms of desired criteria. They are able to work well with new teachers and can provide assistance in guiding the latter in becoming true professionals in the area of teaching. Mentors must be willing to guide and assist new teachers to achieve optimally and well. There must be commitment to truly help new teachers to attain as optimally as possible.

MENTOR TEACHERS AND THEORIES OF LEARNING

Mentor teachers need to have a working knowledge of different psychologies of teaching and learning. Decisions in the classroom should be based on theory. These theories need to be carefully and thoroughly understood so that effective implementation may be an end result. Which theories should be emphasized in teaching and learning ?

B. F. Skinner (1979) and his emphasis upon behaviourism has strong support among numerous educators. He stressed the use of predetermined, measurably stated objectives to be achieved by students. Each objective is precisely written so that teachers may measure if a pupil has or has not attained any single objective of instruction. If learners respond correctly, Skinner advocated reinforcing correct responses with physical prizes or verbal praise. The behaviorally stated objectives movement follows the thinking of Dr. Skinner. The teacher then uses predetermined objectives and announces prior to instruction that which pupils are to attain. Learners are certain as to what to achieve as a result of teaching. Following instruction, pupils reveal what has been learned that was stated inside each behaviorally stated objective.

Piaget (1958) in his research pertaining to studying pupils for over fifty years in Geneva, Switzerland, advocated a theory of maturation in teaching pupils. The first stage is called the sensorimotor stage of pupil development and covers birth to two years of age for the young child. The pre-operational stage covers ages two to seven whereas the stage of concrete operation covers the ages of seven to eleven. Beyond eleven years of age, Piaget emphasized that pupils were in the stage of formal operations. Each stage of pupil development has selected implications for teaching pupils.

Ausubel (1978) in his cognitive theory of pupil development emphasized that the single most salient factor in teaching is to have the teacher start at the entry level of the pupil that he/she is presently at. Each pupil then is ready for new content to be learned which is different from other learners.

Gagne (1977) emphasized that objectives be arranged hierarchically from simple to increasingly more complex when writing and implementing sequential objectives of instruction. Thus at any stage in teaching, if a pupil fails to progress to a more complex objective, the teacher can go back to an earlier objective in sequence. This is done until the pupil is familiar with content being taught by the teacher.

Maslow (1954) offered a theory of motivation based on needs of human beings. Generally the following needs must be met in ascending order of complexity :

1. physical needs such as adequate food, clothing, and shelter.
2. safety and security needs in that adequate protection must be there so that pupils can attain well in school.
3. belonging needs should be met so that pupils feel love and affection.
4. esteem needs stress the importance of status of recognition for something well done individually or within a group.
5. Self actualization in that a person wishes to become the person desired. Thus the actual as perceived and the ideal become closer together, not separate entities.

The above five named needs are to become increasingly realized before a pupil may understand subject matter thoroughly in on-going lessons and units of study. Meeting the needs of pupils should help individuals to attain, achieve, and grow in diverse fields of endeavours. Mentors and beginning teachers must know the relevance of meeting needs of pupils so that they may achieve academically, socially, emotionally, and physically. The self-actualizing person comes about due to having needs met.

Combs (1972) advocates humanism as a psychology of teaching and learning. Here, the emphasis is upon pupils being involved with teacher guidance in choosing objectives, learning opportunities, and appraisal techniques to ascertain progress in learning. Pupil/teacher planning of the curriculum is salient.

Mentor teachers and beginning teachers need to learn upon diverse theories of learning so that individual differences among learners may be provided for and each might attain as much as possible. Theories of learning are not emphasized for the sake of doing so but rather to provide guidance and direction in selecting ends, means, and appraisal procedures in the school curriculum. Pupils possess different talents and each ability and talent must be developed optimally.

IMPORTANT CONSIDERATIONS IN MENTORING

Klug (1990) emphasizes that mentoring can be placed on a continuum from a loosely structured buddy system to a highly structured approach in which designated mentors give all or part of the school day to assist mentees. Differences also exist in terms of involvement of institutions in the mentoring program. Thus there may be collaborative efforts among districts or individual schools. Collaboration might also occur between schools and universities in providing mentor services (Du Bolt 1992). The writer has supervised student and regular teachers for thirty years and has mentored pre-service as well as in-service teachers. When student teachers being supervised have been in one school building or a nearby building, these pre-service teachers were involved in being a community of learners in which they shared experiences and assisted each other in developing quality lessons and units of study. Cooperative endeavours here stressed a mentoring approach. When problems arose in teaching, there was assistance, not only from the cooperating teacher and the university supervisor of student teachers, but also from peers. Crowe (1995), in an essay on mentoring, wrote pertaining to his beginning days as a high school English teacher. His first three days had been a disaster as no one had assisted him in beginning when starting in the middle of the school year upon graduation from college. At the end of the third day, an experienced teacher in the building talked to him and gave assistance. This person who was not designated as a mentor saved him from dropping out of teaching.

It is critical that someone assist the new teacher to secure even the rudiments of information necessary to begin the teaching sequence. Too frequently, beginning teachers enter their first days of teaching with no assistance available. There is no one designated to answer the new teacher's questions, nor to help with the bare necessities of starting the professional career of teaching. In other situations, there are designated mentors with time off from teaching who are assigned to the beginning teacher to offer guidance.

Attrition rates, no doubt, can be reduced when quality mentors are available to help in the induction process of new teachers. Approximately, 40 to 50 per cent of new teachers leave the profession after seven years of teaching. Attrition rates are even greater in urban areas (Haberman and Richards, 1990). Mentor teachers should be able to allay the fears of beginning teachers by offering necessary guidance in the solving of problems pertaining to teaching. The affective or feeling dimension of teachers may be quite strong. When the writer began teaching in a rural two-teacher elementary school, the following were major areas of concern :

1. the other teacher had considerable status with the three members school board. Her actions and deeds were looked upon as being "right" by both the school board members and parents. The writer was new to the rural community and the feelings were that he was not a part of the teaching team. A caring mentor, even with one other teacher in the school, could have made for a marked difference where cooperation, not competition was in evidence.
2. the other teacher sided with pupils continually in the two teacher school. There are rules and regulations, reasonable in nature, that should apply to pupils so that optimal learning may take place. She alone determined what should be done and was fair/right for pupils. My decisions pertaining to an appropriate learning environment were to be ignored unless the other teacher agreed with them. Obviously, quality mentoring was not possible here. A mentor needs to be caring and considerate of the new teacher. He/she needs to assist help, guide, and direct so that a professional induction into teaching is possible.

IN CLOSING

Mentor teachers work in situations involving ambiguity. They do not have measurably stated duties and responsibilities. Thus a mentor must be creative in determining that which will make for an effective role model. There are numerous recommendable philosophies of education. Mentors need to realize that there are diverse acceptable methods of teaching. Within the framework of open endedness and flexibility, the mentor is able to work harmoniously with new teachers in an effective interpersonal manner.

The Kirksville, Missouri R 3 School System lists the following goals for The Beginning Teacher Assistance Program (1995) :

1. promote the personal and professional well being of

beginning teachers.

2. encourage promising beginning teachers to remain in the profession.
3. promise community awareness for beginning teachers.
4. ease the transition for the first year teacher from student teaching to their career in education.
5. enhance teacher performance and improve service to students.
6. foster a better educational environment by breaking down the isolation of classroom teachers and by promoting cooperation among teachers and between administrators and teachers.
7. encourage recognition that the professional development of teachers is an on-going educational process.

'Quality' beginning teachers need to experience growth, development, promise, and encouragement to teach pupils to attain as much as possible. Good mentors have an important responsibility here.

REFERENCES

Ausubel, David (1978). *Educational Psychology* New York : Holt Rinehart and Winston.

Combs, Arthur W. (1972). *Educational Accountability : Beyond Behavioural Objectives.* Washington, DC : Association for Supervision and Curriculum Development.

Crowe, Chris (1995). Mentors : Key to survival and Growth. *English Journal*, 84, 76–77.

Ediger, Marlow (1994) Early Field Experiences in Teacher Education. *College Student Journal.* 28, 302–307.

Furtwengler, C.B. (1993). The Reform Movement : A Fifty State Survey of State Actions for Beginning Teacher Programs. A paper presented at the annual convention of the American Educational Research Association, Atlanta, Georgia.

Ganser, Tom (1995). *Principles for Mentor Teacher Selection*, Clearing House.

Klug, B. J. (1988). *Teacher Induction in South-eastern Idaho*: Preliminary Report, ERIC ED 291–717.

Haberman, M. and W. R. Richards (1990). Urban Teachers Who Quit: Why They Leave and What They Do. *Urban Education*. 25, 297–303.

Huling-Austin L. (1990). Teacher Induction Programs and Internships in *A Handbook of Research on Teacher·Education*. W. R. Houston (editor), 535–548. New York: Macmillan Publishing Company.

Kirksville R3 Professional Development Plan (1995). Kirksville, Missouri.

Maslow, Abraham (1954). *Motivation and Personality*. New York: Harper and Row.

Piaget, Jean (1958). *The Growth of Logical Thinking from Childhood to Adolescence*. New York: Harper and Row Publishers.

Skinner, B. F. (1979) *Beyond Freedom and Dignity*. Columbus, Ohio: Charles Merrill Publishing Company.

INNOVATIVE EVALUATION PROCEDURES

There are numerous techniques to appraise pupil achievement in the science curriculum. Traditional techniques which seemingly have stood the test of time include :

1. Teacher written test items. These include true-false, multiple choice, matching, completion, and essay items.
2. Checklists and rating scales. Specific behaviours are listed and each learner is checked (on the checklist) if more guidance is needed to achieve that objective, or a numerical rating (5-excellent, 4=good, 3=average, 2=below average, and 1=poor) is given in terms of perceived performance on a rating scale.
3. Appraising learner products. Each written paper, art project, or construction item may be appraised in terms of desired criteria.
4. Teacher observation and anecdotal records. What the teacher observes as to representative learner behaviour may be recorded in a behavioural journal. The date shoula also be lsited with the event.

Additional appraisal procedures will be discussed in the remainder of the paper.

INSTRUCTIONAL MANAGEMENT SYSTEMS

A school may utilize instructional management systems (IMS) to appraise pupil progress. To develop an IMS takes considerable time and effort on the part of teachers and supervisors in the school/class setting. Generally, at least a year should be given to writing up the diverse sections of an IMS before its implementation. The very first step to follow in developing an IMS is to write precise measurable objectives for pupils to attain in each curriculum area through the sequential years of schooling. Thus for each grade level and in each curriculum area, there are a certain number of precise objectives that a pupil must achieve. To complete a grade level, a learner then needs to finish the identified number of measurable ends for each subject matter area studied. These are minimal essentials. If a pupil does not complete that which is required for a specific grade level in a given school year, he/she must satisfactorily finish the omitted parts during the next school year. As soon as these have been completed, the learner might then work on measurably stated objectives for the new grade level. Gifted and talented learners, as well as numerous average achievers need to make continuous progress, and thus achieve more objectives than the minimum essentials.

The classroom teacher chooses learning activities for pupils to achieve stated objectives. After which, the teacher measures if a learner has been successful in goal attainment. If so, he/she progresses to the next sequential objectives. If not, the teacher needs to utilize the same or a modified strategy of teaching to guide the learner to be successful in goal attainment.

Advantages given for advocating IMS to evaluate pupil achievement include the following :

1. The teacher can be certain if a pupil has/has not attained any one specific measurable objective.
2. Pupils may know ahead of time what is expected in terms of precise learnings.
3. Parents may also get to know specifically what their offspring are to learn.

4. Verifiable results may be given to supervisors and other responsible evidence is available for each learner's achievement. Teachers may be held accountable for pupils attaining the pre-specified objectives.

Disadvantages given for IMS include the following :

1. It is difficult to pre-plan objectives for pupils to achieve. The objectives may need to be pre-planned a semsester or entire school year before their implementation.
2. Learners having achieved an objective (or objectives) does not guarantee, by any means, the retention of subject matter contained in each end.
3. Emerging objectives in terms of questions and comments come from learners as lessons and units progress. These ends may be perceived by pupils more vital, as compared to adult pre-determined measurable goals.
4. Pupils sequence objectives rather than adults Thus, sequential learnings accrue in the minds of individual learners rather than instructors.
5. Precise measurable goals might measure trivial learnings, such as specific facts, rather than worthwhile values, attitudes, problem solving skills, as well as critical and creative thinking.

Preston and Herman[1] wrote the following involving the use of behavioural objectives:

> Despite the logical appeal of behavioural objectives, many educators and psychologists do not accept them as a final solution of either the curriculum or the evaluation problem. J. M. Stephens, in an intensive analysis of the process of schooling, found that it consists largely of spontaneous, unsophisticated teacher behaviours and that the teacher's effect upon pupil learning is not likely to be improved by most deliberate innovations, including the insistence in some quarters upon behavioural objectives. He contends that teachers who have a lively interest in a subject, but who slight objectives even outrageously, would probably bring about greater subject-matter learning than teachers whose interest is less but who are punctilious about specifying objectives.

LEARNING CENTERS AND EVALUATION

Learning centers may be developed in several ways. The teacher may choose the materials and tasks for each learning center in the classroom. Or, pupils with teacher guidance might plan concrete and semi-concrete items for each center as well as the related learning experiences. In either approach, learners need to sequentially choose tasks to complete. There needs to be an adequate number of experiences in order that learners may omit those tasks perceived as not being purposeful or of personal interest. In a humane curriculum, described by humanism as psychology of learning, pupils need to choose and make decisions. The teacher should not dictate objectives, learning activities, and evaluation procedures. Rather, pupils individually need to achieve self-actualization.

A. H. Maslow[2], late leading humanist, indicates the following needs which need satisfying in order that learners may truly achieve self-actualization.

1. physiological (food, rest, shelter, and water)
2. safety (security from danger)
3. belonging (love and affection)
4. esteem (recognition and status)
5. self-actualization (satisfy one's potential)

Combs, et. al.[3] state the following pertaining to humanism :

> Perceptual psychology is more than the expression of the humanist movement. It is also a frame of reference specially designed to deal with a questions raised by the movement and to contribute to its implementation in the solution of human problems. The humanist movement requires a person-centered psychology, one capable of dealing not only with behaviour, but with the meanings and perceptions that constitute the internal experience of persons as well. Perceptual psychology is uniquely suited to provide this kind of understanding. So it is that the authors of this volume conceive of perceptual psychology as both the expression of the humanist movement and the beginnings of a science through which the humanness of persons can be more adequately understood and the fulfillment of human potential more adequtely achieved.

Knowledge is subjective, not objective, to the learner. Thus, adequate emphasis needs to be given to art, music, drama, literature, creative writing, and the social studies at diverse learning centers in the class setting. Adequate emphasis must also be given to subject matter which is more objective in structure, such as science and mathematics.

Advantages given for utilizing humanism, as a psychology of education, to appraise learner progress include the following :

1. Open-ended flexible means may be utilized to appraise progress. With pupils being involved in choosing objectives, learning activities, and evaluation procedures, ample consideration needs to be placed upon the quality and ability of learners to make decisions.
2. Pupils must have personal needs met to do well in the school/class setting. Thus, adequate stress must be placed in the evaluation process upon meeting needs of learners to achieve self-realization.
3. Learners need to have adequate knowledge of the self and of others. Thus, a quality evaluation program needs to appraise pupil's increasing knowledge, skills, and attitudes in the affective or attitudinal dimensions.

Disadvantages given for humanistic evaluation procedures include the following :

1. Learners are not adequately mature to make choices and decisions in the school/class setting. The school's role is to get pupils ready for adult roles in society.
2. A teacher determined curriculum may meet the personal needs of many learners, especially if learning activities are selected based on motivating achievement.
3. A teacher determined curriculum can be sequentially arranged so that pupils experience continuous progress, thus aiding in affective development of pupils.

IMS VERSUS HUMANISM

Teachers and supervisors need to evaluate rather continuously, appraisal procedures utilized to ascertain learner achievement. Traditional means exist such as using teacher written test items and recorded teacher observations of learner involvement in on-going learning activities.

Relatively recent evaluation procedures have also appeared on the horizon. These include instructional management systems involving behaviourism, as a psychology of learning. The Missouri Department of Elementary and Secondary Education in their recent brochure entitled *Instructional Management, A Priority for Missouri Schools During the 1980's*, lists the following criteria that effective schools follow :

1. High expectations for learning. Teachers and administrators expect a high level of achievement by all students and communicate their expectations to students and parents. No students are expected to fail, and the school assumes responsibility for seeing that they don't.
2. Strong leadership by building principals. The building principal is an instructional leader who participates in all phases of instruction. The principal is a visible leader of instruction, not just an office-bound administrator.
3. Emphasis on instruction in the basic skills. Since mastery of the basic skills is essential to learning in all other subjects, the effective schools make sure students at least master the basic skills.
4. Clear-cut instructional objectives. Each teacher has specific instructional objectives within the overall curriculum which are communicated to students, paretns and the general public. In effective schools, teachers and administrators—not textbooks—are clearly in charge of the curriculum and teaching activities.
5. Mastery learning and testing for mastery. Students are taught, tested, retaught and retested to the extent necessary to assure mastery of important objectives Students are not taught more difficult objectives until pre-requisite objectives have been mastered.
6. School discipline and climate. The effective schools may not be shiny and modern, but they are at least safe, orderly and free of distractions. All teachers and students, as well as parents, know the school's expectations about behavior and discipline.

Humanism has its supporters in the educational arena. Self-actualization is a key concept in the thinking of humanists. Maslow[4] wrote the following :

> Self-actualization is defined in various ways, but a solid core of agreement in perceptible. All definitions accept or imply : (a) acceptance and expression of the inner core or self, i.e. actualization of these latent capabilities and potentialities, "fully functioning," availability of the human and personal essence; and (b) minimal presence of ill health, neurosis, psychosis, or loss of diminuation of the basic human and personal capacities.

IN SUMMARY

Teachers and supervisors need to evaluate and revise the curriculum to provide for diverse needs, interests, and abilities of learners in the school and class setting. Each pupil needs guidance to achieve optimally.

Notes:

1. Ralph C. Preston and Wayne L. Herman, Jr., *Teaching Social studies in the Elementary School.* Fifth edition. New York: Holt, Rinehart and Winston, 1981, pages 12 and 13.
2. A. H. Maslow. *Motivation and Personality.* New York : Harper and Row Publishers, 1954.
3. Arthur W. Combs, et. al., *Perceptual Psychology, A Humanistic Approach to the Study of Persons.* New York : Harper and Row Publishers, 1976, Page xiii.
4. A. H. Maslow, "Some Basic Propositions of a Growth and Self-Actualization Psychology", *Perceiving, Behaving, Becoming,* 1962, Yearbook (Alexandria, Virginia: Association for Supervision and Curriculum Development, 1962), page 51.

REFERENCES

Combs, Arthur W., et. al., *Perceptual Psychology, A Humanistic Approach to the Study of Persons.* New York : Harper and Row Publishers, 1976, page xiii.

Maslow, A. H., *Motivation and Personality.* New York: Harper and Row Publishers, 1954.

Maslow, A. H. "Some Basic Propositions of a Growth and Self-Actualization Psychology," *Perceiving, Behaving, Becoming,* 1962 Yearbook (Alexandria, Virginia: Association for Supervision and Curriculum Development, 1962), page 51.

Preston, Ralph C. and Herman, Jr., Wayne L., *Teaching Social Studies in the Elementary School.* Fifth edition. New York : Holt, Rinehart and Winston, 1981, pages 12 and 13.

IMPROVING SCIENCE CURRICULUM

The science teacher needs to utilize a variety of learning activities to provide for individual differences among students. The less talented as well as gifted students need to achieve optimally in on-going lessons and units. Providing a variety of science activities for learners also has as a goal to provide for diverse styles of learning. Students learn in different ways, such as achieving more from selected kinds of activities, as compared to other experiences, be that concrete, semi-concrete, or abstract experiences. Within each of these—the concrete, the semi-concrete, or the abstract—diversity of activities is also possible. For example, with concrete materials, the following are possibilities to utilize in teaching: seeing actual plants in the classroom, observing plants on the school grounds or city park, making model plants, and seeding/growing selected plants. The semi-concrete may emphasize the use of filmstrips, slides, films, drawings, pictures, transparencies, and study prints of different plants. Abstract learnings may emphasize reading, discussing, listening, and writing to learn about plant life.

With the use of concrete, semi-concrete, and abstract facets of teaching, principles of learning taken from the fields of educational psychology stress that students

1. take interest in learning.
2. attach meaning to what is being learned
3. achieve purpose in on-going lessons and units.
4. sense knowledge as being related, not isolated fragments.

LEARNING ACTIVITIES IN SCIENCE

Activities for students assist in attaining carefully selected goals. Diverse learning opportunities for specific units of study in science will now be discussed.

If a unit on "A Clean Environment" is being taught, students with teacher guidance may pick up litter on and near the school grounds. The collected litter may be classified as being biodegradable as well as non-biodegradable. Ways of controlling and preventing pollution should be discussed. Posters may be developed by students individually or in committees to convey information on the necessity of developing and maintaining a healthy, aesthetically pleasing environment. In a related activity, students may draw a map of the school grounds.

In a science unit on "Weather and How It Affects Us", students may record the temperature reading each hour. It may be necessary to have an alarm clock in the classroom. A bar or line graph should be drawn to show hourly temperature readings.

If a science unit on "Plants in Our Community" is being emphasized, students with teacher direction may in early spring measure the amount of growth of twigs at selected intervals of time. Students can make drawings of and identify selected twigs. Relevant subject matter may be gathered, from a variety of references sources, to understand principles of science involved as to why twigs grow. Leaf scars, lenticels, and buds, among other concepts, may be studied.

Units of study on "Insects in the Community" may capture the interest of many students. Selected insects may be collected and placed in a plastic vial. Diverse parts of insects need classification, such as the head, thorax, and abdomen. The digestive system of these insects and release them when finished. Excursions on and near the school grounds may be conducted to observe and identify insects in the local community.

In a unit on "The Pond Community", students with teacher guidance may observe animal tracks on the pond area. Sounds of animals need to be noticed. Direct observation of plant and animal life is important. Smells in the pond community need to be noticed by students. Students need to record that which the senses experienced. The mechanics of writing (correct spelling, punctuation, and agreement of subject and predicate) may also be stressed.

To extend learning acquired, students may write diverse forms of poetry on the pond community. Students should select which kind of poetry to write whether it be haiku, tanka, quantrains, cuplets, triplets, diamantes, or free verse.

A jar of pond water should be taken along from the excursion. Animal life in the jar needs to be studied over a period of time. Additional contents, such as mud, leaves, and twigs in the jar should also be studied.

In studying a unit on "Nutrition and How It Affects Us", students may study the specific parts of a garden plant that is eaten. Pictures can be collected and drawn pertaining to common garden crops. Learners might then learn to classify if :

a) the seed part is eaten (sweet corn, peas, and green beans).

b) the stalk is eaten (celery and rhubarb).

c) the roots are eaten (onions, radishes, carrots and potatoes).

d) the leaves are eaten (lettuce and spinach).

e) the fruit is eaten (strawberries, apples, pears).

Magnifying glasses should be present in the classroom for students to observe seeds, stalks, roots, leaves and the fruit parts of a plant.

When initiating a unit on "Rocks and Their Uses", the teacher may display igneous, metamorphic, and sedimentary rocks at an interest centre. Students may view slides, filmstrips, and pictures on these three kinds of rocks. For homework, students should locate as many examples of igneous, metamorphic and sedimentary rocks as possible. An individual, committee, or class as a whole collection of rocks can be an end-result in the on-going unit of study. Learners also need to research the diverse use of rocks.

When studying a unit on "Conservation of Natural Resources", students with teacher guidance need to analyze causes for soil erosion on the school grounds or nearby areas. A problem needs solving here in terms of remedying eroded area(s).

For enrichment experiences, students may

1. write any word that starts with the letter A and for each letter of the alphabet. What is recorded must have been experienced through the use of the senses.
2. divide into groups and find one item of each of the following : a seed, a feather, a twig, a rock, a beetle, a nut, a frog or toad, a flower, a caterpillar, and a fern.

IN SUMMARY

Science for students should be interesting. Dull routine activities need to be eliminated. The methods and content of science need to be emphasized in each lesson and unit of study. Each student needs to achieve optimally in on-going lessons and units.

ROLE OF EDUCATIONAL PHILOSOPHIES IN IMPROVING THE QUALITY OF SCIENCE CURRICULUM

Each person lives in a world of science. Teh natural environment operates in terms of scientific principles, theories, and laws. Students living in a world of science need to understand how the natural environment affects them personally. Learners also must understand relevant goals in science for the future which assist in improving the quality of life for each person. A problem solving approach utilizing the methods of science needs to be in the offing in the curriculum.

Diverse philosophies of science will be discussed. Each will be appraised in terms of strengths and weaknesses.

REALISM IN THE TEACHING OF SCIENCE

Realists tend to believe that one can know the natural world in whole or in part as it truly is. One then may receive somewhat of a replica when viewing the totality of what exists in the environment. There are indeed many specifics in the different academic disciplines comprising the world of science. Thus, biology, zoology, botany, chemistry, physics, astronomy, and geology, among others, have their specific objectives to emphasize in the teaching of students. Either a student does or does not attain sequential objectives, as a result of instruction. Observable results are then desired from studetns. What is internal to the learner and cannot be measured by the teacher, as a result of learning opportunities provided, does not count. That which is objective and measurable, regardless of who does the observing, verifies what students individually have learned.

Test results, products made, oral statements made, written reports, as well as objective findings from science experiments and demonstrations pass the requirements for evaluation by realism as a philosophy of education. Students need to reveal, show, and indicate that any single objective has been attained. The teacher determines if verifiable results from students indicate an objective has been achieved.

Realists want to be certain that precise objectives are there for learner attainment in science. These ends can be announced to students prior to instructiion. The next task is for the teacher to teach. Learning opportunities in science must match up directly with the pre-specified objective(s). Thus, the teacher selects the materials and methods of teaching which assist each student to be successful in goal attainment. Appraisal of student progress is strictly in terms of achieving precise ends.

Realism has much to offer in the teaching of science. First of all, the selection of objectives in measurable terms must be done carefully. Vital, significant objectives need to be chosen. Trivia must always be avoided. Secondly, learning activities have a solid basis for selection and that being for students to achieve objectives. Random selection of these activities is not wanted. Thirdly, appraisal of learner progress is accomplished by measuring if students have attained the objectives. In this situation also, appraising is not done at random, but in terms of measuring if objectives have been achieved. Fourthly, parents can be informed of definite student progress as to the number of objectives achieved. Specific information of student achievement is then provided to parents.

Disadvantages may well be given of realism as a philosophy of teaching science. The science curriculum may certainly lack holism. With specific objectives for student attainment, each becomes an entity unto itself. However, knowledge is related and students need to perceive holism in subject matter acquired. Secondly, what is intrinsic may not be observable in a precise manner such as the interests purposes, and meanings adopted by the individual learner. And yet are these inner areas of growth and of utmost importance ? Thirdly, values need to be attached to achievements in science be they the lengthening of human life spans or uses of atomic energy. Values are exceedingly complex to measure. The human being does not live in a vaccum from the obserable accomplishments in science.

EXPERIMENTALISM IN THE TEACHING OF SCIENCE

Experimentalist believe that one can only experience, but not know the natural-social environment as it truly is. With exepriences, problems are recognized and identified. Each problem needs to be clearly identified and be relevant. With clarity of a vital selected problem, information needs to be gathered. The content for solving the identified problem should come from a variety of sources, such as reading materials, audio-visual aids, as well as experiments and demonstrations in science. An answer or hypothesis is developed based on the information obtained. The hypothesis is tentative and in answer to the problem or question. Each hypothesis needs to be tested in a life-like situation. Jumping to hasty conclusions in developing and testing a hypothesis in science is not recommended. The hypothesis is accepted, if verified, through testing. Or, it can be refuted, if evidence warrants. Verification of subject matter is salient in the thinking of experimentalism Verification comes through the solving of problems.

Experimentalists also recommend that school and society be integrated, and not isolated from each other. In the societal arena, many questions and problems about the world of science abound. Problem solving activities involving science are significant in school and in society.

Community endeavors emphasizing problem solving in the science curriculum are important. Individuals interact with each other in society in identifying and solving problems. Community endeavours are therefore utilized in society. The individual student should not be separated from others in the school setting. Community work in science units relates rather than separates human beings.

Experimentalism has much to recommend itself in developing a quality science curriculum. First of all, the learner is the key person within a community to select problem areas for solution. predetermined, measurably stated objectives are definitely not emphasized in on-going lessons and units. Rather, students with teacher guidance select and solve problems. A psychological curriculum is in evidence when the learner is heavily involved in sequencing learning activities. Secondly, student interest in a problem can definitely make for effort in learning. Interest and effort become one and not separate entities. Thirdly, school and society are integrated and not separated. What is relevant in society provides vital content in the science curriculum.

Disadvantages include selected students may not be adequately motivated to identify and solve problems. Other styles of learning might better meet the needs of the motivated student.

IDEALISM AND THE TEACHING OF SCIENCE

Idealists tend to believe that individuals receive ideas about the natural-social environment. Individuals then cannot know the real world as it truly is. Nor can they gain experiences only of the real world. In an idea centered curriculum, advocated by idealists, students need to acquire abstract idèas in terms of relevant concepts and generalisations.

To achieve vital ideas in science, students need to have learning activities, in particular, from carefully selected textbooks, workbooks, and science encyclopedias. Audio-visual aids are utilized as they assist learners to attain ideas. Having a subject centered science curriculum becomes a major objective for students according to idealists.

The science teacher needs to be highly academic and knowledgeable about the diverse science disciplines which provide content for on-going lessons and units. Mind is real and mental development of students is of utmost importance. Each student is a finite individual and needs to àchieve and attain in science to become an increasingly infinite person. A quality science curriculum may well assist students to move away from the finite and toward the infinite.

Numerous strengths can be given for emphasizing idealism in teaching science. First of all, students achieving well in an idea centered curriculum is important. Vital subject matter, such as concepts and generalizations, need attaining by students. All learning ultimately ends with abstract ideas. Secondly, students moving from the finite (being limited) to the infinite (increasingly independent) are musts in science and in life. Thirdly, a highly qualified academically inclined science teacher is a must. To achive excellence in science, students need to have well trained and educated teachers.

Disadvantages in emphasizing tenets of idealism include the strong emphasis of a subject centered curriculum. As a result, hands on approaches in science teaching are minimized. Secondly, idealism emphasizes ultimate reality existing beyond that of data provided by the senses. Thus, meaning, interest, and especially purposes in life exist beyond what can be observed, heard, tasted, smelled, and touched.

EXISTENTIALISM IN THE TEACHING OF SCIENCE

Existentialists believe that one exists first and then finds his/her own essences or puposes in life. There are no a priori rules (that which is prior to experience) given to any individual or group. Each person needs to seek reasons for living as well as goals in life. What is good, true, and beautiful reside within the individual. Truth then resides in the eye of the beholder. Each person evaluates, judges, and perceives merit.

Since each person is responsible for decision making, the science curriculum must present ample opportunities for learners to select, choose, and participate in.

Existentialists adovate that students have much input into the science curriculum. A learning centers approach emphasizes tenets of existentialism. Each student selects the center and tasks to pursue sequentially. An adequate number of tasks need to be in evidence so students may omit the undesired activities. Time on task is very significant. In addition to the implementation of learning centers, student-teacher planning may be stressed to determine what the former should learn. Heavy input from learners must be in evidence when utilizing student-teacher planning of objectives, learning activities, and appraisal procedures in science. A third approach in implementing existentialism would be to develop a contract system. Within the contract, the student with the science teacher's guidance determines what the former is to learn. The due date should appear on the contract in terms of when the student is to fulfil his/her obligations.

Knowledge is subjective to the existentialist. Thus, learning activities such as values clarifications are important. Values are not given to any person. They need to be sought from among alternatives. Values chosen must provide for quality standards used in the societal arena. A commitment must be made to utilize humane values. The consequences of adopted values need to be accepted as the responsibility of the doer. Life itself is absurd and ridiculous to the involved person. Within the absurd, ridiculous environment, the student needs to select values, learning opportunities, and tasks.

THE PSYCHOLOGY OF EDUCATION

Principles of learning from the psychology of education can assist the science teacher in assisting each student to attain in a more optimal manner. First of all, students need to have interesting learning opportunities. The more interested students are in learning, the more likely achievement will take place in science. If interest is lacking, effort will not be in the offing for students to learn as much as possible. With a variety of learning opportunities (reading activities, experiments and demonstrations, as well as the utilization of audio-visual aids), learners may develop and/or maintain interest in learning. Students need to experience interest in learning. The learner and the science curriculum become one when interest in science is inherent.

Secondly, students need to perceive meaning in on-going science lessons and units. If students achieve meaning in learning opportunities, subject matter learned will be understood. With meaning in understanding content, students retain content better than if a lack of understanding is in evidence. Retention of subject matter learned can be a problem for numerous students. Meaning attached to science content can aid in retaining that which has been learned.

Thirdly, learners need to perceive purpose in on-going lessons and units in science. With purpose, students perceive reasons for learning, progressing, and achieving. A deductive procedure can be utilized. With deduction, the science teacher explains to students reasons for learning vital facts, concepts, and generalizations. With induction, the science teacher asks sequential questions of students to have the latter understand reasons for achieving objectives in science. Purpose in learning relates the student to the goals to be attained.

Fourthly, balance among objectives needs to be emphasized. Thus, three categories of objectives may be attained by students. Cognitive ends, as one category, stresses intellectual learning be acquired by learners. These learnings involve acquiring subject matter, skills in creative and critical thinking, as well as problem solving. Affective ends, a second category of objectives, emphasize students attain quality attitudes, values, and moral standards. Psychomotor ends emphasize the use of muscular coordination, such as in using microscopes, making science equipment, and in using the methods of science to acquire useful information. Holism in teaching science is important since one category of objectives affects the others. Thus, for example, affective ends assist in students achieving both cognitive and psychomotor goals. Good attitudes guide students to learn as much as possible in the cognitive domain as well as achieve optimally in psychomotor learnings.

Fifthly, studetns need to perceive appropriate sequence in achieving science objectives. Each objective achieved provides readiness for attaining the next end. The objectives in science then become related and not isolated entities. State mandated and instructional management systems (IMS) can stress isolated precise ends for learner attainment. Unrelated subject matter is difficult to remember. Rather, students need to perceive content in science as being related and integrated with the self. Holism in teaching science strongly advocates that knowledge is related. Students need guidance to perceive relationships in subject matter acquired. Readiness and sequence must be emphasized in on-going lessons and units.

IN SUMMARY

Teachers of science need to select tenets from the philosophy of education which are vital in emphasizing holism in the science curriculum. The writers recommend the following tenets :

1. students attain vital precise objectives in lessons and units, as recommend by realists. However, care must be taken to avoid a fragmented science curriculum. Subject matter is related and must be perceived by learners in its many manifested relationships.
2. students be heavily involved in problem solving in science, as recommended by experimentalists.
3. students acquire vital subject matter knowledge in an idea centered science curriculum, as recommended by idealists.
4. students become proficient in decision-making and in the making of choices, as stressed by existentialists.

The psychology of learning emphasizes guidelines which science teachers should follow to have students attain optimally. These include :

1. securing the interests of students.
2. providing meaningful activities.
3. achieving purpose or reasons for learning.
4. emphasizing balance among objectives.
5. stressing sequence in teaching-learning situations.

REFERENCES

Abruscato, Joseph. *Teaching Children Science.* Englewood Cliffs, New Jersey: Prentice Hall, Inc., 1982.

Beane, James A., et. al. *Curriculum Planning and Development.* Boston: Allyn and Bacon, Inc., 1986.

Carin, Arthur, and Robert B. Sund. *Teaching Science Through Discovery.* Columbus, Ohio: Charles E. Merrill Publishing Company, 1985.

Gega, Peter C., *Science in Elementary Education.* Fifth edition. New York: Macmillan Publishing Company, 1986.

Henson, Kenneth T., and Delmar Janke. *Elementary Science Methods.* New York: McGraw-Hill Book Company, 1984.

Jacobson, Willard J., and Abby Barry Bergman. *Science for Children, A Book for Teachers.* Englewood Cliffs, New Jersey: Prentice-Hall, Inc., 1980.

Moore, W. Edgar, et. al. *Creative and Critical Thinking.* Boston: Houghton Mifflin Company, 1985.

Trojcak, Doris A. *Science With Children.* New York: McGraw Hill Book Company, 1979.

Victor, Edward. *Science for the Elementary School.* Fifth edition. New York: MacMillan Publishing Company, 1985.

FUTURISM IN THE SCIENCE CURRICULUM

Science educators need to study the objectives, learning opportunities, and appraisal procedures in the present science curriculum. The science curriculum is then being evaluated and described in terms of what exists presently in ongoing lessons and units of study. Science educators should not stop with describing what is in the present curriculum. Rather problems need identification and solutions sought in terms of what should be in teaching/learning situations in science. Predictions of the future science curriculum is a necessity. Science instruction needs to move away from the present to a better future. Futurism and its studies are necessary in order to develop excellence in the science curriculum.

THE SCIENCE CURRICULUM OF THE FUTURE

The teacher will have more adequate opportunities to determine where a student is in science achievement presently. To start where a learner is achieving and work for optimal continuous student progress is an ideal for the science teacher to follow. A futuristic science programme will emphasize determining a student's entry level of achievement with ordered opportunities for optimal achievement.

Second, better approaches in sequencing student learning will be in evidence, be it a psychological or logical science curriculum. Students then will experience increased success in sequential lessons and units. The lack of ordered learnings will be minimized while appropriate sequence in achievement will be optimalized.

Third, learners will perceive increased purpose in learning. Thus, students will accept inherent reasons for acquiring facts, concepts, and generalizations. Science teachers will have definite knowledge and skills pertaining to assisting learners to perceive purpose in learning.

Fourth, materials and methods of teaching will assist science teachers to secure student interests more effectively. With increased interest in science lessons and units, the student will put forth increased effort to learn. Increased interest in science will make for more effort to attain relevant goals of instruction. Interest and effort will be one and not separate entities.

Fifth, harmonious balance among diverse categories of objectives will be in evidence. Knowledge objectives stressing students acquiring vital subject matter will become increasingly salient. Skills ends are equally significant for student attainment. With skills objectives implemented, learners apply content acquired within the framework of knowledge objectives. The last of the three categories of objectives—attitudinal—are the most significant. With quality attitudes, students are positive in their wanting to achieve knowledge and skills ends. Science teachers in the future will become increasingly professional in guiding optimal student progress in knowledge, skills, and attitudes. Improved philosophies, psychologies, and research results will assist teachers to increase learner progress in science.

Sixth, new materials and procedures of teaching science will assist teachers to individual instruction more thoroughly. With more knowledge available to teachers in providing for diverse achivement levels, each student regardless of past levels of progress will be guided increasingly to attain as much as possible. Developing, growing, learning and achieving in science lessons will become more optimal for each student.

Seventh, science achievement of essentials will be a life-long process. Growth in science learning will have no end beyond itself.

Achievement is continuous and cumulative. Development in knowledge, skills, and attitudes has no ends in the science curriculum. Knowledge for its own sake as well as for utilitarian purposes will become a goal in science for each person. School and society will both emphasize vitality in its diverse manifestations of life-long learning in science.

Eighth, school and society will increasingly integrate its goals in science instruction. What transpires and occurs in science in the societal arena will provide content in the school curriculum. The realness and rality of scientific phenomena will provide objectives for instruction, learning opportunities to attain objectives, as well as appraisal procedures.

Ninth, more appropriate means to ascertain student attainment in science will be in the offing. These appraisal procedures will appraise not only cognitive learnings, but also skills and attitudes. Skills to be appraised include critical and creative thinking, as well as problem solving. Appraising student progress in the attitudinal dimension will include determining the quality of feelings, beliefs, and appreciations of contributions of science.

Tenth, quality in-service means of updating science instruction will be in the offing. In-service education programmes will be varied, purposeful, and provide for individual needs of science teachers. The major objective of in-service education will be to provide the best possible objectives, learning opportunities, and appraisal procedures in actual classroom teaching situations.

IN-SERVICE EDUCATION AND THE SCIENCE TEACHER

Each science teacher should provide for individual differences in the classroom to provide the best science curriculum possible for students. In-service education in its diverse manifestations many well assist each science teacher to do the best possible in teaching-learning situations.

First, a quality professional library needs to be in evidence for science teachers in the school setting: Teacher education textbooks, professionals journals for teachers, as well as audio-visual materials need to be available to teachers to benefit from. Science teachers should have time to read and view these materials to update the profession of teaching science.

Second, techers should attend state and national education conventions devoted to the teaching of science. Each teacher needs to attend meetings in conventions which assist to provide quality ends, means, and appraisal procedures for students. Attendance at these meetings for science teachers should be fully funded.

Third, science teachers should be involved in a local school district or in a regional meeting involving a planned series of meetings to improve the curriculum. With interaction among participants, quality science lessons and units should be in the offing. Each science teacher has opportunities to share with others means of improving teaching-learning situations.

Fourth, workshops should be conducted to provide science teachers with opportunities to identify and solve problems in teaching studnets. A general session with all participating should emphasize teachers selecting problems areas. The general session should be followed by committee endeavours. Here, each participant works on his/her chosen problem(s) to solve in the committee setting. Ample opportunities should be provided for teachers to work on individual tasks, projects, and endeavours. Feedback from committee and individual endeavours should be shared with the general session. Practical situations should be emphasized in the workshop whereby each secures valuable suggestions to improve the teaching of science.

Fifth, faculty meeting conducted withi a school should assist in identifying and solving problems related to the general areas of curriculum and instruction. These problems could involve discipline, inductive teaching, inquiry learning, as well as utilizing a variety of materials in on-going lessons and units. The general areas of curriculum development in terms of problem areas identified should also relate to teaching science in the school setting. Hopefully, solutions decided upon will improve the teaching of science.

Sixth, departmental meetings might be an excellent means in improving the science curriculum, Stimulating discussions on new methods in teaching science should aid in curriculum improvement. Content taught in science also needs appraisal to determine if key generalizations, concepts, and structural ideas are being emphasized in on-going lessons and units.

Seventh, team teaching is a way of learning from others in the teaching of science. With team teaching, member splan cooperatively objectives, learning opportunities, and appraisal procedures. In large group instruction, each team member may appraise and provide feedback to the teacher teaching students. Quality criteria need to be utilized in the feedback. Small group work as well as individual projects and activities for students provide teaching team members ample opportunities to work with learners in committees as well as in individual endeavours.

Eighth, models in teaching science may come from selected audio-visual materials such as video-tapes, films, filmstrips, and slides. Teachers need to analyze and appraise each method, prior to its implementation in the classroom.

Ninth, student teachers, when assigned, are a source of new ideas, methodology, and content for the regular science teacher. The student teacher and the regular teacher need to plan ends, means, and appraisal procedures cooperatively. Each new approach having quality criteria needs to be tried out in actual teaching situations. Feed-back from students provides information as to the effectiveness of new approaches utilized.

Tenth, science teacher sneed to have paid leaves of absence to secure advanced degrees in their area of expertise on a college/university campus. The advançed degree, be it a Specialist in Educaiton or a Doctorate, should assist the science teacher to become increasingly professional and competent in teaching. Achievement, growth and development are key concepts to emphasize when a science teacher works on and secures an advanced degree.

IN CLOSING

A forward looking science programme will emphasize :

1. determining specifically where a student in presently achieving.
2. sequencing learning opportunities for optimal student progress
3. feelings of purpose on the part of the student for learning.
4. securing the interests .of students in on-going lessons and units.
5. emphasizing balance among diverse categories of objec-

tives in teaching-learning situations. Thus, each category of objectives—knowledge, skills, and attitudes—will receive appropriate emphasis.

6. providing for individual differences in order that each student may achieve as much possible.
7. learning as being life-long and continuous.
8. integrating school and society.
9. appraising student progress for diagnostic purposes as well as to determine progress of learners.
10. increasing opportunities for in-service education for teachers.

Inservice education opportunities for science teachers will mphasize :

1. quality libraries in the school setting. Content will be readily available for teachers to use to improve the science curriculum.
2. attendance at state or national professional teacher education conventions to improve science teaching.
3. regional meetings convened to develop quality objectives, learning opportunities, and appraisal procedures.
4. workshops emphasizing large group and small group sessions as well as individualized study for participants to solve problems in the teaching of science.
5. faculty meetings scheduled to plan a quality science curriculum.
6. departmental meetings to view present trends in teaching with effort put forth to upgrade the curriculum.
7. teach teaching as a means of learning from each other in developing the science curriculum.
8. observation of audio-visual materials to update content and methodology.
9. cooperative planning with an assigned student teacher.
10. work toward an advanced degree in science teaching on a college/university campus.

REFERENCES

Beane, James A. et al. *Curriculum Planning and Development*. Boston: Allyn and Bacon, Inc., 1986, pp. 241-42.

Cruickshank, Donald R. *Teaching is Tough*. Englewood Cliffs, New Jersey: Prentice-Hall, Inc., 1980.

Ebel, Robert and David A. Frisbie. *Essentials of Educational Measurement*. Fourth edition. Englewood Cliffs, New Jersey: Prentice-Hall, 1986.

Esler, William K. *Teaching Elementary Science*, Belmont, California: Wadsworth Publishing Company, Inc., 1973

Friedl, Alfred E. *Teaching Science to Children: The Inquiry Approach Applied*. New York: Random House, Inc., 1972.

Gronlund, Norman E. *Measurement and Evaluation in Teaching*. New York: Macmillan, 1985.

Henson, Kenneth T. *Secondary Teaching Methods*. Lexington, Massachusetts: D.C. Heath and Company, 1981.

Herman, Jerry J. *Developing an Effective Elementary Science Curriculum*. West Nyack, New York: Parker Publishing Company, 1969.

Joyce, Bruce and Marsha Weil. *Models of Teaching*. Third edition. Englewood Cliffs, New Jersey: Prentice-Hall, Inc., 1986.

Joyce, Bruce et al. *The Structure of School Improvement*. New York: Longmans, 1983.

Kuslan, Louis I. and A. Harris Stone. *Teaching Children Science: An Inquiry Approach*. Belmont, California: 1972.

Lewis, June E. and Irene C. Potter. *The Teaching of Science in the Elementary School*. Englewood Cliffs, New Jersey: Prentice-Hall, Inc., 1970.

Mehrens, William A. and Irvin J. Lehmann. *Measurement and Evaluation in Education and Psychology*. Third edition. New York : Holt, Rinehart and Winston, 1984, pp. 14-15.

National Society for the Study of Education. *Staff Development*, Part II. Chicago, Illinois : The Society, 1983.

National Society for the Study of Education. *The Humanities in Precollegiate Education*, Part II. Chicago, Illinois: The Society, 1984.

PROJECT 2000+

Project 2000+ is a novel collaborative venture based on a partnership between a group of major inter-governmental organizations and agencies and non-governmental organizations with special concerns and responsibilities in the field of science and technology education and research. In July 1993 they convened an International Forum and invited the participants to establish an agenda for action, supporting steps that individuals, institutions, organizations and governments can take together in working to reform and revitalize science and technology at all levels.

The 400 participants from some 80 countries who attended the Forum enthusiastically demonstrated their commitment to the task of achieving scientific and technological literacy for the people of all nations. The Declaration they adopted by consensus at the close of the meeting found its driving force in the World Declaration on Education for all and in the Rio declaration. It constitutes a challenge to both governmental and non-governmental bodies worldwide to work together to promote scientific and technological literacy for all.

The full text of the Declaration is reproduced in the following pages together with a series of proposals for action to reach its goals. They are an invitation for us all to work together to quickly bring about through educational means of all kinds, formal and non-formal, a society which is enriched by a conscious sense of the scientific and technological dimension of its culture. The challenge is to make a reality of scientific and technological literacy for all children, youth and adults and throughout the world.

DECLARATION

We, participants in the Project 2000+ Forum, meeting at UNESCO, Paris, France, from 5 to 10 July, 1993:

1. *Recalling* the World Declaration on Education for All, in particular its recognition that 'sound basic education is fundamental to the strengthening of higher levels of education and of scientific and technological literacy and capacity and thus to self-reliant development' and, further recalling recent worldwide expressions of concern for the environment and for the quality of human life, especially those contained in Agenda 21, the output of the United Nations Conference on Environment and Development, Rio de Janeiro, 3-14 June 1992,
2. *Believing* that scientific literacy and technological literacy are essential for achieving responsible and sustainable development.
3. *Declare* our full commitment to the promotion of science ad technology education for all in keeping with the World Declaration on Education for all, and our readiness to contribute through Project 2000+ to the concerted action set out in the Framework Action to Meet Basic Learning Needs;
4. *Call* on Governments, industry, public and private sector interests, and education and other authorities in all countries to:
    a) Review critically existing provisions for science and technology education at all levels and in all settings with the aim of giving appropriate attention to development and maintenance of learning programmes responsive to the needs of individuals and communities;
    b) assign priority to the development and introduction of programmes leading to scientific literacy and technolog-

ical literacy for all with the aim of achieving responsible and sustainable development;

c) take such as steps may be necessary to ensure equity of access for everybody to science and technology education, notably for women and girls, young children and other under-represented groups;

d) develop appropriate in-school and out-of-school opportunities, programmes, curricula and assessment procedures for science and technology education responding to the human needs of a scientific and technological society;

e) ensure and support appropriate pre-service and continuing in-service provisions for those responsible for all forms of science and technology education;

f) encourage and support evaluation, research and development in science and technology education in both formal and non-formal sectors;

and to this end:

g) establish and support task forces involving partnership with public and private educational bodies and councils; these might include universities and other institutions of higher and further education, research institutions, libraries, interactive science centres, environmental areas and nature reserves as well as public and private bodies active in the fields of agriculture, natural resources, environment, health, industry, commerce and the media, and also organizations and individuals specially concerned with science and technology education;

h) recognize the central role of teachers in achieving scientific literacy and technological literacy for everybody, and enhance the status of careers in science and technology education at all levels:

i) recognize the capital role of institutions of non-formal education, such as museums and scientific centers, of the media (radio, television and the press) and of all other out-of-school channels for communicating knowledge of science and technology, in fostering scientific and technological literacy for all; and develop activities designed to set science and its applications in a wider social and cultural environment;

j) ensure that adequate resources are available to achieve these aims;

5. *Urge* United Nations Agencies and other inter-governmental organizations to work together to initiate and support programmes which will advance the ability of countries and of populations to shape their worn future in a scientific and technological society and which will increase the capacity of countries for designing, planning and implementing scientific literacy and technological literacy programmes;

6. *Urge* non-governmental organizations active in fields of science and technology education, as well as the social sciences, and professional associations of teachers and educators and educational organizations at all levels to:

   — enter into partnership with, and make their knowledge and experience available to, united Nations and other inter-governmental bodies as well as establish innovative programmes in a common effort to achieve the goal of scientific literacy and technological literacy for all; and

   — participate in national, regional and international programmes for the enhancement of scientific literacy and technological literacy for the improvement of the quality of life in all societies and for the achievement of sustainable development;

7. ***Recommend*** that UNESCO makes provision, within its Medium Terms Plan (1996-2001) in the field of education, and in the context of Project 2000+, for an international programme to develop co-operation among all countries in the field of science and technology education, with particular reference to the promotion of scientific literacy and technological literacy for all:

   This programme, conducted in partnership with the relevant and competent governmental and non-governmental organizations and agencies, should focus on regional and subregional co-operation and on strengthening networks for exchange of ideas, informations, human and material resources for science and technology education, and actively seek to promote world-wide:

a) understanding of the nature of, and the need for, scientific literacy and technological literacy in relation to local culture and values and to the social and economic needs and aspirations of each country and its peoples, and also in accord both with the general aims of education for the all-round development of human personality and with human rights and basic freedoms;

b) identification of those issues concerning the applications of science and technology which are of special importance for personal, local and national development and their embodiment in educational programmes;

c) establishment of teaching and learning environments as well as supporting structures conducive to the achievement of scientific literacy and technological literacy for all;

d) formulation of guidelines for the preparation and continuous professional development of science and technology educators and leadership coupled with assistance to countries in giving effect to them:

e) development of effective communication, both verbal and visual, assessment strategies and evaluation programmes designed to enhance general levels of scientific literacy and technological literacy;

f) support for the non-formal and informal sector in its own right and support for development strategies which will help to stimulate and maintain lifelong scientific literacy and technological literacy;

8. *Recommend* that by the year 2001 there should be in place appropriate structures and activities to foster scientific literacy and technological literacy for all, in all countries.

THE WAY FORWARD

1. THE NATURE OF PROJECT 2000+

The target has been set:

> appropriate structures and activities to foster scientific literacy and technological literacy for all, in all countries, should be in place by the year 2001.

There is, therefore, urgent need not only for action but also for reflection on current practices in formal, informal and non-formal education at all levels as well as on the meaning to be attached to scientific and technological literacy in different national settings.

To this end Project 2000+ is working to:

- identify ways of promoting the development of scientific and technological literacy for all;
- put forward educational programmes (formal and non-formal) which will empower all to satisfy their basic needs and productive in an increasingly technological society;
- provide guidelines for continuous development of science and technology educators and leaders;
- encourage the formation of broadly based national task forces to initiate programmes for greater scientific and technological literacy;
- support the development of a wide range of projects designed to promote solidarity and co-operation in achieving scientific and technological literacy for all;
- support the evaluation of existing and projected programmes in this vital area.

Project 2000+ involves a long-term co-operative effort to move forward on a broad front developing and strengthening interlocking links between the United Nations and other intergovernmental agencies, governmental bodies, bilateral donors and non-governmental organizations.

Time is now short.

2. WHAT DOES THE DECLARATION MEAN IN EACH NATIONAL CONTEXT ?

To implement the Declaration and promote action, it is proposed that national task forces be set up to work closely with existing Education for All task forces or to form an integral part of them. Although the structure of Project 2000+ task forces may vary from one country to another, all should involve partnership between public and private educational bodies, governmental and non-governmental organizations concerned with science and technology education and institutions of both formal and non-formal education. They should also have links with those other sectors of the economy underpinned by science and technology, including notably, agriculture, natural resources, environment, population and health, commerce and the media.

The first function of national task force would be to analyse the Declaration in terms of the country's national and local needs and to identify priorities for action. These priorities should take into account both qualitative and quantitative factors.

Qualitative issues to be considered might include the following:

- Science and technology education which does not lead to *understanding* cannot lead to scientific and technological literacy. Is the science and technology education now being given in the schools leading to such understanding and if not why not?
- Scientific and technological literacy implies and science and its applications should be set in the wider context of the *social and cultural environment*. Are activities being undertaken to achieve this?
- The role of *teachers* is central to the achievement scientific literacy and technological literacy for everyone. Is their training adequate ? Is their career status appropriate ?

In quantitative terms, scientific and technological literacy for *all* calls for an outreach through *non-formal education* of many kinds. Institutions providing non-former education have a capital role to play in this regard. They include: museums, science centers, the media (radio, television and the press) and other out-of-school channels for communicating knowledge and understanding of science and technology and of their applications.

- How can the impact of such institution and bodies be enhanced ? It also implies outreach to groups which are often under-represented in both formal and non-formal science and technology education—women and girls, ethnic minorities, the disabled, the poor, refugees and those who live in remote rural areas.
- What can be done to engage such groups more effectively ?

The second function of the task force would be to draw up on overall strategy for establishing the structures that are deemed necessary to prepare projects for action. It may, for example, be necessary to:

- create centres or facilities (or reinforce, adapt, equip, or restructure those already existing) for supporting the improvement of science and technology education throughout the country;
- provide support for the establishment or reinforcement of science and technology teachers' professional associations which will make important contributions to achieving both the qualitative and quantitative goals of Project 2000+;
- provide support for groups or institutions working or willing to engage in the popularization of science and technology (museums, exhibitions, the media, etc.) particularly for helping them to focus on people's needs and to establish good links with the educational system.

Relevant projects may include:

- revising school science and technology curricula and assessment procedures to make them more relevant to national needs, problems and priorities;
- revising pre-service and in-service teacher-training programmes, paying special attention to re-shaping the institutional culture so as better to prepare teachers to deal with current scientific and technological issues and face the challenge of those which may arise in the future;
- developing teaching and learning materials suited to local needs, both for use in schools and in the training

of teachers;

- integrating knowledge about relevant science and technology into literacy, post literacy and adult education programmes;
- promoting and supporting activities designed to improve and participation of women in scientific and technological occupations and professions and to open to them the benefits that they can derive for themselves, their families and society at large from better access to a basic understanding of science and technology.

3. FINANCE

To accomplish this task, it will be necessary to mobilize financial resources from both public and private sources. Although the pattern of financing education is specific to each country, channels exists in all countries for requesting international and bilateral funding. If high priority is accorded to scientific and technological literacy in national plans, United Nations agencies, such as UNESCO and the United Environment Programme (UNEP), are willing to support well-prepared projects in co-operation with the United Nations Development Programme (UNDP) or under funds-in-trust arrangements. UNESCO's own Regular and Participation Programmes are also able to provide seed money for the support of task forces, while programmes developed with World Bank loans may also have a scientific and technological literacy component.

4. SECRETARIAT

Communications should be addressed to:

Project 2000+ Secretariat
Science and Technology Education Section
UNESCO Place de Fontenoy, 75352 Paris 07-SP
FRANCE

Fax: 33-1-40659405
Telephone: 33-1-45 68 08 37/8
E Mail: EDEAP @ FRUNES 21.BITNET

Contact may also be made with UNESCO regional and subregional offices (Addresses may be obtained from UNESCO National Commissions) or with any of other members of the Steering Committee.

LEARNING WITHOUT BURDEN

PART-A

REPORT OF THE NATIONAL ADVISORY COMMITTEE
APPOINTED BY THE
MINISTRY OF HUMAN RESOURCE DEVELOPMENT

I. INTRODUCTION

Concern regarding academic burden on students and satisfactory quality of learning has been voiced time and again in our country during the past two decades. The question has been discussed extensively by several committees and groups. The Ishwarbhai Patel Review Committee (1977), National Council of Educational Research and Training (NCERT) Working Group (1984) and National Policy on Education (NPE) Review Committees (1990) made several recommendations to reduce the academic burden on students. The curriculum development agencies are generally in agreement with the recommendations of the committee and assure the public that these would be kept in view at the time of the forthcoming revision of curricula, But the Problem, instead of being mitigated, becomes more acute when a new curriculum is introduced. This has happened in the case of new curriculum introduced in the wake of implementation of NPE (1986). With a view to a have a fresh look on the problems of education, particularly with regard to the problem of academic burden on students, the Ministry of Human Resource Development, Government of India, set up a National Advisory Committee in March 1992 with the following terms of reference:

> To advice on the ways and means to reduce the load on school students at all levels particularly the young students, while improving quality of learning including capability for life-long self-learning and skill formulation.

Before starting its work, the Committee decided the parameters of its work and also the methodology for completing the task entrusted to it. With a view of keeping a national perspective in view, the Committee decided not to confine its work to the Central Board of Secondary Education (CBSE) or NCERT syllabi and textbooks but to take into account the textbooks used in different states and union territories also. Secondly, the Committee decided to base its recommendations on the data obtained through perception survey, wide-ranging consultations with teachers and analysis of textbooks and other instructional materials. Thirdly, the Committee decided to look at the work of agencies/organisations doing innovative programmes.

The process of consultation was initiated with a meeting with a few faculty members of NCERT followed by meetings with teachers and principals working in different states at four places in the country, viz. Delhi, Thiruvananthapuram, Pune and Calcutta. The consultation meetings were also held with voluntary organisations engaged in innovative programmes, syllabus and textbook writers, private publishers, and Chairpersons of Boards of Secondary Education. Some members of the Committee organised meetings with parents, teachers and students at Bombay, Nasik, Baroda and Calcutta. Surveys to ascertain the opinions of teachers and parents were conducted with the help of questionnaires at Bombay and Delhi.

To involve the whole country in the exercise of looking at the problems of school education from the perspective the mechanical load studies on children, views and suggestions were invited from the students, teachers, parents and general public through advertisements in the newspapers and special announcements by all India Radio and Doordarshan. The Committee received more than 600 memoranda, letters and write-ups from students, teachers, parents and professionals interested in children's education.

The wide-ranging consultations with knowledgeable people, analysis of the existing instructional materials and reactions of the teachers and students have enabled the Committee to understand the function of the present educational system which forms the basis of its recommendations.

In its work, the Committee received cooperation from a large number of teacher, principals, syllabus and textbook writers, organisations, associations and departments. We gratefully acknowledge their contribution in our work. Particularly, we are grateful to the State Council of Educational Research and Training (SCERT), Delhi, where the Committee's office was located, for providing all types of administrative support with tremendously facilitated our work. We are also thankful to NCERT and its Department of Social Sciences and Humanities for providing finances and other facilities for holding meetings of the Committee. The education departments of the states of Kerala, Maharashtra and West Bengal, and the NCERT Field Advisors in these states deserve appreciation for hosting the regional consultation meeting held at Thiruvananthapuram, Pune and Calcutta. Special thanks are due to voluntary organisations, Alla Rippu, Digantar and Eklavya for sharing their experiences with members of the committee. We express our sense of gratitude to the authorities of Doordarshan and Akashwani for making special announcement requesting the audience to send their view and suggestions to the Committee. Above all, we are extremely grateful to hundreds of parents, students and teachers who responded to our invitation and sent their view in writing, in many a times after holding meetings/workshops at their places.

Smt. Meenu Taneja, stenographer, SCERT, Delhi deserves a pat for providing all sorts of secretarial assistance and for typing minutes, discussion papers and finally the report.

II. THE PROBLEM OF CURRICULUM LOAD

1. Preamble

Our Committee was concerned with one major flaw of our

system of education. This flaw can be identified briefly by saying that a "a lot is taught, but little is learnt or understood". The problem manifests itself in a variety of ways. The most common and striking manifestation is the size of the school bag that children can be seen carrying from home the school and back to home everyday. A survey conducted in Delhi revealed that the weight of school bag, on a average, in primary classes in public schools in more than 4 kg while it is around 1 kg in MCD schools. Nevertheless the load we want to discuss is not only the physical load but the load of learning which is there for all children irrespective of the category or type of schools where they study. Eminent writer R.K. Narayan had drawn the country's attention to this daily sight by making a moving speech in the Rajya Sabha a few years ago. The situation has become worse over these years, with even pre-school children a carrying a bag of books and notebooks. And the sight is not confined to metropolitan cities alone; it can be seen in small towns and the bigger villages too.

The weight of the school bag represents one dimension of the problem; another dimension can be seen in the child's daily routine. Right from early childhood, many children specially those belonging to middle classes, are made to slog through home work, tuitions and coaching classes of different kinds. Leisure has become a highly scarce commodity in the child's, especially the urban child's life. The child's innate nature and capacities have no opportunity to find expression in a daily routine which permits no time to play, to enjoy simple pleasures, and to explore the world.

2. Joyless Learning

It is hard to reconcile the rigorous 'academic' regime that is imposed on children from an early age with the widespread complaint made about the declining norms and performance of the formal system of education. Teachers routinely complain that they do not have enough time to explain anything in detail, or to organize activities in the classroom. 'Covering' the syllabus seems to have become an end in itself, unrelated to the philosophical and social aims of education. The manner in which the syllabus is 'covered' in the average classroom is by means of reading the prescribed textbook aloud, with occasional noting of salient points on the blackboard. Opportunities for children to carry out experiments, excursions, or any kind of observations are scarce even in the best of schools. In the average school, especially the school located in a rural area, even routine teaching of the kind described above does not take place in many cases. In several states, school teachers encourage children to attend after-school tuition given for a fee while regular classroom teaching has become a tenuous ritual.

One message of this situation is that both the teacher and the child have lost the sense of joy in being involved in an educational process. Teaching and learning have both become a chore for a great number of teachers and children. Barring those studying in reputed or exceptional institutions, the majority of our school-going children are made to view learning at school as a boring, even unpleasant and bitter experience. They are daily socialized to look upon education as mainly a process of preparing for examinations. No other motivation seems to have any legitimacy.

The contribution that teachers, make towards this kind of socialization is especially worrisome. Trained teachers are expected to be aware of the wider aims of education; Indeed, aims like 'development of the child's total personality' are the shibboleths of teacher training institutions everywhere in the country. It appears that teachers feel they can do little to pursue such lofty aims in any realistic sense under the harsh circumstances created by factors like excessively large classes, a heavy syllabus, difficult textbooks, and so on. Moreover, majority of them neither know nor have the necessary skills to realise the goals of education. The recommended pupil-teacher ratio of forty to one is now more an exception than a norm, and in many parts of the country it is customary to have sixty to eighty students in one class. The Committee learnt that in many states senior secondary classes often have one hundred or more students. Many of them spilling into the corridor. In the national capital, many 'model' secondary schools, Central Schools, and several elite 'public' schools have classes, including primary classes, with more than sixty students.

This kind of class-size understandably generates a feeling of helplessness among teachers, but why much teachers feel helpless in the face of curriculum-related problems such as heavy syllabi, poorly produced textbooks, etc.? Why don't they act in more vocal ways and involve themselves in curriculum reform? Apart from the fact that there are very few forums encouraging curriculum inquiry and reform in any systematic manner, it seems to be an entrenched attitude among teachers to regard all decisions about curriculum and textbooks as the responsibility of 'authorities'. The fact is that while the teachers' involvement in the preparation of syllabi and textbooks is verbalized as a matter of principle, in practice it takes the shape of token involvement of a handful of teachers. Most teachers have reason, therefore, to think that they have little to say about the changes made from time to time in syllabi and textbooks. Even in such extreme cases where a textbook has a factual mistake, no complaints are made by teachers asking for correction of error. There is no established procedure or official forum to mobilise teacher vigilance had participation in curriculum improvement. On the contrary, there are cases where an individual teacher who complained about an error in a state-published textbook, was taken to task. Even if such cases can be described as rare or exceptionally unfortunate, they explain why the majority of teachers intuitively feel that it is not their business to critically examines the syllabus and texts they teach.

3. Examination System

Much has been written by various official committees on the ills of our examination system. The major, well-understood defect of the examination system is that it focuses on children's ability to reproduce information to the exclusion of the ability to apply concepts and information on unfamiliar, new problems, or simply to think. The pubic examinations taken after Classes X and XII have assumed the importance of major events which have a set character or culture of their own. The awe they generate, the response they trigger, and the kind of preparation they demand have all got so entrenched into the social lore that minor improvements in the style of question papers do not make difference to the dominant influence that the examination system has on the processes of learning and teaching. The influence is so strong that school start holding a formal written examination several year prior to Class X indeed, in the primary classes in many parts of the country. And children receive the message almost as soon as they start attending school that they only thing which matters here is one's performance in the examination.

Both the teacher and the parents constantly reinforce the fear of examination and the need to prepare for it in the only manner that seems practical, namely, by memorising a whole lot of information from the textbooks and guidebooks. Educated parents, who have themselves gone through examinations, and the uneducated parents, whose knowledge of the examination system is based on social lore, share the belief that what really matters in education is the score one gets in the final examination. This belief is undoubtedly rooted in social or market reality. Percentage of marks obtained in the high school, higher secondary, or BA/B.Sc examinations is what ultimately matters in determining a student's chance of being called for an interview for admission to a university or for employment. Since the examination score is what a candidate carries with him or her as the key authoritative record of school or college performance, higher level institutions or employing agencies understandably rely on it. It is a process in which no beginning or end can be meaningfully established. Changing the system of examination in a structural or even in a merely procedural sense does not require that a source outcome or cause effect relationship be established; yet, the examination system goes on, apparently with the help of energies or rationales located in the system of education itself.

4. Textbook as the 'Truth'

The pervasive effects of the examination system can be seen in the style and content of textbooks, and not just guidebooks which are specifically manufactured to help children pass an examination. If 'facts' or 'information' constitute the main burden of an examination, the same is true of textbooks. Barring exceptions, our textbooks appear to have been written primarily to convey information or 'facts', rather than to make children think and explore. Over the years some attempts have been made to incorporate a certain amount of reflective writing in textbooks. Such writing is so exceptional that its examples can be spotted and named without difficulty. 'How leaves are designed' in a Class VIII textbook is one such piece of writing*. It stands out from among the thousands of pages of textbooks in different subjects that our teachers and children have to go through painstakingly so that they can retain the information recorded in those pages in highly compressed, usually abstruse manner. The more common style used in the textbooks is exemplified by passages of the following kind**:

---

* Class VIII science textbook prepared by NCERT

** We have decided to cite such examples without giving a reference in order to avoid the impression that we are criticising certain specific titles, authors, publishers or organisations. Our aim is to highlight certain common tendencies in the style of textbook writing.

> The term pH is defined as the negative logarithm to the base 10 of the hydrogen ion concentration expressed in gram ions per liter or moles per liter. (Class X)
>
> Fatty acids are slowly hydrolysed during digestion in the small intestine to form glycero and fatty acids through the enzyme action of lipase which is secreted by the pancreas. (Class X)
>
> We find that while dividing a decimal by a multiple of 10,000 or 1,000, we first move the decimal point to the left as many places as there are zeros in the number and then divide the resulting decimal by the second factor of the divisor (Class V)

The problem of readability in textbooks becomes grim in the context of a system which often leaves the child with no resource other than the prescribed textbook. The extent to which the child can rely on a teacher to elucidate tersely written text material is dependent on the quality of teachers, their training, and their accountability. From what impression the Committee could form about these aspects of the system, it seems valid to say that the child is very often helpless in the face of a style of teaching that is far from being interactive, let alone the absence or irregular presence of teachers. (And we are not saying that the teachers alone are responsibie for the kind of teaching that takes place daily in lacks of classrooms that have hardly any equipment and often not even a proper means of ventilation or lighting.) Under the circumstances that are widely prevalent in our country, a child is more likely than not to mug up the definition of 'pH' quoted above without grasping it. And mugging does get the child through the examination !

Textbooks and guidebooks form a tight nexus. In some parts of the country children are compelled to buy the guidebook (or 'key') along the textbook. The economic and business aspects of this pairing apart, the academic function of the textbook has become quite dubious indeed. It is *not* perceived as one of the resources for learning about a subject, but as the *only* authoritative resource. This kind of sanctity distorts what useful purpose the textbook could serve. Teachers see it as a body of 'truths' which children must learn by heart. This perception and urge to 'cover' the chapters of the prescribed textbook, turn all knowledge into a load to be borne by the child's memory.

The distance between the child's everyday life and the content of the textbook further accentuates the transformation of knowledge into a load. We are not talking here about advanced science or mathematics, but about elementary science, social subjects in a manner that leads to alienation of knowledge from the child's world. This tragic phenomenon takes different forms in different subjects. In the natural sciences, it takes the form of esotericisation of the subject. In the social sciences it becomes manifest in the coating of every inquiry in didacticism, suggestive of one preferred answer to every question. A common source of alienation of subject-matter from the children's perspective and life is the presentation of the life-style and world view of the urban well-off class. This life-style is characterized by access to concrete housing, modern kitchens, electrical gadgets, and so on. Of course there is nothing 'wrong' with this life-style; but the symbolization of this life-style in every illustration and description that concerns a child's home life alienates millions of children who live in houses with traditional kitchens, or with no separate kitchens. Objects of daily use in common Indian homes, such as a broom or clay pitcher, are seldom seen in textbooks. One wonders whether the common Indian broom, which could be a versatile resource for learning about the social and physical environment, is perceived by our textbook writers and illustrators with a sense of stigma or as a symbol of backwardness. Or could it be that it is simply too common to be seen as being of any use in an educational material ? Neither of the two guesses is totally irrelevant in view of the complete absence of common objects of ordinary Indian life in the world depicted in textbooks.

The most common message that children get from the textbooks is that the life ordinary people live is 'wrong' or irrational. And this kind of didactic rejection does not apply to non-middle class life alone. All simple joys of childhood are also criticized. No better example of this can be given than the message conveyed in a Class V exercise which asks children to decide whether the statement 'Road is also a playground', is correct or wrong. The right response is that this statement is 'wrong, the message of the lesson being that playing on the street can be dangerous. This message is of course true in a normative sense, but it ignores the reality of the overwhelming majority of urban children who have no other space except the street to play. The moot point is not the scarcity of space, but rather the need to accept the universally valid fact that children enjoy playing on the street. This joy must be respected in a text written from a child-centered point of view. To argue that a respectful acknowledgment of this joy will amount to sanctioning carelessness, or to say that children must be warned about the risks of playing on the street is to trivialise the issue. Every child who plays on the street fully knows the dangers involved in it. Science textbooks need not waste valuable pages on such trivial preaching which is precisely what they do throughout the elementary classes in place of using these golden years of childhood to arouse curiosity about things and ideas.

5. Language Textbooks

We hardly need to assert that our textbooks are not written from the child's viewpoint. Neither the mode of communication, nor the selection of objects depicted, nor the language conveys the centrality of the child in the world constructed by the text. This last dimension of language deserves some elaboration. The vocabulary and syntax used in the textbooks in the Hindi region were critically referred to by a number of individuals and groups whom the Committee met during the course of its deliberations. Not just the textbooks used for the teaching of the natural and the social sciences, but even the textbook used for the teaching of mother tongue are written in such stylized diction and sentence-structure, that children cannot be expected to see the language used in them as their own. Words, expression and nuances commonly used by children and others in their milieu are all absent from textbooks. So is humour. An artificial, sophisticated style dominates textbooks lessons, reinforcing the tradition of distancing knowledge from life. The language used in textbooks, thus, deepens the sense of 'burden' attached to all school-related knowledge.

6. Observation Discouraged

A highly disturbing tendency we discovered in next writing, which excerbates the problem we are discussing, is that of treating pictures as substitutes for experience. We found textbooks asking children to observe a picture of the object under study rather than asking children and the teacher to go out and observe the object itself in nature. For example, a Class V science text says: 'Look at the picture of a cactus plant. Observe the thick green structure...' Such an instruction prompts what motivation there may be in a teacher or child to bring an actual cactus plant to the class or to grow one. The most painful example of this phenomenon brought to our attention was one in which private publisher claimed that he had made the teacher's task 'easier' by turning an official 'Teacher's Guide', which suggests that the teacher should take children outside the school and identify some common birds, into a text where the pictures of all the common birds with their names were provided for ready use. This case is especially painful as it shows how even a specific instruction given in a Teacher's Guide (Teacher's Guides are themselves rare; and in subjects in which they have been prepared in certain states, circulation has not been satisfactorily looked after) to encourage teachers to extend the lesson beyond the four walls of the classroom is co-opted within the dominant, traditional approach of teaching everything verbally from a text-book. Over the recent years, some textbooks have adopted the vocabulary of observation and exploration or discovery as a necessary part of science teaching, but even here, virtually all commands for observation conclude with statements about what will be seen if an observation is actually made, thereby making it unnecessary for the teacher and children to find an object and actually observe it.

7. Structure of Syllabus

The absence of the child's viewpoint is also reflected in the organisation of syllabi in different subjects. We received a large number of complaints from parents as well as teachers that the content of syllabi lacks an overall organisation or coherence. Gaps in the syllabi between the lower and the higher secondary stages are as common as repetitions of the same content. These weaknesses of organisation apparently lead to memorization and poor comprehension, both exacerbating the sense of curriculum load. Gaps between the secondary and the senior secondary stages seem to be glaring in the science syllabi. When students come to Class XI, they often find themselves without a clue even if they have done well in Class X. The level of abstraction attempted in the senior secondary stage science syllabi and textbooks, especially the physics text-books, represents a jump in many topics. Apparently, those preparing the senior secondary syllabi and texts lacked adequate familiarity with the syllabi and texts used in the earlier classes. In fact, they had no occasion to interact with the persons involved in the preparation of syllabi and textbooks for secondary classes (IX and X)

Repetitions of concepts and information also leads to boredom and a sense of load. The need to repeat is rooted in the flawed structure of syllabi. In the primary classes, ideas and information are presented in a synoptic manner, making the text look deceptively simple. In the later classes, the same ideas are repeated, with some elaboration which does not prevent the child from viewing the ideas as trivialised by repetition. In the study of nutrition and health, for example, virtually the same ideas and information are given in the syllabi and texts of Class III, IV, V, VII and X. Even the questions given at the end of the lessons in the tests are almost of the same kind. Apparently, the structure of syllabi is not carefully thought out. Indeed, our Committee was told by senior experts, who have been involved in syllabus and textbook preparation, that experts working on the syllabus of different levels (secondary and senior secondary) had no contact with each other. Reference to such procedural lapses, however, is not necessary to explain the tendency towards repetition that is embedded in the structure of the syllabus and has been reinforced by tradition.

History is the most clear case in point. Although it forms one part of the subject called social science, it offers a prime example of curriculum load. Despite many changes that have come about in the style of history texts, the history syllabus continues to be a frustrating and meaningless experience for children. The aim of teaching history is defeated because children are not enabled to relate to their own heritage. Traditionally, it requires children to form an overall picture of the 'whole' of India's known history, from ancient to modern times, during the three years from Classes VI to VIII. Since the texts for these classes are required to cover such a vast span, the density of these texts becomes extremely high which means that historical time is greatly compressed, i.e. a few sentences are deemed to 'cover' several decades. The synoptic style forces the child into 'accepting' whatever is narrated. There aren't enough details that a child could use to work out some kind of argument or interpretation, but the sheer volume of text (which is supposed to 'cover' 'all' of India's history in three years) forces the child (and the teacher) to 'take in' as much text as possible without 'wasting' time in studying or constructing an argument.

This common problem of the history syllabus apart, we found that the content of the history syllabus in certain states was conceived as a densely packed box of informations. The syllabus of history in West Bengal illustrates this tendency in tragically exag gerated proportions. For example in Class VIII, children are re quired to learn 17 topics in all which are:

> 1. Modern age; 2. Renaissance in Europe; 3. Europeans widen the world; 4. Reformation in Europe; 5. The English Revolution in the 17th century; 6. India; 7. Foundation and growth of the British power in India til 1857 in short narrative form; 8. World in the 18th century; 9. Europe since 1815; 10. (a) Developments in China till 1911; (b) Rise of Japan as a great power till 1914; 11. India under the crown 1858-1914; 12. The First World War; 13. The Bolshevik Revolution; 14. Europe 1919-1939; 15. Second World War; 16. India 1919-1947; 17. (a) Revolution in China 1911-1949; (b) Revolution in South East Asia after 1945; (c) Spread of nationalism and unrest in subject countries during the Second World War.

The entire syllabus is to be covered in 135 pages of a text, according to the instruction given in the syllabus itself. Apparently, the syllabus makers believe that compression of information in terms of page-space does not affect the readability, let alone comprehensibility, of a text.

8. Teaching Everything

The problem of densely packed syllabi like this one cuts across disciplines. In geography, it takes the form all the continents being 'covered' under regional geography between Class VI and VIII. In mathematics and the natural sciences, the packing of details makes any kind of learning with understanding, leave alone enjoyment, virtually impossible. Numérous example could be given from these disciplines to illustrate the problem. In one page of a class VII science textbook we find all these items 'covered': definition of time period, how to find the number of oscillations per second, definition of frequency, 'Hertz' unit of frequency, the idea that vibrations have amplitude and frequency, definitions of these, the concept of sound as vibration, loudness and pitch, and finally frequency/pitch and its relation to speed of rotation and tension. WE are not citing this example as a specific case to be looked into, but as evidence of a deeply rooted tendency, rather an ideology, which impels syllabus and textbook planners to include 'everything' without any regard for children's ability at different ages to learn and the time available in an average school for teaching a subject. Class XI and XII textbooks of science, prepared recently with a view apparently to implement the National Education Policy, have been widely criticised on these scores. Children studying science subjects have been asked by their teachers to look for private tutors, the rationale being that there may not be enough time in the class to cover the syllabus, and some of the syllabus being beyond the capacities of the teacher. The terse content of these texts was apparently edited and reviewed in some haste, we were informed, due to constraints of time while sending the manuscripts for publication. Perhaps it can argued that these textbooks are liked by the highly motivated and the brightest among the students and teachers. If this indeed is the case, it gives all the more reason to worry about the fate of the overwhelming majority of children studying in ordinary schools.

In mathematics, the situation seems to be grim right from the start of the child's school carrier: Far too many abstractions are introduced all at once with scant attention paid to well-known facts about development of mathematical thinking in children. To begin, with children are expected to handle arithmetical operations on a very large numbers early. In Class I, they are supposed to go up to 100 (compared to this a British child in this class spends the whole year working with numbers up to 20), in Class II up to 1000, in Class III, up to 10,000 in Class IV up to a million, and in Class V up to a crore. Even though the conservation of volume and weight are known to emerge in the child's mind after the conservation of length is fully established, all three are introduced simultaneously (usually in one unit of study) at the young age of seven or eight years, with the expectation that children will compute with standard units. Concrete operational thought, which is characteristic of elementary school children, demands manipulation of objects and activities using a variety of materials (to enable 'elaboration' of a concept, i.e. its dislocation from any one material or object). Such activities become impossible to organise under a curriculum which 'progresses' so swiftly from concept to concept. Also, children of this stage find proportional reasoning difficult yet percentage and ratio are introduced in Classes IV and V. In the middle and higher classes, the tendency to follow the logic of the discipline of mathematics rather than psychology of learning as the basis of the curriculum becomes even more dominant. Mathematics, thus, acquires the image of an esoteric discipline which has little application in the real life of the child.

9. Starting Early

The general problems of curriculum conceptualization that we have discussed in this part of our report can all be seen reflected in the emerging pre-school sector of the education system. Despite official stipulations that no textbooks be used at this stage, pre-school teachers and parents in the urban centre are feeling 'compelled' to burden the young child with textbooks and the formal learning they represent. The sense of compulsion comes from a widespread feeling that unless academic training of a child starts early, he or she cannot cope with the fast-paced pedagogy and the competitive ethos of the later school years. The pernicious grip of this false argument manifests itself in absurd, and of course deeply harmful, practices in pre-schools and primary schools, such as early emphasis on shapely drawing, writing, and memorising information. Intrinsic motivation and the child's natural abilities are being smothered at a scale so vast that it cannot be correctly estimated. Out national commitment to the development of human resource is daily challenged in our nurseries and primary schools.

10. Not just as Urban Problem

The problem we have tried to identify in this part of the report is not confined to urban areas as some people think. It is deeply relevant to children's education in rural India although there, more basic problems- such as abysmally poor condition of schools, absenteeism among teachers, etc. may cloud the problem of curriculum load. In our view, the problem of a high drop-out rate, which was rightly preoccupied our policy-makers for a long time, has one of its origins in the curriculum scenario we have portrayed. A curriculum policy that takes away the elements of joy and inquiry from learning obviously contributes to the rate at which children leave school in the early years, undoubtedly under the force of economic and social circumstances. As we have indicated earlier, symbolic tilt towards an urban, middle class way of life in textbooks can also be expected to make the rural child's association with his or her experience at school thin and brittle. Quality of teachers and the equipment available to them also make an impact on the tenuous and fragile link that the first-generation learner in many parts of rural India tries to establish with the system of education.

III. ROOTS OF THE PROBLEM

1. Knowledge vs Information

In our discussions with people directly involved in syllabi and textbook preparation all over the country, we found one argument repeated over and over again as the main justification for the phenomenon we have described in Chapter II. The argument was that India has to catch up with developed countries where an explosion of knowledge has occurred; therefore, our children must learn a lot more than they used to, which mean that new topics, new concepts and information have to be added to the syllabi and textbooks. This argument seems to be so widespread and so tenacious that those who believe in it use it as an undebatable 'given'. When it is pointed out to them that children of the so-called developed countries learn certain concepts a lot later than our children do (for example, in chemistry, the concept of valency is now taught in our schools in class VII whereas European children do not hear about it till they are in Class IX), supporters of the 'explosion of knowledge' argument simply say that the European societies are already way ahead of us, so they can afford to instruct their children at a relaxed pace. In geography, when it is pointed out that European and North American children do not have to study every continent (only selected countries are intensively studied instead), the answer given is that in Western societies children have access to many resources of learning outside the school whereas the majority of our children are dependent on the school for getting to know about the world. The idea entrenched in the 'explosion of knowledge' theory finds similar justifications for present state of syllabi and texts in other school subjects.

The notion that there has been an explosion of knowledge apparently treats knowledge and information as synonymous. It is true that the twentieth century has been a period of massive expansion in human capacity to find new facts and to store them, but the concepts and theories that assist in the generation and organisation of information can hardly be said to have multiplied at an 'explosive' rate. (It is another matter that in an ex-colonial society it often looks as if all new 'knowledge' in being produced by 'others' and our job is simply to 'learn' and consume this knowledge). Also, the important thing in children's education ought to be concept-information and growth of capacity for theory-building, rather than possession of vast amounts of information. The 'explosion of knowledge' idea prevents us from appreciating that learning in childhood is not the same thing as storing information about different subjects. If we say that a child has knowledge of phenomenon 'x', we can anticipate three possible ways in which this statement will be interpreted:

i) the child has been given information about phenomenon 'x',

ii) the child can reproduce information about phenomenon 'x',

iii) the child has understood phenomenon 'x' and he or she can apply this understanding on other phenomena.

It is mostly the first two meanings that hold in the context of formal education in our country, the first being used as a basis for the second. 'Understanding' is often confused with 'acquisition of facts'.

Such as confusion leads to the neglect of 'understanding' as an aim of education. It would be correct to say that this neglect of understanding has gone so far and deep in our education system that a child can pass almost any examination without any understanding of the phenomena he or she has been told about in books or in the classroom. To a great extent, this paradoxical situation can be attributed to the excessive emphasis placed in our syllabi and textbooks on information or 'names' of things. Children have no choice but to memorise all the 'names' in order to 'prove' at an examination that they have 'understood' a phenomenon. Despite all kinds of claims that examinations have been reformed, they continue to focus on testing the possession of 'correct' information (i.e. the names of things, definitions, examples etc.). Recall-type questions outnumber the questions that test the child's capacity to speculate, evaluate or judge, and to apply an idea in an unfamiliar context. Board examinations, taken at the end of Class X and Class XII, have remained rigid, bureaucratic and essentially inductive (as the child never sees why he or she was marked in a certain way), and mainly a source of awe because of the amount of information they demand in a manner ready for instant recall. Such a system obviously influences the tests and annual examinations taken by schools in earlier classes as well as the daily pedagogy practised in classrooms. The fact that entrance tests of prestigious institutions like the Indian Institutes of Technology have less focus on recall (although they put a premium on speed) is ignored, and even these tests are cited for justifying the excessively large syllabi in certain subjects in the senior secondary classes.

2. Isolation of experts from Classroom Realities

The new topics and information put into the syllabus and textbooks at the time of each successive revision are usually added at the behest of experts of different subjects. These experts are university-level teachers, sometimes including individuals of high stature in the research world. Their involvement in the writing or revision of textbooks is indeed appreciable but they have little exposure to children in classroom situations. Their exposure to school teachers is also confined to interaction with the few teachers who are selected as members of syllabus and textbook committees. Several factors, such as the difference of social and official status, make it difficult for school teachers serving on these committees to freely put across their feelings and experiences regarding the teachability of a syllabus or the style of a textbook.

Teachability can be defined as the quotient of content that an average teacher can put across at a comfortable pace in a thirty-five minute school period. If our textbooks were to be judged in the light of this criterion, most of them especially in the sciences, mathematics, and the social sciences, would appear as unteachable. The amount of information and concept-load they present are far in excess of the amount that can be put across in any meaningful way in thirty-five minute periods allotted for a school subject in one academic session. It appears that no rigorous count, using the thirty-five minute period as a unit, of the total teaching time available for a subject in any year is used as basis for determining syllabus and text content. Indeed, the syllabi and textbooks are evidence to say that the experts involved in preparing them have little knowledge of school and classroom realities. This limitation of the experts extends to their possible ignorance of children and of the processes that children use for learning new ideas. Textbooks simply do not reflect the versatile search of the ordinary child for clues to make sense of natural or social phenomena. Typically, school texts proceed in a linear fashion, adding bits of information in, and concepts as they go along. The linear patterns they follow often spill across school years, i.e. something left off in Class VII is picked up again in Class IX, and so on. Very seldom is an effort made to construct knowledge-patterns in non-linear ways.

We feel that if experts involved in the preparation of syllabi and textbooks had the opportunity to work with children and their teachers, they would have a chance to develop some insight into children's learning strategies. This would have helped them to develop the ability to emulate such strategies in script-writing for textbooks. Interaction with children might enable experts to develop a certain amount of sensitivity towards the living and versatile approaches used by children. Also, in the course of interaction, the experts might also perceive the need to equip themselves with knowledge of children's psychology, particularly the psychology of learning, before venturing out on the task of textbook preparation. This, of course, implies that the job of syllabus and textbook preparation be perceived as a serious professional activity, not as a part-time obligation.

3. Centralised Character

In the specific context of the curriculum planning and textbook production, we feel, the system invites a number of problems upon itself on account of being unnecessarily centralised. It seems there is a widespread misconception which justifies centralization in this matters. This misconception treats the content of syllabus and textbooks as synonymous with learning and testing norms. On the basis of the confusion, it is argued that syllabi and textbooks should be the same all over a state, even all over the country, in order to ensure uniformity of standards. This kind of argument completely overlooks the lopsided manner in which standards are set under the present system by an examination system which focuses on information rather than on skills and capacity to apply skills. Indeed, there is a 'catch 22' situation: the examination system ignores skills, concentrating on memorized information, definitions and descriptions; therefore, syllabus and textbooks, which cannot do justice to diversified milieux, varying needs and facilities, become necessary to ensure that all children 'know' the same 'fact'.

This circular argument has created a situation in which curriculum and textbook preparation is confined to the state capitals and New Delhi. At regional and local levels, teachers do not perceive curriculum development and preparation of educational materials as part of their job. And indeed, the way these tasks has been defined and traditionally carried out in our country, they are not the teacher's job. The teacher sees his or her role as one of elucidating whatever content of knowledge is prescribed in the syllabus. At the primary and lower secondary stages, teachers come to know the syllabus through the textbook which acts as the *de facto* syllabus. Covering' the syllabus means 'covering' or finishing the textbook. This kind of perception results in the confinement of classroom life to a narrow orbit. Classroom knowledge assumes total independence from the child's own experience and knowledge of the world. *As a consequence of this de-coupling, children begin to compartmentalize knowledge into two categories: that which has currency in the school and classroom, and the other which has uses and relevance outside the school.* Necessarily, the knowledge in the first category ceases to have any 'life' and becomes increasing ritualistic and burdensome.

Teachers also carry the same kind of categorization in their mind; very few of them are able to help the child make bridges between what is learnt at school and what is required to face real-life situations. One teacher who tried to make such a bridge in a lesson about letter-writing was asked by a Class VI child: " Madam, shall we write it the way we write at home or in the school way?"

While several factors, including those related to the training of teachers, can be held responsible for this aspect of the situation, we feel that the centralised structures of syllabus and textbook preparation set the tone. Howsoever 'good' a textbook produced at central level may be on professional standards, it cannot reflect the subtler nuances of life in village of Kashmir or Assam. Adaptation to local conditions is indeed officially carried out to match the content of textbooks with local conditions, but it does not change the basic character of a textbook. Adaptation of syllabi to local conditions is even less effectively possible.

4. Convention of 'Teaching the Text'

Lack of adequate opportunities for teachers to participate in the processes of syllabus and textbook preparation is a major factor indirectly responsible for the problem of unrealistic syllabi or curriculum load. Teachers perform a more direct role in the rigid boundary or definer of their work in the classroom. Boredom is the inevitable outcome when a tersely written textbook is taught in a rigid, mechanical manner. Poor grasp among teachers of their role as translators of the curriculum into classroom activity is a widely prevalent characteristic of our system. We are citing this as a relevant aspect of the phenomenon of curriculum load *without* suggesting that there is a vicious cycle here, i.e. teaching cannot improve unless there are better textbooks, etc. We feel that strategies to improve textbook writing and production must work parallel to strategies for improvement in teacher training and for creating an ethos in which teachers would feel motivated to take an academic interest in their work. The perception that a teacher can do little in the classroom that is different from what the textbooks says is part of historical legacy. This legacy must be transcended and the self-perception rooted in it must be changed. Teacher training institutions and the mass media, both can assist in making this change possible.

In the context of constructing a new self-image of the teacher, pre-service training is a key but elusive area of reform. Past attempts to improve teacher training programmes and institutions have met with rather limited success. By and large, teacher training continues to be isolated from mainstream academic areas related to education. In-service training too in most of the places, has assumed the character of a ritual devoid of academic substance or the capacity to stimulate. The current efforts to provide statutory status to the National Council for Teacher Education (NCTE) (as envisaged in the National Education Policy) may perhaps make some impact on the weak training that is generally available in the country to people who want to work with children, especially young children.

Administrative and legal concern needs to be applied to several training programmes running as commercial success stories, such as those offering a degree by correspondence. Similarly, there is need to examine existing policies with regard to nursery teacher training courses and institutions. Indeed, what is required is a review of the overall training policy which permits the traditional bifurcation of degree programmes from non-degree programmes, and their application to different stages of school education. We hope that after acquiring statutory status, the NCTE will work out a comprehensive training programme to cover all stages of schooling, ending the bifurcation we have mentioned above. Such a programme will have to be radically different from the present ones which are anchored in the culture of late nineteenth century normal schools, and are sadly lacking both in perspective and means to equip teachers with the capacity to understand children and their learning processes in a professional manner.

5. Competition-based Social Ethos

Our social ethos, particularly in the urban areas, are now fully entrenched in the competitive spirit which is fast becoming our way of life. The desire to catch up with the industrially developed countries has given it further impetus. Rising aspirations of people in all sections of the society and the growing realisation that education is an important instrument to fulfil their aspirations have resulted in a craze for admission to English-medium schools which start imparting formal education too early in the child's life.

The educated sections of the society believe that command over English is the key to upward mobility in social life. This has led to unprecedented growth in the number of private schools where English is not only taught as subject but is also used a medium of education in all subjects right from Class I. It is a well-known fact that young children studying in English-medium schools mug up the content of science and social sciences without understanding. It is an accepted principle of pedagogy that whatever is memorized without understanding proves burdensome for children. Any language other than the mother tongue of the child, if used as medium of instruction, is a big source of academic burden on children. Most of the parents in urban and semi-urban areas do not realise it, in fact they try to promote the use of English as medium of education. Unfortunately, instead of resisting the pressure of the competitive spirit prevalent in the society or directing it is appropriate channels, our educational system has succumbed to it. The most conspicuous manifestations of this phenomenon in education are upgradation of content of syllabus by advancing introduction of many topics and subjects in utter disregard of the process of maturation. The entrance tests for admission to professional courses like engineering and medicine have influenced the objectives, content and methodology of education in many ways. The 'quiz culture' which has taken roots in education, can be attributed to these tests.

With a view to provide incentives to 'high achievers' and 'talented' in different fields, high profile competitions are organised by different departments and institutions in the name of 'talent search', which at the most provide moments of brief glory to the winners but damage the 'ego strength' of numerous others who participate in the contents at the cost of leisurely pursuit of knowledge at their own pace and in their own ways. The experience of the ignominy of failure on the part of millions of children have long-term deleterious effect on the personality of the individual and the matrix of society. It would be better to reward group performance so as to convey the message to everyone that excellence in group work rather than individual effort should be the target.

6. Absence of Academic Ethos

Adequate time, staff, accommodation, and its maintenance funds, pedagogical equipment, playgrounds are essential prerequisites for effective curriculum transaction but, unfortunately, an overwhelming majority of schools do not have even the minimum essential facilities. It is a matter of great concern that the number of teachers with a sense of commitment is gradually shrinking while cynicism, feelings of helplessness and hopelessness are on the rise. Lack of adequate infrastructural facilities, rigid administrative structures and growing cynicism are responsible for the absence of academic ethos in majority of schools.

The methods of teaching used by majority of teachers are devoid of any type of challenge for the students. Transmission of information rather than experimentation or exploration or observation characterizes the teaching-learning process in most of the classrooms. We have no reason to believe that there is something wrong with our children, rural or urban. Luckily they have not compartmentalized knowledge; they are interested in seeking understanding rather than mere information. As they are educated by us, while they grow older, freshness goes away, as does romance and curiosity. Before anything is learnt they want to find out why they need to know. Must we, in the name of so-called 'proper education' go on committing the murder of their innate desire to discover and to learn on their own?

Children are not allowed to observe and explore natural phenomena, but at the same time they are also not provided opportunity to explore the world of books. The concept of library as a readily available resource for learning simply does not exist in most schools. Even those rare schools that do happen to have a library stock little more than copies of prescribed textbooks, often stored behind locked doors. If children are to be prepared for experiencing the beauty and richness of nature and the fascination of ideas without feeling the curricular load, priority has to be given to developing school libraries and their adequate and appropriate utilisation.

Similarly science laboratories even in the few cases where they are adequately equipped are not used for experimentation and discovery. A laboratory is not perceived as a place where children can conduct even those experiments which are not prescribed in their syllabi and come out with novel observations that need exploratory frameworks. The main purpose of a laboratory programme is to visualize children's natural talents and develop their ability to learn through observation and exploration. Over-regimentation of prescribed experiments which the entire emphasis on getting the final result, is contrary to this spirit. Laboratories should be conceived as exploratories, and schools should have the freedom to structure experiments to suit the needs of their children.

IV. RECOMMENDATIONS

We have come to the conclusion that the problem of the load on school children does not arise only from over-enthusiastic curriculum designers, or poorly equipped teachers, or school administrators, or book publishers, or district, state or central education authorities. Yes, what all these groups, agencies and administrators do can exacerbate or alleviate the problem. But, there is a deeper malaise in our society, which impacts our young children. If we continue to value a few elite qualifications far more than real competence for doing useful things in life, and if the economic distance, between those who can manage to cross some academic hurdles and those who can't, continues to widen, we will probably continue to spend our effort in designing hurdles, instead of opportunities for children to learn with joy. As the body of the Report analyses, a major problem is connected with the notions of 'knowledge explosion' and the 'catching up' syndrome. We believe that these problems cannot be fully addressed through easily managoable administrative actions. They need wider discussions because they are centrally connected with images of our civilization, self-esteem and societal goals. Such a wide discussion can come about through publication of this Report, and through a set of seminars, meetings and media discussions. Academics, thinkers, need to pour over this basic problem.

The question of medium of instruction, particularly in early life, will not be fully resolved till the time our dominant and externally connected sections of society continue to give more importance to elementary graces in a foreign language, than to intimate connections with the 'vernacular' knowledge with our children gain during every week of their growing up before they go to school. It is because of this reason that we have restrained ourselves from repeating the recommendation that mother tongue alone should be the medium of instruction at the primary stage.

1. A number of organisations and departments organise competitions as district, state and national level for students in various fields such as school subjects, exhibitions, essay writing, elocution, etc. Perhaps the spirit behind these activities is to recognise and reward the talent in diverse fields. But, unfortunately this tends to produce somewhat unhealthy singling out of people for their brief moment of glory. Competitions where individual achievement is rewarded need to be discouraged since they deprive children of joyful learning. However, groups activities and groups achievements must be encouraged and rewarded to give a boost to cooperative learning in schools.

2. (a) The process of curriculum-framing and preparation of textbooks of decentralized so as to increase teachers' involvement in these tasks. Decentralisation should mean greater autonomy, within state-level apparatus, to district-level boards or other relevant authority, and to heads of schools and classroom teachers to develop curricular materials on their own, best suited to the needs of local environment. All the schools be encouraged to innovate in all aspects of curriculum, including choice of textbooks and other materials.

(b) Voluntary organisations with a specific commitment to pedagogical innovations within the formal or non-formal system be provided greater freedom and support in development of curriculum, textbooks and teacher training. A suitable and adequate mechanism be evolved for wider dissemination of the experiences of such organisations.

(c) We endorse the idea of setting up education committees at village, block and district level to undertake planning and supervision of schools under their jurisdiction.

(d) Sufficient contingency amount (not less that 10 per cent of the total salary bill of the school) be placed at the disposal of heads of schools for purchase, repair and replacement of pedagogical equipment.

3. The culture of writing textbooks be changed so as to involve a much large, number of teachers in the preparation of textbooks. The scientists and experts in various disciplines may be associated with the preparation of textbooks as consultants and not as writers of the books. Initiative in this regard should rest with groups of enlightened and innovative teachers who should be provided training in book writing.

4. At least three parallel system of school education (syllabus, textbooks and examination) are running concurrently in different states. In each state majority of schools are affiliated to the State Board of Eduction while a few are affiliated to either CBSE or Council for the Indian School Certificate Examination (CISCE). The schools affiliated to CBSE in the states other than Delhi enjoy the prestige of being elite schools. The CBSE curriculum becomes a trend-setter for the State Boards leading to heavier curriculum for majority of children. Therefore, the committee recommends that jurisdiction of CBSE be restricted to Kendriya and Navodaya Vidyalays and all other schools be affiliated to the respective State Boards.

5 (a) Appropriate legislative and administrative measures be adopted to regulate the opening and functioning of early childhood education institutions (pre-schools). Norms regarding accommodation, staff, apparatuses, play materials be laid down for the recognition of these schools. It

should be ensured that these institutions do not perpetrate violence on young children by inflicting a heavy dose off 'over-eduction' in the form of formal teaching of Reading, Wrinting and Numbers. The practice of holding tests and interviews for admission to nursery class be abolished.

(b) Norms for granting recognition to private schools be made more stringent. This will prove conducive for improving the quality of learning on the one hand and arrest growing commercialisation on the other. The norms, thus developed, be made uniformly applicable to all schools including the state-run institutions.

6. There is no justification for torturing the young children by compelling them to carry very heavy bags of books everyday to schools. Textbooks should be treated as school property and thus, there should be no need for children to purchase the books individually and carry them daily to homes. A separate time-table for the assignment of home work and for the use of textbooks and notebooks be prepared by the school and be made known to the children in advance.

7. The nature and character of homework needs a radical change. In the primary classes, children should not be given any homework, save for extension of explorations in the home environment. In the upper primary and secondary classes, homework, where necessary, should be non-textual, and textbooks, when needs for work at home should be made available on a rotation basis.

8. The existing norm for teacher-pupil ratio (i.e. 1:40) should be enforced and an attempt should be made reduced this to 1:30, at least in the primary classes, as a basis for future educational planning.

9. Greater use of the electronic media be made for the creation of a child-centered social ethos in the country. A regular television programme addressed to students, teacher and parents and possibly called 'Shiksha Darshan' be launched, along the lines of 'Krishi Darshan' programme.

10. (a) Inadequate programme of teacher preparation leads to unsatisfactory quality of learning in schools. The B.Ed.

programme should offer the possibility of specialization in secondary or elementary or nursery education. The duration of the programme should either be one year after graduation or three-four years after higher secondary. The content of the programme should be restructured to ensure its relevance to the changing needs to school education and to make it more practicum-centred. The emphasis in these programmes should be on enabling the trainees to acquire the ability for self-learning and independent thinking. Pre-service teacher education programme, being a professional course has to be a rigorous, thorough and intensive programme. Therefore, B.Ed degree courses by correspondence be derecognised.

(b) The continuing education of teachers must be institutionalized. The organisation of in-service education programmes and other activities aimed at professional growth of teachers be systematically designed and conducted imaginatively.

11. The public examinations taken at the end of Class X and XII be reviewed with a view to ensure replacement of the prevailing textbased and 'quiz type' questioning by the concept-based questioning. This single reform is sufficient to improve the quality of learning and save the children from the tyranny of rote memorization.

12. (a) A project team with a number of sub-groups be set up in each state to examine the syllabi and textbooks for all school classes. The sub-groups be required to decide the following:

i) The minimum number of topics required to be taught.

ii) The minimum number of concepts to be introduced with each topic.

iii) The total time needed for teaching this minimum number of concepts comfortably by a teacher in the total working days realistically available in a year.

(b) Mathematics curriculum for primary classes in all parts of the country be reviewed with a view to slowing down the place at which children are required to learn basic mathematical concepts, and broadening the scope of primary mathematics to include areas other than number work (e.g. space-and shape-related concepts and problem solving). The tendency embedded in the syllabi and textbooks of primary mathematics to accelerate children's mathematical skills by teaching the mechanical rules at the expense of understanding and intelligent application ought to be discouraged in future syllabi and texts.

(c) Language textbooks should adequately reflect the spoken idiom. An attempt should be made in future textbooks to give adequate representation to children's life experiences, imaginary stories and poems, and stories reflecting the lives of ordinary people in different parts of the country. Pedantic language and excessive didacticism ought to be avoided.

(d) Science syllabi and textbooks in the primary classes should provide greater room and necessity for experimentation than they do at present. In place of didacticism in areas like health and sanitation, the texts should emphasis analytical reflection on real-life situations. A great deal of trivial materials included in primary-level science texts should be dropped.

(e) The syllabi of natural sciences throughout the secondary and senior secondary classes be revised in a manner so as to ensure that most of the topics included are actively linked to experiments or activities that can be performed by children and teachers.

(f) Besides imparting knowledge of history and geography, the social sciences curriculum for Class VI-VIII and IX-X should convey the philosophy and methodology of the functions of our socio-political and economic system and enable the students to analyse, understand and reflect on the problems and priorities of socio-economic development. The repetitious nature of history syllabus should be changed. The history of ancient times should be introduced for systematic study in secondary class (IX and X). The history syllabus for Class VI-VIII should focus on the freedom struggle and post-independence developments. The civics, as it is taught today, puts a great load on children's capacity to memories. Therefore, it may be dropped in its present form and be replaced by contemporary studies' The study of geography be related to contemporary reality.

PART-B

REPORT OF THE GROUP TO EXAMINE THE FEASIBILITY OF IMPLEMENTING THE RECOMMENDATIONS OF THE NATIONAL ADVIRSORY COMMITTEE SET UP TO SUGGEST WAYS TO REDUCE ACADEMIC BURDEN ON SCHOOL STUDENTS

A National Advisory Committee was set up on 1 March 1992 by the Ministry of Human Resource Development under the chairmanship of Prof. Yash Pal, former Chairman of the University Grants Commission (UGC), to advise on the ways and means to reduce the academic burden on school students. The Committee submitted its Report to the Ministry on 15 July 1993.

2. On receipt of the Report of the National Advisory Committee, a decision was taken by the Ministry to set up a Group under the Chairmanship of Shri Y.N. Chaturvedi, Additional Secretary, Department of Education of the Ministry, to examine the recommendations of the Committee, give its views on the feasibility of implementing them and a time schedule of implementation. The Group was set up on 25 August 1993 and a copy of the Government Order giving the composition and terms of reference of the Group is given in Annex A.

3. The Group held two meetings on 23 and 24 September 1993 in which it examined the recommendations made in the Yash Pal Committee Report. The Group had the benefit of advice of Shri R.C. Tripathi, Adviser (Education), Planning Commission; also. The list of members who participated in the deliberations is given in Annex B. In addition to participation by two senior functionaries of the National Council of Educational Research and Training (NCERT), the Group had the benefit of a detailed critique of the Yash Pal Committee Report prepared by the NCERT plays in curriculum development, textbook preparation and other aspects of school education.

4. General Observations

The Groups has observed with considerable appreciation the participative nature of the Yash Pal Committee Report about the load of curriculum on school students. While discussion on curriculum load has been extensive over the years in the mass media, it has been largely confined to the physical load of the school bag which a student has carry. Many have felt that there has been a lot of generalisation in such discussions on the basis of the size of the school bag seen in metropolitan cities and particularly in regard to students studying in public schools even at the pre-school stage. The Report has taken note in the beginning itself that "a survey conducted in Delhi revealed that the weight of school bag, on an average, in primary classes in public school is more than 4 kg, while it is around 1 kg in MCD schools". This finding of the Yash Pal Committee is in tune with the information with the educational managers that firstly, the load of the school bag is not a forbidding one in schools in villages and in small towns and secondly, even in big towns, the problem is in its most aggravated form in regard to students of public schools and children of pre-school classes. Luckily, there are signs recently of the more enlightened public schools de-emphasizing subject-matter learning at pre-school stage as also de-emphasising the need to prescribe a lot of books and exercise books at pre-school stage. Since such schools are pace-setters, it is hoped that this example will soon influence other pre-primary schools. This Group is recommending subsequently some specific measures in pursuance of one the recommendations of the Yash Pal Committee to accelerate this process.

The Yash Pal Committee has instead taken the problem at more elevated plane by observing that in the present school "a lot is taught but little is learnt or understood". It has, therefore, inferred that the load of non-learning or non-comprehension is the real load one should be concerned about. This approach of looking at the problem of academic burden has imparted to the Report of the Yash Pal Committee a great deal of significance.

Simultaneously, the Group noted that there are a few things to which the Yash Pal Committee could have given specific attention. The National Policy on Education (NPE) and the programme of Action (POA) enuciate the need to have a national core curriculum and have spelt out some of the features of this. The policy also strongly enunciates a child-centered approach to education. It is in pursuance of this that the NCERT framed a curriculum framework for the school stage which has been accepted by all the states. The NCERT has also developed the levels of competencies to be attained at the end of primary stage. These exercises with a lot of validity in them have been the basis for developing syllabi and textbooks for different stages of school education. While there may be some flaws in the syllabi and the textbooks prepared by the NCERT, it does not seem that they can be accused of being grossly unsuitable or overloaded. In regard to curriculum load, the NCERT had carried out a study in mid-eighties which identified the physical overload of curriculum at some stages of school education and also pointed out that inadequate teacher competency, insufficient teaching days, and inadequate classroom facilities, transfer the curriculum load to the students as well as indirectly to parents. The Yash Pal Committee has not referred to this work and the facts stated in the preceding statements. While the main argument forming the basis of the Yash Pal Committee Report is eminently sound, with regard to the main thrust of its recommendations, some of the statements in the Report do not indicate the data or basis on which the Committee has relied. Similarly, some of the recommendations like the one concerning affiliation of schools to the Central Board of Secondary Education (CBSE) are not accompanied by corresponding consideration in the main body of the Report. In a few cases like in regard to medium of instruction in schools, the Committee has noted in the main body of its Report: "the educated sections of the society believe that command over English is key to upward mobility in social life.....It is a well-known fact that young children studying in English medium schools mug the content of science and social sciences without understanding. It is an accepted principle of pedagogy that whatever is memorised without understanding proves burdensome on children. Any language other than the mother tongue of the child, if used a medium of instruction, is a big source of academic burden on children". However, such strong statements do not have a corresponding recommendation. The Report also ignores the fact that for most of our students, medium of instruction is the mother tongue or regional language at all stages of school education. Overall it is an important Report which has brought to the fore an understanding about curriculum load which one does not frequently come across. For this it is bound to raise the level of debate about the curriculum load to a qualitatively higher level. It is expected that this Report would lead to meaningful and adequate reform in curriculum formulation, textbook preparation, teacher training, etc. The Group feels that the nature of the problem is different for each stage of school education but the Committee has not specifically referred to the distinct problems of each stage and ways of dealing with them. The views of the Group in regard to individual recommendations made by the Yash Pal Committee are given below.

Recommendation No. 1

A number of organisations and departments organise competitions at district, state and national level for students in various fields such as school subjects, exhibitions, essay writing, elocution, etc. Perhaps, the spirit behind these activities is to recognise and reward the talent in diverse fields. But, unfortunately this tends to produce somewhat unhealthy singling out of people for their brief moment of glory. Competitions where individual achievement is rewarded need to be discouraged since they deprive children of joyful learning. However, group activities and group achievement must be encouraged and rewarded to give a boost to cooperative learning in schools.

Comments

The Group is of the view that group activity and individual effort are not mutually exclusive or antagonistic. Rewarding individual achievement does not take away the joy of learning and is also a means to motivate towards higher achievement. In the view of the Group, the educational system should promote performance of the students both as an individual and as a member of the group.

Recommendation No. 2 (a)

The process of curriculum framing and preparation of textbooks be decentralized so as to increase teachers 'involvement in these tasks. Decentralisation should mean greater autonomy, within state-level apparatus, to district-level boards or other relevant authority, and to heads of schools and classroom teachers to develop curricular materials on their own, best suited to needs of local environment. All the schools be encouraged to innovate in all aspects of curriculum, including choice of textbooks and other materials.

Comments

The Group noted that the curriculum and syllabi are designed by the NCERT/CBSE at national level and by the State Boards of Secondary Education/SCERTs at state level by involving teachers and through teachers. However, the number of teachers associated with this exercise is limited to the number of members of the Committee or the Board. The Yash Pal Committee has rightly underlined the need to increase teachers' participation in curriculum development. The Group feels that while the size of committees at national or state level cannot be increased beyond a limit, meaningful way of improving teachers' participation would be for either the NCERT/CBSE/State Boards/ SCERTs to prepare the draft syllabus and finalize it after subjecting it to regional or, in the alternative, to get multiple syllabi developed at regional and district levels on the levels on the basis of which the final syllabi could be prepared at the state/national level. The Group, however, does not recommend decentralisation in the preparation of syllabus or textbooks at the district or school level because it will be difficult to ensure adequate projection of national identity and of composite culture of India. Also, in such a situation, the adherence to even minimum standards in all parts of the country may become difficult.

In regard to textbooks, the Group agrees with the Yash Pal Committee that the primary responsibility for preparing textbooks, particularly for the lower classes should be that of teachers. It may, however, be remembered that the involvement of experts since the early 1960s led to qualitative improvement in school textbooks. They helped in weeding out dead wood, brought in new perspectives in tune with contemporary knowledge. The Group, however, shares the concern of the Yash Pal Committee that many textbooks presently tend to project predominantly the urban middle class life style. Therefore, the Group recommends that:

(a) the writing of textbooks as far as possible, should be assigned to school teachers and to those who have developed professional expertise in the area. Subject-matter specialists should be engaged as consultants or advisers to vet the content and presentation of subject-matter to ensure its accuracy.

(b) In states which have distinct socio-cultural geographical zones, different and parallel sets of textbooks with the same learning objectives should be prepared and used in schools for each such distinct socio-cultural geographical region.

(c) A conscious effort should be made by the textbook preparation agencies to take examples from rural areas for illustrating various points because a large majority of students are in rural areas.

(d) The textbook preparation agencies should undertake systematic review of all textbooks in a time-bound manner to ensure that any trivial matter which may have got included in the textbooks is weeded out. Similarly, such a review should also try to eliminate elements of repetitions of the topics covered in previous classes.

(e) The group noted that, in some cases, the textbooks for subjects other than languages in some classes are written in a language which is considerably more complex and difficult than the language used in textbooks for that class. It, therefore, recommends that the group which writes a textbook should include one language teacher who should vet the manuscript to ensure that the degree of difficulty of the language used in the subject-matter is not more than the degree of difficulty designed for language competency for that class. In regard to curriculum transaction and teaching materials, the Group noted that there are no restrictions on schools and teachers to innovate. Indeed, the teacher training courses have consistently advocated this and many organisations have introduced special programmes to promote this. Needless to say that school and teachers should be motivated to innovate to the fullest extent in regard to teaching methods and use of teaching materials.

Recommendation No. 2 (b)

Voluntary organisations with a specific commitment to pedagogical innovations within the formal or non-formal system be provided greater freedom and support in development of curriculum, textbooks and teacher training. A suitable and adequate mechanism be evolved for wider dissemination of experiences of such organisations.

Comments

The Group fully agrees that voluntary organisations with a commitment to education should be encouraged in all possible manners. The Group also noted that the governments, both at the national and the state levels have, in recent past, made a substantial move to expand such cooperation. The process needs to be continued. However, for reasons mentioned in 2 (a), the Group does not favour decentralisation in curriculum development and textbooks preparation to the extent of entrusting it to voluntary organisation because of the sensitivity of the matter.

Recommendation No. 2 (c)

We endorse the idea of setting up education committees at village, block and district levels to undertake planning and supervision of schools under their jurisdiction.

Comments

This is acceptable in principle. This has been strongly advocated in para 10.8 of the NPE, 1986. Following the Constitutional Amendment for decentralisation at Panchayat level, the Central Advisory Board of Education (CABE) has already constituted a Committee on Decentralized Management of Education to examine and recommend measures for effectively carrying out the desired involvement of the local committees. Therefore, this recommendation should be implemented in the light of the recommendations of the CABE Committee.

Recommendation No. 2 (d)

Sufficient contingency amount (not less than 10 per cent of the total salary bill of the school) be placed at the disposal of heads of schools for purchase, repair and replacement of pedagogical equipment.

Comments

This is acceptable. The State/UT Government and autonomous bodies of the Central Government controlling their respective chain of schools (Kendriya Vidyalays, Navodaya Vidyalayas, Central Tibetan Schools, Railway Schools and Sainik Schools and other schools run by the Defence establishments) should be urged to give authority to the Principals/ Headmasters of the schools to make repairs to school buildings, purchase, repair and replace pedagogical equipment and books and also to carry out innovative projects, subject to the control of the local education committees. The organisations controlling the schools and the State Governments should categorically specify higher educational authority and the School Management/advisory Committee for using the available money for these purposes.

Recommendation No. 3

The culture of writing textbooks be changed so as to involve a much larger number of teachers in the preparation of textbooks. The scientists and experts in various disciplines may be associated with the preparation of textbooks as consultants and not as writers of the books. Initiative in this regard should rest with groups of enlightened and innovative teachers who should be provided training in book writing.

Comments

The group agrees with the purport of this recommendation—greater involvement of teachers—and the view of the Group on this recommendation is included in the comments on 2(a).

Recommendation No. 4

At least three parallel systems of school education (syllabus, textbooks and examination) are running concurrently in different states. In each state majority of schools are affiliated to the State Board of Education while a few are affiliated to either CBSE or ICSE. The schools affiliated to CBSE in the states other than Delhi enjoy the prestige of being elite schools. The CBSE curriculum becomes a trend-setter for the State Boards leading to heavier curriculum for majority of children. Therefore, the Committee recommends that jurisdiction of CBSE be restricted to Kendriya and Navodaya Vidyalayas and all other schools be affiliated to the respective State Boards.

Comments

The Group has been unable to appreciate the arguments put forth by the Yash Pal Committee in this recommendation. The choice of educational boards that the schools have is already very limited—there is no free choice—and it can be exercised only with the approval of the State Government. Therefore, if a school in any part of the country has the choice of affiliating with one Board or the other, it should be generally good for education. As for CBSE, it relies heavily on the NCERT for developing syllabi and preparing textbooks. The NCERT, in turn, operates within the national policy framework and on the basis of guidelines contained in the National Curriculum Framework. Rightly the NCERT keeps in view the existing standards in the country, the capability of students, and standards in developed countries because the syllabus and textbook must take not of all these. If there is unnecessary material in some of the NCERT books, it should be eliminated as the Group has suggested in the preceding recommendations. However, there is not adequate material on record to substantiate that CBSE syllabi or NCERT books *per se* are overloaded. Also, the Yash Pal Committee has recommended that affiliation to CBSE should be restricted to Kendriya and Navodaya Vidyalayas with all other schools being affiliated to respective State Boards. If affiliation to the CBSE is good for Kendriya and Navodaya Vidyalayas it cannot be bad for other schools.

Recommendation No. 5 (a)

Appropriate legislative and administrative measures be adopted to regulate the opening and functioning of early childhood education institutions (pre-schools). Norms regarding accommodation, staff, apparatuses, play materials be laid down for the recognition of these schools. It should be ensured that these institutions do not perpetrate violence on young children by inflicting a heavy dose of 'over education' in the form of formal teaching of Reading, Writing and Numbers. The practice of holding tests and interviews for admission to nursery class be abolished.

Recommendation No. 5. (b)

Norms for granting recognition to private schools be made more stringent. This will prove conducive for improving the quality of learning on the one hand and arrest growing commercialization on the other. The norms, thus developed, be made uniformly applicable to all schools including the state-run institutions.

Comments [5 (a) and 5 (b)]

The Group is in agreement with the recommendations. While the NCERT has prepared some norms for the staff, nature of curriculum and educational material for pre-primary stage, this sector of education in the country is largely unsupervised and unregulated. It is also a known fact that most of these schools are loading the students with the burden of formal teaching of various subjects. The Group advised that an appropriate regulatory mechanism should be urgently set up in the country to ensure that learning at this stage is by play way method and formal teaching of subjects is scrupulously prevented. Similarly, the Group agrees that recognition and affiliation of both private and government schools should be made more stringent so that schools lacking in minimum essential facilities are not allowed to function because it really means punishment to the students. Although there is a well set arrangement for recognition and affiliation of schools but due to extraneous pressures the standards sometimes are not observed. The Group would like to suggest that the possibility of having a legislation to specify norms of facilities in schools and providing for powers to prevent opening of schools which do not have facilities should be seriously considered.

Recommendation No. 6

There is no justification for torturing the young children by compelling them carry heavy bags of books everyday to schools. Textbooks should be treated as school property and thus, there should be no need for children to purchase the books individually and carry them daily to homes. A separate time-table for the assignment of homework and for the use of textbooks and note-books be prepared by the school and be made known to the children in advance.

Recommendation No. 7.

The nature and character of homework needs a radical change. In the primary classes, children should be given any homework, save for extension of explorations in the home environment. In the upper primary and secondary classes, homework, where necessary, should be non-textual, and textbooks, when needed for work at home should be made available on a rotation basis.

Comments (6 and 7)

The Group has already agreed that there should be no formal teaching of subjects in the pre-school stage. The Group also feels that there should be no homework and project work at the primary stage (Class I-V). However, it is an extreme point of observation that textbooks should be treated as school property. Besides the financial implications arising out of the burden on schools to purchase the textbooks and the concomitant responsibility on the schools to store the books when most of the schools of the country do not have either the financial resources or storage capacities, the children would be devoid of the opportunity to refer to the textbooks in their homes. For an overwhelming majority of school students of the country, the textbooks remain as the only source of reading material. The Group recommends that the class routine for the upper primary, secondary and higher secondary stages should be drawn up in such a way that every subject is not required to be taught everyday. This should be included in the norms for compliance by every school which the Group has suggested in para 5 (a) and 5 (b) above.

Recommendation No. 8.

The existing norms for teacher-pupil ratio (i.e. 1:40) should be enforced and an attempt should be made to reduce this to 1:30, at least in the primary classes, as a basis for future educational planning.

Comments

The Group agrees with a higher teacher-pupil ratio with improved teaching and standards of education. It understands that in reality the existing teacher-pupil ratio is around 1:40 in most part of the country. Attempts should be made bring it to 1:30 over a period of time. Such change in ratio would have a very large financial implication because of the need to induct a large number of extra teachers and, therefore, this can be done only over a period of time. Efforts should be made to ensure that the class size does not exceed 40.

Recommendation No. 9.

Greater use of the electronic media be made for the creation of a child-centred social ethos in the country. A regular television programme addressed to students, teachers and parents and possibly called 'Shiksha Darshan' be launched, along the lines of the 'Krishi Darshan' programme.

Comments

Greater use of electronic media for education is an essential part of modernizing the educational system. A regular programme on TV addressed to students, teachers and parents would be very welcome. The Group took note of the fact that the Ministry of Human Resource Development, Department of Education, has already made a request for allocating one channel for education out of 15 or 16 channels which have recently become available with the commissioning of INSAT 2-A. The Group strongly suggests that an educational channel should be operationalised at the earliest and this channel should include a programme of the nature suggest by the Yash Pal Committee.

Recommendation No. 10 (a)

Inadequate programme of teacher preparation leads to unsatisfactory quality of learning in schools. The B.Ed. programme should offer the possibility of specialization in secondary or elementary or nursery education. The duration of the programme should either be one year after graduation or three-four years after higher secondary. The content of the programme should be restructured to ensure its relevance to the changing needs of school education and to make it more practicum-centered. The emphasis in these programmes should be on enabling the trainees to acquire the ability for self-learning and independent thinking. Pre-service teacher education programme, being a professional course, has to be a rigorous, thorough and intensive programme. Therefore, B.Ed. degree courses by correspondence be de-recognised.

Comments

There is a lot of merit in the argument advanced by the Yash Pal Committee for having a programme of B.Ed. aimed at elementary or secondary education. In metropolitan cities, a large number of teachers are actually getting recruited for pre-school and elementary and schools with B.Ed. qualifications. Recruitment in KVS and NVS is also, in practice, based on B.Ed. qualifications. Therefore, this reality needs to be taken cognizance of and the present practice of focussing on secondary education in B.Ed. needs to be given up by enabling B.Ed. to be pursued with either specialization in secondary or in elementary or in pre-school education. In any case the existing arrangements, including the District Institutes of Education and Training (DIETs) for preparing primary school teachers need to be continued and strengthened.

The recommendation of the Yash Pal Committee, for de-recognizing B.Ed. degree by correspondence course is more problematic, while the National Council for Teacher Education (NCTE) has earlier made recommendations on these lines and the UGC has been interacting with the concerned universities during the last ten years on that basis, such courses are continuing. A recent expert committee of the UGC has expressed that for women candidates and for people from rural areas, B.Ed. correspondence course opens up valuable career opportunities. Also, in a large number of countries, B.Ed. through correspondence course is one of the prominent courses in distance mode. These arguments cannot be totally ignored. The Group understands that the matter is at an advanced stage of consideration in the UGC. Also the NCTE as a statutory body is expected to become operational in the near future. The Group recommends that this matter should be referred to the UGC and the NCTE for appropriate decision.

Recommendation No. 10 (b)

The continuing education of teachers must be institutionalized. The organisation of In-service education programmes and other activities aimed at professional growth of teachers be systematically designed and conducted imaginatively.

Comments

The emphasis given by the Yash Pal Committee to continuing education of teachers is totally unexceptionable. Thus DIETs are being set up in the country primarily to meet this need. Distance education system also is coming up in the country which can be used to meet the needs of in-service education. However, the progress in this regard has been slow. The Group fully endorses the need to set up arrangements for regular and periodic in-service training of teachers and recommends that the DIETs should be operationalised as early as possible and the distance mode of education should be used extensively to strengthen in-service training of teachers.

Recommendation No. 11

The public examinations taken at the end of class X and XII be reviewed with a view of ensure replacement of the prevailing text-based and 'quiz type' questioning by the concept-based questioning. This single reform is sufficient to improve the quality of learning and save the children from the tyranny of rote memoriza-tion.

Comments

The Group feels that the Yash Pal Committee's reference to the concept-based questioning perhaps advocates greater importance to questions of higher ability. The Group agrees with this but it should be remembered that assessment should test various kinds of abilities and not just of one kind. The Group also feels that the Boards of School Education should emphasize Continuous and Comprehensive Evaluation (CCE) that incorporates both scholastic and non-scholastic aspects of education, spread over the total span of instructional time as stipulated in para 8.24 (iii) of the NPE, 1986.

Recommendation No 12 (a)

A project team with a number of sub-groups be set up in each state to examine the syllabi and textbooks for all school classes. The sub-groups be required to decide the following:

(i) the minimum number of topics required to be taught.

(ii) The minimum number of concepts to be introduced within each topic.

(iii) The total time needed for teaching this minimum number of concepts comfortably by a teacher in the total working days realistically available in a year.

Comments

The Minimum Levels of Learning (MLLs) for language (mother tongue), mathematics and environmental studies for Class I-V have already been prepared at the national level in 1990 and the NCERT, the Boards of School Education and the SCERTs have developed their resources to introduce the MLLs at the primary stage. Therefore, setting up another Project Team for the same purpose would amount to avoidable duplication. The Group feels that though in para 5.4.5 (vii) and para 21.3.1 (a), the POA, 1992 has called for laying down MLLs at the upper primary stage and in para 21.3.1. (b), the POA, 1992 has urged the Boards to lay down expected levels of attainment at Classes IX-XII, the reasonableness of laying down MLLs at the upper primary stage and above deserves a careful reconsideration since knowledge base is supposed to grow at a fast pace after the primary stage. Moreover, with emphasis shifting to subject-matter learning at the upper primary stage and above, the idea of laying down uniform MLLs after primary stage does not seem to be a viable proposition. However, at the time of curriculum renewal and preparation of textbooks, the curriculum/textbook designers should systematically check that those can be covered within the instructional time available to teachers. The NCERT at the national level and the State Boards/ SCERTs/SIEs at the state level may consider the desirability of reviewing the school curricula/textbooks to ensure that non-essential matter and repetitive treatment of concepts in subjects in different classes is minimized as far as possible without sacrificing the requirements of cognitive development.

Recommendation No. 12 (b)

Mathematics curriculum for primary classes in all parts of the country be reviewed with a view to slowing down the pace at which children are required to learn basic mathematical concepts, and broadening the scope of primary mathematics to include areas other than number work (e.g. space-and shape-related concepts and problem solving). The tendency embedded in the syllabi and textbooks of primary mathematics to accelerate children's mathematical skills by teaching them mechanical rules at the expense of understanding and intelligent application ought to be discouraged in future syllabi and texts.

Comments

The Group endorses the recommendation that mathematics and syllabi for other subjects should be reviewed to assess whether they are overloaded. But it would not like to state at this stage that they indeed are overloaded. The MLLs adopted by the MHRD are now being tried out and the question of review should be considered only on the basis of the feedback. As has been referred to in the preceding recommendations, syllabi have to be designed keeping in view the existing standards, and capacity of students and standards in developed countries. However, the Group endorses the statement of the Yash Pal Committee that the syllabus should emphasize understanding and intelligent application rather than memorising without understanding.

Recommendation No. 12 (c)

Language textbooks should adequately reflect the spoken idiom. An attempt should be made in future textbooks to give adequate representation to children's life experiences, imaginary stories and poems, and stories reflecting the lives of ordinary people in different parts of the country. Pedantic language and excessive didacticism ought to be avoided.

Comments

These recommendations are acceptable. The NCERT and the Boards including CBSE and Council for the Indian School Certificate Examination (CISCE) should review their respective language textbooks from these angles.

Recommendation No. 12 (d)

Science syllabi and textbooks in the primary classes should provide greater room and necessity for experimentation than they do at present. In place of didacticism in areas like health and sanitation, the texts should emphasize analytical reflection on real-life situations. A great deal of trivial material included in primary-level science texts should be dropped.

Comments

The Group has already given its views that all the existing textbooks should be screened in a time-bound manner for eliminating trivial matter and repetition. The Group endorses the recommendation that there should be greater scope for experimentation at the primary stage. This should be systematically promoted through a large programme of in-service education of teachers.

Recommendation No. 12 (e)

The syllabi of natural sciences throughout the secondary and senior secondary classes be revised in a manner so as to ensure that most of the topics included are actively linked to experiments or activities that can be performed by children and teachers.

Comments

The Group is of the view that while experiments and activities at all levels are important, the selection of topics in science curriculum at higher stages cannot be determined by the criterion that they are linked to experiment, etc. Every effort should however, be made to see that experiments and activities, as much as possible. Depending on the nature of the topic, are made a part of science teaching even at higher levels.

Recommendation No. 12 (f)

Besides imparting knowledge of history and geography the social sciences curriculum for Classes VI-VIII and IX-X should convey the philosophy and methodology of the functions of our socio-political and economic system and enable the students to analyse, understand and reflect on the problems and priorities of socio-economic development. The repetitious nature of history syllabus should be changed. The history of ancient times should be introduced for systematic study in secondary class (IX and X). The history syllabus for Classes VI-VIII should focus on the freedom struggle and post-independence developments. The civics, as it is taught today, puts a great load on children's capacity to memorize. Therefore, it may be dropped in its present form and be replaced by 'contemporary studies' The study of geography be related to contemporary reality.

Comments

As regards the Committees' suggestion that history syllabus for Class VI-VIII should focus on freedom struggle and post-independence developments, the Group holds the view that a large majority of children drop out at the end of Class VIII, which is also the last year of compulsory education and, therefore, it would not be educationally sound to allow such a big section of our children to remain oblivious of the entire heritage of India before the freedom struggle. The Committee seems to have linked spiral approach (which is based on a well-established principle of curriculum construction) with repetition which 'leads to boredom and load and trivialisation of ideas'. The Group feels that in geography greater importance should be given to study of contemporary problems. The context or implications of the Committee's recommendation for replacing 'civics' by 'contemporary Studies' are not clear

Additional Suggestions of the Group

The Yash Pal Committee has made many thought-provoking

recommendations which the Group has tried to recommend for implementation in a more specific manner. If these are implemented efficiently, the standards of school education will undoubtedly improve and as the Yash Pal Committee has envisaged alienation of students from education and the burden of 'non-understanding' on them would effectively diminish. However, in addition to the recommendations made by the Yash Pal Committee, there are a few more issues which immediately present themselves for consideration while considering any exercises for reducing the load of curriculum. The Group would like to suggest these also for implementation.

1. Age of Entry

It is a known fact that in India children join school at a rather early age than their counterparts do in most of the developed countries. At the age of 4 and 5, a difference of one year in age makes a lot of difference in the mental capability of a child. A more mature child can easily cope with the learning requirements. The effect of early admissions of children in schools, particularly at the pre-primary stage, is that she/he is unable to cope with the demands that the syllabus makes and consequently she/he starts in a situation of personal inadequacy. This contributed significantly to the load of non-learning. It is, therefore, desirable that the minimum age of admission to pre-primary classes and in primary classes should be reconsidered for being raised by one year.

2. Teaching Days

Kothari Commission recommended 210 teaching days but the actual number of school days are 125-150. Since the syllabi are framed on the basis that 210 days will be available, this only means that either a part of syllabus is not covered by the teacher or that she/he covers the syllabus in a hurried manner which creates difficulty for students for being able to cope with a lot of content in a limited time. Effective action to increase the number of teaching days to 210 in a year would undoubtedly very substantially reduce the daily learning load and would also improve standards.

3. Classroom Facilities

In large number of schools in the country not only the facilities in the classroom but the classroom themselves are grossly deficient.

This inevitably affects the quality of teaching and, therefore, of learning. The Yash Pal Committee has recommended and we have endorsed that recommendation earlier in this Report that norms for school facilities should be effectively and strictly enforced for recognition/affiliation. However, since government is the major funding agency for most schools there should be a positive movement for improving availability of classrooms and improving availability of educational aids in schools. For primary schools the Government of India is implementing a large programme of Operation Blackboard and in the Eighth Plan it is being extended to cover upper primary classes also. At secondary level, the Government of India is implementing a scheme for assisting schools for improving science equipment. However, a much large effort needs to be made. It would be imperative that the effort of the government is supplemented by individuals and philanthropic bodies because the requirement is large. It would be appropriate that the governments and the school systems consider how best they can encourage such individuals and philanthropic bodies to help schools to develop.

4. Strengthening of the Professional Support System

An area which needs to be looked into is the qualitative improvement of professional bodies like the SCERTs, Textbook Bureaus and Boards of School Education who are primarily responsible for curriculum, textbooks and examinations. It is these bodies which will ultimately have to reckon with the problem of load. Under the centrally sponsored scheme of teacher education, there is a component of strengthening of SCERTs which should be taken up on a priority basis.

5. "*...........impact of examinations, admission to higher education institutions, including professional courses*"

This was one of the terms of reference of the Committee which has not been dealt with in the Report. The CABE may consider to refer this matter to a committee drawn from school and higher education. Another term of reference of the committee related to "the measures such as formal recognition and weightage to sports and games and co-curricular and extra-curricular activities....." A CABE committee is looking into this matter and its report is expected to be presented to the CABE shortly.

Time schedule for Implementation

As regards laying down a time schedule for implementation of the recommendations found feasible, the Groups felt that the recommendations are of long-term nature. Moreover, the report of the National Advisory Committee as well as this report of the Groups would be placed before the CABE in its meeting scheduled to be held on 15.10.1993. As such, it would be advisable to wait for the CABE's approval to Committee's recommendations and then draw up a time schedule for implementation of the recommendations accepted by the CABE.

Index